READ THE REVIEWS

"This book provides a comprehensive understanding of industry best practices, key issues, and process and technology considerations for deploying an effective purchase order management process. I find it a valuable resource for practitioners, consultants and students."
— **Aamer Rehman**, *Vice President of Consulting*
Factory Logic, Inc.

"The key to sound management, in both thought and action, in the current day world is the integration of business practice with technology and behavioral science. This is exactly what the authors of this book have done. They have not only presented the best practices for managing the purchase order process, but have also highlighted the role of technology and change management in that process. This is 'the book' for practitioners of the purchasing function."
— **Vidyaranya B. Gargeya**, Ph.D., *Director of the MBA Program*
and Professor of Operations Management at
Joseph M. Bryan School of Business and Economics
University of North Carolina at Greensboro

"The authors clearly reveal the recipe of success for managing supply and give practical tools for IT and business managers to make better management decisions. Truly a survival guide for executives and managers as they struggle to cope with mounting competition between supply chains, especially at the execution level. This book is a must-read for every manager who affects the purchase order management process and change management."
— **Aditya Srivastava**, *Senior Vice President of Research*
and Development, i2 Technologies, Inc.

Purchase Order Management Best Practices

Process, Technology, and Change Management

Purchase Order Management Best Practices

Process, Technology, and Change Management

Ehap H. Sabri
Arun P. Gupta
Michael A. Beitler

J.ROSS
PUBLISHING

Copyright ©2007 by Ehap H. Sabri, Arun P. Gupta, and Michael A. Beitler

ISBN-13: 978-1-932159-63-9
ISBN-10: 1-932159-63-0

Printed and bound in the U.S.A. Printed on acid-free paper
10 9 8 7 6 5 4 3 2 1

Library of Congress Cataloging-in-Publication Data

Sabri, Ehap H., 1967-
   Purchase order management best practices : process, technology, and change management /
by Ehap H. Sabri, Arun P. Gupta, and Michael A. Beitler.
       p. cm.
   Includes index.
   ISBN-13: 978-1-932159-63-9 (hardcover : alk. paper)
   ISBN-10: 1-932159-63-0 (hardcover : alk. paper)
   1. Industrial procurement--Management. 2. Business
logistics--Technological innovations. I. Gupta, Arun P., 1954- II. Beitler,
Michael A. III. Title.
   HD39.5.S24 2006
   658.7'23--dc22   2006025682

Phone: (954) 727-9333
Fax: (561) 892-0700
Web: www.jrosspub.com

To Sawsan, Jana, Jude, Alia, and Hisham
Ehap H. Sabri

To Anshu, Avni, and Ankit
Arun P. Gupta

To my wife Danyang Peng
Michael A. Beitler

FOREWORD

By writing *Purchase Order Management Best Practices: Process, Technology, and Change Management,* Ehap Sabri, Arun Gupta, and Michael Beitler have created the definitive standard reference book on purchase order management as well a guide to new procurement management practices.

This comprehensive text on purchase order management covers all of the management practices and process steps in purchasing and provides valuable guidance as well as a checklist of best practices. Some companies will find this book useful for reviewing their purchase order practices and processes to identify opportunities for improvement. Other companies will find it useful as a training aid to help increase understanding of effective purchase order management and processes. Due to the comprehensive nature of this text, I would also expect many professors and instructors to find this book valuable as a teaching resource for college students or for those just starting or looking to advance their careers in purchasing management. This book combines a solid review of the most important concepts with examples of practical application, and the case studies provide additional insight into the practical application of the concepts discussed throughout the book.

Purchase Order Management Best Practices: Process, Technology, and Change Management is a useful reference beyond the topic of purchase order management because it sets the context for purchasing within the broader framework of supply chain management. An example of this is the discussion of innovative strategies for selecting the right replenishment program with suppliers. The summaries of vendor management inventory (VMI) and Just-in-Time (JIT) programs provide the context for today's procurement management. The overview of these practices is excellent and will be useful for anyone who is involved in supply chain management.

The chapter on purchase order management at the execution level is the most comprehensive treatment of this topic I have ever read. It covers the entire process thoroughly from beginning to end, omitting nothing. For this reason alone, anyone involved in purchasing should keep this book on hand as a valuable desk reference. However, the authors also provide a good overview of the technologies that will shape the future of purchase order management. They review the evolution of technologies such as SOA and RFID and then go on to describe how these and other technologies will impact procurement processes.

The final section of the book shows you how to actually implement best practice, process, and technology changes. Change management will be necessary to remain competitive, and this book with its many useful tips will help guide you through the landmines of implementation and help lead you to a path of success.

Supply change management, including purchasing, is entering an entirely new generation of management practices, which will transform the way we manage supply chains in the future. Driven by new technologies such as SOA and business process platforms, supply chain management will become much broader, more integrated, and real-time. How a company works with its suppliers will change dramatically. This important reference book is also a guide to that transformation.

Overall, *Purchase Order Management Best Practices: Process, Technology, and Change Management* is a must read for everyone involved with the practice or study of purchasing management and for many in the field of supply chain management. It should become a standard reference on this topic and be widely used for many years.

Michael E. McGrath, CEO and President
i2 Technologies, Inc.

Michael McGrath is President and CEO of i2 Technologies, Inc., the leader in supply chain solutions, and author of five books, including *Product Strategy for High Technology Companies*. He is a pioneering expert in the field of product development and supply chain management and was co-founder and Managing Director of Pittiglio, Rabin, Todd & McGrath (PRTM), where he developed the original concept for the Supply Chain Operations Reference (SCOR®) model in 1993. In 1996, McGrath's consulting firm (PRTM) and AMR Research organized the Supply Chain Council, a not-for-profit association, which initially included 69 volunteer member organizations. The SCOR® model has since become the standard process reference model for supply chain management and continues to evolve to meet the needs of business.

TABLE OF CONTENTS

INTRODUCTION

Although improvement of the purchase order management (POM) process is desperately needed in today's competitive environment, decision-makers and operations managers may find themselves asking the most fundamental questions: How can we do it? What is the best practice in moving to a proactive mode instead of the reactive mode when dealing with supply problems? How can we spend more of our energy on making improvement rather than on managing transactions? How can we improve POM? What new technology best suits us? What is the best way to quantify and then maximize the value from implementing the technology? How can we drive the change successfully?

This book brings together the latest advances in POM, providing business professionals with a comprehensive framework for driving out costs, improving efficiency, eliminating non-value added activities, and optimizing a transformation program for POM process. The framework is applicable for every industry. This book also offers practical, proven tactics and detailed guidance about every aspect of POM process redesign, intelligent leveraging of new technologies, building a strategy for strengthening the relationship with suppliers, identifying comprehensive related metrics, and much more, including industry success stories and lessons learned.

POM process transformation is a hot topic, but as of yet no single book has focused directly on a recipe for success in a POM transformation program. This text will fill that gap by providing a breakthrough, start-to-finish roadmap for organizations to use in implementing a POM transformation program successfully. The strengths of this book are in its focus on management and the unique inclusion of all elements that are needed during process improvement—best practices, benefits, technology, business justification, and ongoing support strategy. This book will also enable readers to better understand:

- The challenges in a conventional POM process and how the conventional approach compares to the best practices

- The benefits of implementing the best practices enabled by the right technology
- How to leverage innovative strategies for selecting the right replenishment program with suppliers, strengthening trust in the supply chain, selecting the right software provider, rolling out the solution to all suppliers, providing ongoing support for the solution, and establishing a consistent process for metrics tracking and publishing
- A framework for organizations to improve the POM process efficiently and with lower risk

Concepts in this book are presented in an easy-to-understand manner that is intended for all readers who are interested in learning about POM. Because POM is involved in several functions within an organization, this text has been written for a wide audience which is interested in learning concepts that will optimize the POM process and slash waste from it. This text has been written for those who work with POM on a daily basis as well as those who are interested in entering the field of POM.

Strategies are provided for senior managers for use in planning for transformation programs. Middle managers are also provided with tools to effectively manage and implement the best practices. Graduate students may use this book to gain a more thorough understanding of how POM functions and use this knowledge to extend research in the field of POM or to implement the concepts in industry.

The book is divided into three parts—Process Best Practices (Part I), Enabling Technologies (Part II), and Change Management (Part III)—which are considered to be the "ingredients" of the "recipe for success" in a POM transformation program (Figure 1).

POM is defined in this book as the process of issuing a purchase order (PO) and tracking its life cycle and related schedules until receipt of the PO into a buyer's inventory or until consumed by production. Part I provides best practices for the POM process at the operational and execution levels. Return (reverse logistics) and PO settlement subprocesses are included in the life cycle. Many challenges exist in the POM process today, which means many potential benefits can be gained when these challenges are addressed by adopting best practices.

An effective solution incorporates a best practices proven process and its supporting technologies, which address all of the varied organizational requirements. As communication technologies have improved, the POM process has adapted these technologies. Maturity of the POM process has also followed the maturity of communication technologies. Any POM component that requires visibility has been positively impacted by technology that provided better ways to communicate. Internet technology is an enabler of the best practices POM process, which allows

Part I Process Best Practices		Part II Enabling Technologies		Part III Change Management	
1	POM: Challenges and Solutions	4	EDI, the Internet, and e-Hubs	8	Planning Change
2	POM at the Operational Level	5	Identification Technologies: Barcodes and RFID		
3	POM at the Execution Level	6	Web Services and SOA	9	Implementing and Sustaining Change
		7	POM Software Vendors		

Figure 1. Organization of the Book.

enterprises to integrate and collaborate with their suppliers, provide visibility, automate the paper-driven business subprocesses, and interconnect inventory, logistics, and planning systems.

Current state-of-the-art POM-related technologies are presented in Part II. An environment of uncertainty and doubt exists today in many organizations in regard to new technologies. The appeal of best practices and the benefits of implementing the new technologies are clear, yet enterprises struggle in integrating new technology into supply chain operations and change management. If POM change has been properly planned, implementing and sustaining the change becomes easier. Yet even when POM change planning has been conducted in a thorough and systematic manner, inevitably problems will still arise during the implementing and sustaining phases.

Part III provides guidelines for implementing a POM transformation program (process improvement) successfully. Part III also provides a template to calculate the return on investment (ROI) for a POM process.

This book has also been organized to fit the needs of many readers. Chapter 1 of Part I is an executive summary of POM challenges and solutions. If all a reader needs is the "big picture," Chapter 1 will provide this information. Chapters 2 and 3 in Part I provide vital information for operation and supply chain managers to read and master.

Part II dives deep into leading-edge technologies related to the POM process. For IT managers, Part II will be an important source of information to "get up to speed" with the latest technology. Others readers may decide to study Part II, skim it, or even skip it.

Transformation managers and change management consultants may prefer to go directly to Part III first and then read Part I and Part II.

ABOUT THE AUTHORS

EHAP SABRI

Ehap H. Sabri has a doctorate in Industrial Engineering from the University of Cincinnati in Ohio. He has fifteen years of professional experience in management consulting, leading large process improvement programs, software development, project management, advance planning and scheduling, and e-business solutions in a variety of industries, with a proven record of success in adding value and achieving cost reductions. Dr. Sabri currently holds the position of Solution Strategist at i2 Technologies, Inc., in Dallas, Texas, a well-known leader in supply chain and e-business solutions. He is also an Adjunct Professor at the University of Dallas, Dallas and the University of Texas at Dallas, teaching advanced supply chain management and logistics courses for the MBA and Ph.D. programs. He is a PRACTX author for CAPS (the Center for Strategic Supply Research), has given presentations at several industry meetings, and has published several conference and journal papers. Dr. Sabri's research focus is on order management, value chain management concepts, process improvement, performance management, demand planning, strategic sourcing, and lean manufacturing.

ARUN GUPTA

Arun P. Gupta has a doctorate in Computer Science Engineering from the University of Texas at Arlington. He has sixteen years of professional experience in academia, IT, and management consulting. As a consultant, Dr. Gupta has architected e-business solutions, led process improvement workshops, directed large IT projects, developed software, acted as a business analyst, and trained in the NA, APAC, and EMEA areas. He has a proven track record of success in various types of industry. Dr. Gupta is currently acting as a trusted advisor for a large industrial manufacturing organization. For the past five years he has also been a research associate at the Supply Chain Resource Consortium at North Carolina State University, Raleigh, developing a supply chain maturity model. Dr. Gupta's research focus is on architecting multiorganization e-business solutions, supply chain maturity, fuzzy models for supply risk, predictive modeling, and distributed order management. He has given presentations at conferences and has published several conference papers.

MICHAEL BEITLER

Michael A. Beitler is Professor of Business Practice in the MBA program of the University of North Carolina-Greensboro and a Visiting Professor of Management at the University of Mannheim's Business School (a number-one-ranked business school). He has thirty years of professional experience as an executive, consultant, and university professor and has earned an international reputation as a keynote speaker, workshop leader, and author. His clients include Fortune 100 companies and mid-sized manufacturing, distribution, retailing, banking, and publishing companies. Dr. Beitler is the author of two books, including the best-selling *Strategic Organizational Change*. His books and articles are used at leading universities in the United States, Canada, and Europe and at leading corporations including Coca-Cola. His research focuses on organizational change, leadership development, and self-directed learning.

ACKNOWLEDGMENTS

The authors have countless people to thank. During the writing of this book we have received valuable comments and suggestions from clients, colleagues, and students on an almost daily basis. Dr. John Besaw provided invaluable insight and suggestions throughout our writing. He was available from the very beginning with ideas and encouragement. We sincerely appreciate his contributions to this book.

Although acknowledging the contribution of everyone is impossible, several individuals provided invaluable suggestions and encouragement throughout this project:

Mrs. Sawsan Abublan	Sanjay Jain
Dr. Amr AbuSoliman	Aamer Rehman
David Beitler	Aditya Srivastava
Prof. Vidya Gargeya	Eyas Sabri
Ankit A. Gupta	Samuel Straight
Dr. Robert B. Handfield	Bill Tasker

Web
Added
Value™

At J. Ross Publishing we are committed to providing today's professional with practical, hands-on tools that enhance the learning experience and give readers an opportunity to apply what they have learned. That is why we offer free ancillary materials available for download on this book and all participating Web Added Value™ publications. These online resources may include interactive versions of material that appears in the book or supplemental templates, worksheets, models, plans, case studies, proposals, spreadsheets and assessment tools, among other things. Whenever you see the WAV™ symbol in any of our publications it means bonus materials accompany the book and are available from the Web Added Value™ Download Resource Center at www.jrosspub.com.

Downloads for *Purchase Order Management Best Practices: Process, Technology, and Change Management* include PowerPoint® slides that illustrate purchase order management (POM) best practices, POM technology architecture, and an effective change management template derived from the 60 years of combined experience of the authors. Downloads are available from the Web Added Value™ Download Resource Center at www.jrosspub.com.

PART I:
PROCESS BEST PRACTICES

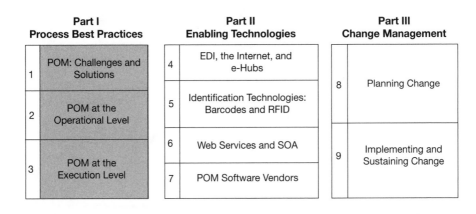

Part I Process Best Practices		Part II Enabling Technologies		Part III Change Management	
1	POM: Challenges and Solutions	4	EDI, the Internet, and e-Hubs	8	Planning Change
2	POM at the Operational Level	5	Identification Technologies: Barcodes and RFID		
3	POM at the Execution Level	6	Web Services and SOA	9	Implementing and Sustaining Change
		7	POM Software Vendors		

Figure 1. Organization of Part I.

Survival in today's business environment has become extremely challenging because of the level of coordination that is required. Companies must eliminate barriers between the functional "silos" within their own organizations. They must replace traditional supplier relationships with win-win relationships, which requires collaboration. Executives and operations managers must understand how to make the supply chain as efficient and effective as it can be in order to give their companies a good chance to succeed in today's competitive business environment.

1

Part I will provide best practices for improving the POM process between companies and their suppliers and for strengthening relationships at the operational and execution levels. Part I is divided into three chapters (see Figure 1). Chapter 1 provides an executive briefing on POM—the process, challenges, solutions, success stories, lessons learned, and the recipe for success for process improvement.

Chapter 2 describes the POM process at the operational level and discusses replenishment philosophies, best practices replenishment programs, and other processes that are directly related to POM such as contract management, material planning, and transportation scheduling. Closing the loop between these processes is crucial in achieving a lean and agile supply chain.

Chapter 3 discusses the life cycle of a purchase order (PO) at the execution level, which includes PO communication, shipment preparation, advanced shipment notice (ASN), receipt, return, and settlement. This discussion is followed by a case study from a large telecommunications company. A list of POM technology requirements that are needed to support process best practices will also be presented.

POM: CHALLENGES AND SOLUTIONS

SCOPE AND VALUE

To survive competition in today's business world, an organization must stay ahead of its competitors. Effective purchase order management (POM) is key to staying competitive and gaining critical core competency in today's business world—something organizations have begun to realize. In all different types of businesses—from the relatively slow-moving ones such as businesses in the utilities and cement industries to rapidly changing ones such as businesses in the high-tech industry—the POM process has become a critical part of achieving a competitive advantage by enabling lean and agile supply chains.

In some companies, traditional purchasing strategies such as aggressive negotiation to reduce unit price have shifted to new initiatives such as collaboration and lean supply in order to lower transaction and operational costs and to improve response capabilities. Supply chains of the future will be leaner and faster (Johnson 2003). The POM process will grow in greater importance for several fundamental reasons:

- Global competition is exerting pressure to reduce costs, which contributes to the growing importance of POM.
- Strategic outsourcing is creating a need for improved information sharing and collaboration with suppliers.
- Firms are extending the POM process outside their "four walls" to include contract manufacturers, third-party logistics providers, and service providers, with a desire to regain direct visibility of the inbound supply that has been lost through expansion.

- A top priority for firms in today's dynamic business environment is making well-informed and timely decisions. The POM process is key to providing real-time information about the in-bound supply, which aids making correct decisions.
- Demand is increasing for building faster responsiveness, for increasing flexibility, and for having proactive management of internal and external process changes. POM can help achieve these objectives by managing and monitoring incoming material effectively.
- Supply chains are vulnerable to the variability of downstream and upstream activities. A relatively small delay in an upstream process can propagate downward throughout the entire supply chain, negatively affecting production scheduling, shutting down assembly lines, and preventing any number of deliveries. Effective POM can control and manage the impact of upstream variability, which is critical for the success of the supply chain.
- Firms are in a better position to drive improvement upstream rather than downstream in the supply chain because they have more "clout" with suppliers than with their customers. Therefore process improvement and cost reduction initiatives are more likely to succeed in processes that are related to suppliers (such as POM) than in processes that are related to customers.
- Over recent years, supply replenishment has become increasingly more complex, resulting in increased time requirements, costs, and errors, which lead to more expedited and "rush" orders.

The biggest challenge for companies in the competitive environment of today is to deliver products to their customers when and where the customers need them, exactly as the customers want them, but to also have a competitive price and to make deliveries in a cost-effective manner. Companies will not be able to address this challenge without having tight integration with their supplier bases as well as efficient order management operations.

Managing the supplier base is becoming more complicated due to globalization, the increasing complexity of supply chains that is caused by outsourcing, the need for shorter times to market, the shift from vertical to horizontal supply chains, and the move to mass customization and build-to-order (BTO) environments. As a result, operations managers are continually looking for ways to improve the conventional order management process or to replace it with a new process.

The importance of a structured methodology for tackling the order management process cannot be overemphasized. Therefore achieving an effective POM process to reduce operating expenses, to improve supply replenishment efficiency, and to obtain and sustain a competitive advantage is essential. Yet to date no studies in the literature directly relate to this important issue. Effective POM will therefore be the focus of this chapter.

The Conventional POM Process

POM of direct material can be defined as the process of issuing a purchase order (PO) and tracking its life cycle until receipt of the ordered material into a buyer's inventory or until the ordered material has been consumed by production. Returns (reverse logistics) and PO settlement subprocesses are also included in the life cycle. Depending on the arrangement between a buyer and a supplier, PO settlement can be triggered by any of these events—supplier's order acknowledgment, an advanced shipment notice (ASN), an invoice, a warehouse receipt from the buyer's receiving system, or an inventory consumption notification (in the case of a co-assignment arrangement). The trigger for a PO settlement subprocess is considered to be the handoff between the physical supply chain and the financial supply chain.

Although there are major events (or milestones) in the PO life cycle, such as PO communication or ASN generation, some companies track more granular (smaller) events, especially for international shipments, such as manifest filing, arrival at a consolidator, when loaded on a vessel, vessel departure, arrival at destination port, customs clearance, when loaded onto a truck, etc.

In a conventional POM process, the first step is for a buying organization to send a PO for goods or services to a specified supplier and then to expect the supplier to ship the goods (or provide the services) based on the PO. After the shipment, the supplier generates invoices on a periodic basis and waits for payment notifications to arrive. These are fragmented processes in which each party has no visibility of what is happening at the other end in the time that passes between the initial steps. Lack of visibility between purchasers and suppliers is the main driver for premium freight expense. Yet changes to the conventional process order routine are very difficult to assimilate by the buyer and the supplier. Changes may include:

- Modifying a PO by the buyer (e.g., sending a PO change request): the supplier must identify and adjust the existing PO before sending the shipment; the buyer must check the received goods against the modified PO.
- Partially fulfilling a shipment: partial fulfillment of an order will generate a discrepancy during check-in of the received goods by the buyer. The buyer will then expect a back-order shipment from the supplier.
- Returning some of the received material by the buyer

- Changing pricing: a different price on the invoice compared to the price on the PO or contract will generate a discrepancy during invoice settlement.

A significant amount of time and manual effort is required to monitor the PO and in-transit shipment of the ordered goods, to match received goods against partial shipments and PO modifications, and to resolve discrepancies.

The conventional POM process has critical links, which are missing at the execution level:

- Timely ASNs: crucial for providing visibility of in-transit goods
- An audit trail: makes proving whether or not a supplier received a PO amendment easier
- Support for matching ASNs to POs: necessary to provide an accurate "picture" of incoming material to the planning engine
- Timely and clear communication of a PO or a firm's required schedule: some suppliers may not always know if the date on a PO is a shipment date or a delivery date
- Support of new, emerging settlement programs (e.g., evaluated receipt settlement, ERS, which is a significant step in eliminating non-value added activities and facilitates paying suppliers faster): many suppliers reporting more than a 60-day delay in receiving payments from buyers; many buyers reporting a significant delay in receiving invoices from vendors
- Monitoring: returns, receipt confirmations, and payment notifications

The conventional POM process also has critical links, which are missing at the operational and tactical levels:

- Real-time collaboration on changes
- Tight integration with material planning (MP) to obtain material requirements and to adhere to suppliers' constraints
- An ability to negotiate program parameters during contract processing
- An ability to "close the loop" by updating supplier and buyer performance scorecards

Figure 1.1 illustrates a best practices process for POM (highlighted in dark gray) that addresses the missing links in the conventional POM process. (*Note:* Figure 1.1 will be discussed in detail in Chapters 2 and 3.) The process in Figure 1.1 can have several variations, but regardless of the type or size of the variation, all interactions between the subprocesses presented in the figure should be available and streamlined for the process to be considered a best practices process.

For example, one variation would be to outsource the transportation function to a supplier. This variation would be a good practice if the transportation function is not a core competency of the buyer and if a supplier can manage

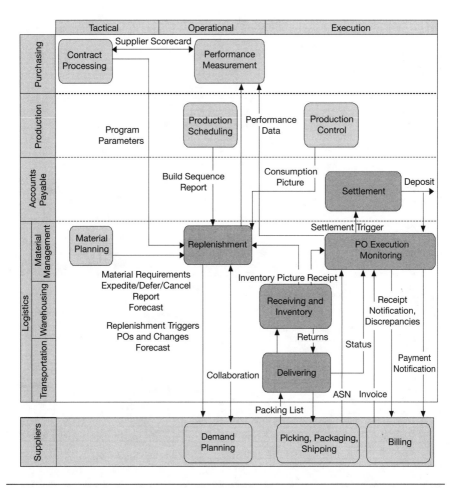

Figure 1.1. Best Practices: POM Process and Related Interactions with Supply Management Processes and Functions.

transportation more efficiently and provide more granular (specific) status information. In this case, the delivery subprocess under the "Transportation" function in Figure 1.1 would be in the supplier "swim-lane" (the horizontal row) as shown in Figure 1.2. Another variation would be to outsource the warehouse function to a third-party logistics provider for some or all items. In this scenario, a third-party logistics provider would provide receipt information and an updated inventory picture. In yet another variation, a production scheduling process would need to be included in the POM process to support sequence-driven programs (e.g., to provide an assembly line schedule). This type of variation is mainly adopted in the automotive industry and in line assembly environments. Therefore, a link or integration between production scheduling and POM may not be needed if a sequence-driven variation is not adopted.

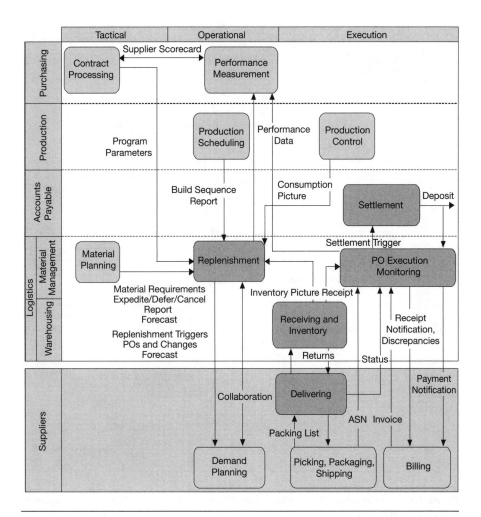

Figure 1.2. Best Practices: POM Process with Transportation Function Outsourced to the Suppliers.

Vendor-managed inventory (VMI), sequence-driven processes, and other advanced replenishment programs have recently become more common in the supply chain. Yet many replenishment programs are implemented without a strategy, without a well-defined process, or without the enabling technology that is required to achieve the promised benefits, which creates strategic missing links in the conventional POM process.

In summary, many challenges exist in today's POM process, yet numerous potential benefits can be gained if these challenges are addressed.

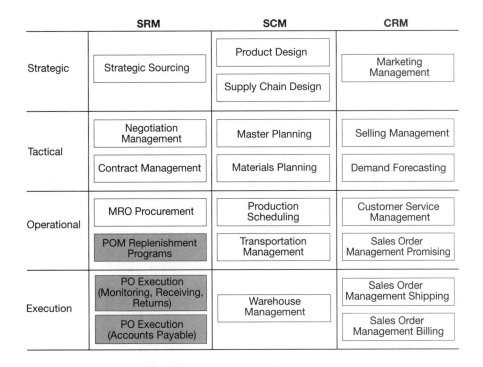

	SRM	SCM	CRM
Strategic	Strategic Sourcing	Product Design Supply Chain Design	Marketing Management
Tactical	Negotiation Management Contract Management	Master Planning Materials Planning	Selling Management Demand Forecasting
Operational	MRO Procurement POM Replenishment Programs	Production Scheduling Transportation Management	Customer Service Management Sales Order Management Promising
Execution	PO Execution (Monitoring, Receiving, Returns) PO Execution (Accounts Payable)	Warehouse Management	Sales Order Management Shipping Sales Order Management Billing

Figure 1.3. Value Chain Processes.

The Big Picture

Although Figure 1.1 illustrates a comprehensive picture of supply management, in which a POM process and its related interactions encounter other processes such as material planning and contract processing, Figure 1.3 illustrates the position of POM in the "big picture." Figure 1.3 presents all of a buyer's processes that add value to the product throughout the supply chain until the product reaches a customer. (In Figure 1.3, POM-related subprocesses are highlighted in dark gray and MRO represents maintenance, repair, and operating supplies.) These value chain processes can be grouped into three "super" processes: supplier relationship management (SRM), supply chain management (SCM), and customer relationship management (CRM):

- SRM: a super process of effectively managing supply by using several processes, including the POM process
- SCM: a super process that has a main objective of achieving balance between supply and demand and optimizing it if possible

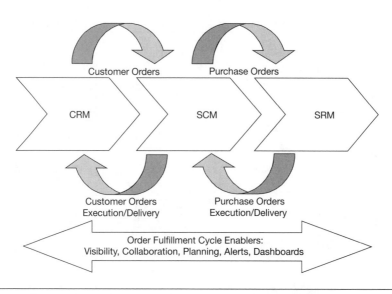

Figure 1.4. Order Fulfillment Cycle.

- CRM: a super process of managing customer relationships by effectively supporting marketing, sales, demand forecasts, sales order promises and management, and service processes

Another way to link POM to the customer is through the order fulfillment cycle, which spans the CRM, SCM, and SRM super processes and is considered to be one of the major differentiators for best-in-class (BIC) companies. As illustrated in Figure 1.4, an order fulfillment cycle links sales order management processes to supply management processes. Order fulfillment cycle "enablers" are real-time *visibility* in the supply chain, effective *collaboration* with suppliers and customers, an efficient supply chain *planning* cycle with "what if" analysis capabilities, intelligent *alerts*, and *dashboards* to monitor performance of the fulfillment cycle.

A Lean and Agile Supply Chain

Considering the current market pressures on margins, lean strategy provides an excellent framework for "squeezing" costs out of supply chains. Lean strategy provides a strong infrastructure to support many innovative manufacturing methods, including engineer to order (mass customization), build to order, and assemble to order. Lean strategy reduces the lead time of any process and minimizes costs from activities that do not add value. Yet with today's supply and demand volatility, supply chains must be agile in addition to being lean to be able to react quickly to changes and even to be able to detect changes before they occur. Variability will continue to exist, but agility will help to control it.

Managing the supply chain is also becoming more complicated due to globalization, increased complexity with outsourcing, and a need for shorter times to market. As a result, senior managers are considering the benefits of moving toward a lean and agile supply chain (LASC) in order to address today's challenges, which have caused managers to be in unfamiliar situations such as needing to manage with less waste, inventory, personnel, and resources, while simultaneously giving customers more configuration options, more delivery flexibility, and shorter lead times.

Being "lean" means working with limited inventory, having no waste, and reacting without delay to changing conditions. Lean strategy was shaped largely around the 35-year-old Toyota Production System and was originally based on two core assumptions—low demand fluctuation to ensure smooth production and a network of local suppliers to ensure short lead times and Just-in-Time (JIT) deliveries. Yet neither of these assumptions exists in today's dynamic and global environment of fluctuating demand with suppliers that are scattered all over the world. The leaner a supply chain is, the greater the impact of disruptions will be.

Conversely, being only agile is not a good option either. As well, the old concept of building excess capacity, adding inventory, or increasing labor to solve problems is very expensive and does not solve the root cause of the problem.

LASC enables businesses to be flexible in various aspects such as providing an ability to rapidly determine customer needs, to respond to volume and mix changes, and to rapidly respond to a crisis. Yet LASC does not include providing flexibility by maintaining a high stock of raw material or spare production capacity because those conditions conflict with lean strategy. LASC is based on pull, not push philosophies. Therefore, pull-based replenishment is a standard technique of LASC operations. LASC provides an ability to profitably replenish the supply chain while responding effectively to supply and demand variability. A detailed comparison between lean supply chains (LSC) and LASC is shown in Table 1.1.

With globalization, supply chains are becoming more fragile and a small disruption can cause catastrophic results. Therefore, it is essential to detect disruptions proactively and have the necessary flexibility to diminish disruptions at their source. LASC requires constant plan changes and very short lead times. However, LASC cannot only be about processes. LASC must be supported by enabling technology so it will be broadly applicable and scaleable. LASC-supported technology should be able to provide visibility to all relevant players, proactively capture and manage exceptions, and generate alerts when performance approaches set thresholds. LASC-supported technology encourages reevaluating traditional processes and relationships with partners, suppliers, and customers and collaborating with them in real time. (*Note:* The POM process is a key process that can also benefit from a collaborative environment.)

Table 1.1. Comparison of Lean Supply Chain and Lean and Agile Supply Chain

	Lean Supply Chain	Lean and Agile Supply Chain
Primary Focus	**Factory**	**Customer and Supplier**
Strategy	Reducing waste and excessive materials, inventory, labor, and capital equipment	• Customer focus: quicker response, greater flexibility, quicker adaptation to changing customer demands • Extends lean strategy
Complement Techniques	• Direct replenishment to the factory with no intermediate storage • Rapid setup • Just-in-time shipping and receiving	• Postponement (delaying final assembly until the most optimal point) • Frequent deliveries of small quantities • Supply chain collaboration with customers and suppliers
Prerequisites	• Strong operational control • Timely visibility of inventory and production • Automated data collections and real-time communications	• Extremely strong operational control • Timely and intelligent visibility of inventory and production • Automated data collections and real-time collaborations • Tight system integration
Critical-to-Success Metrics	• Inventory turns • Asset utilization	• Response time
Pioneers	Toyota, others	Dell, Wal-Mart, others
Industries	Automotive	Retail, high-tech (electronic)

LASC is not only fast and flexible, but it is also transparent—managers can "see" through the systems what is coming, be proactive, and make the needed adjustments to keep supply chain processes aligned with customers' needs and the managers' own bottom lines. In the past decade, Internet technology has radically transformed the supply chain from being in a world of POs and bills of lading to having a competitive advantage. According to Mayor (2004), "The challenge now, as CIO 100 honorees demonstrate, is to use the opportunities presented by advances like real-time data availability, global communication and business-partner alliances to create a supply chain that's not simply fast, but agile as well."

In summary, the LASC concept is not a fad. Even firms that do not formally adopt the entire philosophy of LASC are implementing certain lean and agile principles. LASC is a strategic philosophy that is not only making a lasting impact on industry, but is also helping to achieve a competitive advantage. (*Note:* An effective POM process should also follow lean and agile principles to be effective and to also be an integral part of LASC.)

IMPROVEMENT CHALLENGES AND SOLUTIONS

An effective solution incorporates a best practices proven process and its support-ing technologies, which will address all of the varied organizational requirements. Internet technologies act as an enabler for the best practices POM process by allowing enterprises to integrate and collaborate with their suppliers thereby pro-viding visibility, automating paper-driven business processes, and interconnecting inventory, logistics, and planning systems. Having an effective POM solution can make a significant impact on an industry by providing needed benefits in:

- Inventory reduction: visibility reduces "nervousness" in the supply chain
- Logistics improvements and procurement cost reductions, which reduce stock-outs, premium freight charges, and discrepancies and increase user productivity
- Integration of streamlined processes and elimination of non-value added activities
- Flexibility and speed, which enable enterprises to shift to mass-cus-tomization or build-to-order (BTO) environments, which are consid-ered to be significant differentiators in today's business environment
- Improvement of service levels and reduction of fulfillment lead time
- Reduction of risk
- Quality improvement
- "Early adopter" benefits for companies using e-business technology in improving POM processes to realize a competitive edge, to have a head-start over their competitors, and to be able to set rules and standards for new technology instead of following rules established by others

Although the benefits of improving the POM process are clear and are desperately needed in today's competitive environment, decision-makers find themselves ask-ing the most fundamental questions: "How can we do it? What is the best practice and does it apply to us? Does technology add value? If so, what is the best way to quantify technology and then maximize it? Many have failed in achieving value, so how can we ensure that we will not be one of them, but instead will be able to minimize risk? What does senior management need to do to support transforma-tion initiatives?"

Currently, uncertainty and doubt continue to exist among organizations in regard to new Internet technologies. Although the appeal of best practices and the benefits of implementing Internet technologies are clear, enterprises struggle to integrate Internet technologies into their supply chain operations. Challenges related to the Internet that are encountered by businesses can be grouped into three categories—process, enabling technology, and change management.

Process Challenges and Solutions

Deciding When to Improve, When to Redesign, or When to Keep

Deciding when to improve, redesign, or keep a process is a challenge encountered in a POM improvement initiative. Radical change (redesign) may lead to better results than attempting incremental improvement. For example, Dell redesigned its business model to move to BTO, while Compaq made incremental improvements. Dell is currently the leader in the market, but achieving this result is not always the case.

Benchmarking involves a thorough analysis of the best practices used by competitors or other industries and helps gain an understanding of market dynamics. Benchmarking can help companies decide when to improve, redesign, or keep their processes. Yet the difficulty encountered in benchmarking supply performance and the need to gain a deep understanding about how data is calculated and presented can slow down a program transformation initiative and prevent a company from identifying the "low-hanging fruit" processes, which can bring the highest and fastest value if improved first.

Major providers in the telecommunications industry have created a benchmarking program in which industry suppliers routinely report performance data to Quest, an independent third party. Quest compiles the data and reports it back to suppliers and their customers. The data allows a company to compare a given supplier's performance with an industry benchmark, giving both parties valuable information on which to base future corrective actions (Carter, Monczka, and Mosconi 2005).

However, having obsessive focus on the technology platform alone, without ensuring that processes are efficient before applying automated solutions, is a recipe for failure. Many misconceptions such as "more technology is better" and "just automate the process and keep the business running as usual" exist and represent related challenges.

When considering process improvement, consider several important questions:

- Is automation possible and appropriate?

- If automation is possible, can off-the-shelf software be used?

- Will employees need to learn new skills?

- Will managers need to change the measures they currently use to control the activities they manage?

- Will the entire management hierarchy need to realign the metrics it uses?

These issues will be addressed in the next two sections.

Supply Chain Configuration and Strategy

Supply chain configuration and strategy may vary at the product and/or supplier levels, which will add complexity to managing the POM process. For example, products with short life cycles, such as fashion clothing or consumer electronics equipment, cannot be combined in the same strategy with long life cycle products such as paper. The same can be said about combining stock products with BTO products. The "product portfolio mix" trend requires having multiple supply chains to effectively and efficiently manage products that have different characteristics. Yet, often the same supply chain strategy and configuration is applied to all products in spite of their different characteristics, which causes shortages and loss of flexibility. Continuing to follow the path of "one supply chain strategy fits all" is a recipe for loss of competitive advantage and market share.

A single supply chain may typically involve hundreds to thousands of suppliers and span multiple tiers of suppliers. Tier 1 suppliers are suppliers who have a direct relationship with the buyer. Suppliers in other tiers have an indirect relationship with the buyer. In the automotive industry, a supply chain can be deep, e.g., it has four or more tiers. Multiple tiers add another dimension of complexity to the POM process.

Another challenge to POM process improvement is having a functional structure in the organization that blocks supply chain integration. Many organizations have a function-oriented structure and have not moved to a process-oriented structure. A function-oriented structure can block information sharing and workflow automation, restrict the optimization of the entire supply chain, and increase the complexity of material flow. As a PO moves across departmental boundaries from one function to another, the PO will gradually lose visibility and "fade from sight." Management is no longer able to see the status details of the PO. Continuing to view the supply chain as a series of functional activities rather than viewing it as several processes that span functions and organizations allows companies in the supply chain to only optimize locally, not globally.

Another related challenge is lack of overall coordination. For example, information technology (IT) managers often complain that line (or business) managers do not understand the complexities that are faced by IT. Yet line managers frequently complain that IT process modeling techniques only focus on automation and software integration and do not focus on the needs of users or on other nonautomated considerations. This situation usually turns into a struggle between the two groups.

Pull-Driven Replenishment Programs

Improvement in order management, inventory management, and purchasing processes by using pull-driven replenishment programs, such as vendor-managed inventory (VMI) replenishment, Just-in-Time (JIT) replenishment, and sequence-driven replenishment programs, is a practice that many successful firms have adopted.

A VMI replenishment program allows a supplier to manage and restock inventory physically located at a factory, until the factory pulls parts for production. VMI can improve visibility across the supply chain, increase material planning efficiency, reduce inventory, and improve stock availability.

In a JIT replenishment program, the basic premise is to have just the right levels of inventory, whether raw materials or subassembly goods, available to meet the demands of a production process or an end customer—no more, no less. This type of inventory status will allow a company to carry a lower inventory, to have less capital tied up in raw materials, and to have less obsolescence to write off.

A sequence-driven replenishment program, which was derived from the JIT replenishment program, was introduced by automotive manufacturers and their suppliers in the early 1990s. Depending on the manufacturer and the industry, a sequence-driven replenishment program is known by different names and acronyms, such as ILVS (in-line vehicle sequencing), sequenced part delivery, and Just in Sequence. The essence of a sequence-driven replenishment program is that as vehicle production is scheduled at a plant, the required components and subassemblies from suppliers are sequenced and brought to the production line just in time to meet assembly requirements as requested by the customer.

The drawback of pull-driven replenishment programs is that having too little inventory and resources will leave a company more vulnerable to any variability in supply. Because it is impossible to anticipate every unforeseen event in the real world, there is no guarantee that synchrony with the plan will always exist. Additionally, the leaner the program, the more subject it is to exceptions. Therefore in today's dynamic environment, *lean* needs to be supported by *agility* in order to react rapidly and effectively to change. Agility requires a thorough understanding of the business environment, an ability to connect in real time with people and systems, an early warning system for potential problems, and a capability to analyze events across the supply chain using technologies that enable quick and effective responses.

Pull-driven replenishment programs along with adoption of Internet technology and agility principles are becoming an integral part of LASC. The benefits of these programs are tremendous, e.g., the ability to have minimum inventory levels, better space utilization, higher quality, increased productivity, and increased flexibility. The next 5 years are expected to result in an expansion of these programs and concepts in many more industries.

Enabling Technology: Challenges and Solutions

Scaleable, Affordable, and Replicable Integration
Other major challenges to technology are the costs and complexity associated with the integration of enterprise applications. Generally, enterprise applications address the needs of a particular department or a related group of departments.

Yet most business processes, particularly processes such as the POM process that interact directly with suppliers, are cross-departmental. As a result, companies must develop enterprise application integration (EAI) solutions for multiple systems to automate multiple business processes. EAI solutions have recently emerged that introduce a "middleman" into the infrastructure, which translates the language of one application into the language of another application. This translation of application languages is neither fast nor easy. In many cases, an organization will revert to an earlier method such as point-to-point batch processing for a simple integration exercise just to get a particular task done.

Because EAI solutions are costly and complex, in many situations, an organization will simply defer automation of processes that span multiple applications to a later time, which also defers potential cost savings and other benefits that would have been realized from the automated processes. Additionally, many partners of the organization such as suppliers become concerned about whether they will incur a charge for systems integration or not and whether employees will receive training to use the new or modified processes and systems.

Integration options should be tailored to the product and standardized to allow integration to be scaleable, affordable, and replicable. Some buyer organizations assume responsibility for developing and maintaining multiple integration links for their suppliers and partners and for setting standards for data definitions and communication protocols to make the suppliers' rollout smooth and replicable. Electronic communication (commerce collaboration) becomes the norm for communication protocols, regardless of the level of integration—simple browser access, electronic data interchange (EDI), or system-to-system integration using Web services.

Select the Right Software Partner

Selecting the right software provider is a challenge for IT and for business managers. A particular implementation may not work because software vendors have failed to fulfill their promises or because of difficulties that have been encountered in installation, testing, customization, and migration of the software. For example, although 80% of the POM process is the same in different industries, the remaining 20% is different, making it the most difficult piece! It is the 20% that causes projects to fail or succeed. In addition to the common process (the 80%), a software provider must be able to address this specific 20% piece in each company or industry.

Internal IT department resistance is a related challenge that must be managed when a company is looking for an external software provider. Usually IT development departments want to manage most projects internally to justify a larger budget, to get more exposure to leading edge technology, and to have greater control over the direction of a project.

At the end of the 1990s, there was significant hype about the huge value that a company could add to its purchasing and supply management processes by leveraging the marketplaces. This hype has subsequently been tempered by negative reports from clients. Many online marketplaces had failed to deliver the level of expected value because expectations were very high, budgets were tight, and the return on investment was overestimated. Another significant reason for failure was that the focus was on the technology rather than on the process. Many managers thought that technology would be a "silver bullet" that would solve all their problems. Software providers did not do much to correct this misperception. Their focus was only on "selling" and they had little experience in implementing the new technology. Additionally, incorrectly setting expectations shifted focus from adding value by improving the process to "going live," which might lead the organization to never use a new process solution. Change management was also underestimated by everyone—another major reason for failure.

Many companies are not certain about the best way to proceed with online marketplaces. For some companies, the best way is thought to be to adopt a new technology as quickly as possible rather than to risk being left behind. Some companies continue to see little value in the online marketplace. Yet others are totally confused about what to do and remain paralyzed.

In the last 5 years, three online marketplaces models have emerged to leverage the opportunities of Internet technologies through streamlining and automating processes. The POM process is impacted by these models:

- Public online marketplaces are independently owned and developed by a third party. Public marketplaces represent a many-to-many relationship. Their primary focus is to find the lowest prices. As an example, Medibuy Marketplace connects healthcare providers to suppliers and service providers. (Note: It is important to mention that many public e-marketplaces have stopped operations and tried to change their model.)

- Industry-sponsored online marketplaces (also consortia) are jointly developed and owned by several specific industry players. Sometimes they are called "captive exchanges." Consortia also represent a many-to-many relationship. Functionality focuses mainly on addressing industry-specific processes and standards. Several consortia now offer hosted private exchange services that allow members to obtain value from tailored technology and/or confidential one-to-many relationships, e.g., Covisint provides procurement, supply-chain management, and other services to the automobile industry and Aeroxchange is an industry-sponsored online marketplace. Aeroxchange has a spare parts inventory visibility tool for the airline industry that can hold $55 billion in inventory. The biggest challenge for an airline is ensuring that the right part for each of the many types of airplanes in use will be available when needed for routine and unscheduled maintenance or for routine maintenance that is required in between scheduled flights. The Aeroxchange tool has the potential to significantly reduce costs in the airline industry by facilitating finding a needed part faster, reducing administrative costs, and reducing required inventory levels (CAPS Research and McKinsey & Company 2002).

- Private online marketplaces are owned by a single company. Private online marketplaces represent a one-to-many relationship that is used to manage processes with key trading partners. A private online marketplace requires partners to integrate with an owner's technical application standards in order to participate in system-to-system integration and/or to use an Internet website browser. Dell, Boeing, and Daimler Chrysler are examples of companies using a private online marketplace.

In most cases, the POM process is best addressed in the private online marketplace model because of the nature of the PO process. A PO is considered to be the heart of any business transaction. Therefore, established processes have been built around the PO process in each company, which makes it difficult for a marketplace company to enforce the use of its tool without tailoring it. (*Note*: With that said, the process owner of POM should consider using an industry-sponsored online marketplace if POM is not considered to be a core competency of the company, if the marketplace POM process is close to the company's process, and if the marketplace POM represents the best practice in the industry.) If a company is considering using a private online marketplace, it should also consider developing its technology in-house if managing technology is a key to its competitive advantage. Otherwise, outsourcing technology and management is a valid option.

BIC companies use new technology to promote improvement in POM. Yet while transitioning to a new technology, a company should review and reengineer its processes in order to achieve the maximum benefits from implementing POM technology, i.e., "improve before automate." At each step in the POM process, supply chain managers have an opportunity to ask if a step can be improved through automation or eliminated altogether with a new technology and process.

For example, Daimler Chrysler's pilot tool not only distributes forecast information to Tier 1 suppliers, replacing the information previously sent by EDI, but the pilot tool also simultaneously sends forecast information to suppliers throughout the supply chain to reduce delays that were occurring at each stage of the supply chain and limiting the ability of lower-tier suppliers to receive information in timely fashion (CAPS Research and McKinsey & Company 2002).

Stanford Medical is another buying organization that has successfully improved their POM process by using e-business (Internet) technology. Over 8 years Stanford Medical has improved their purchasing process for more efficient materials management. For example, transactions from nursing stations are automated through point-of-use systems, delivered from central storage centers, and then restocked by a preferred supplier. The complete order cycle captures all data electronically and requires no human intervention beyond the initial order. The new process saves invaluable time for nurses, reduces regular stocks (i.e., stocks that provide protection against running out of stock during the time it takes to replenish inventory), reduces processing and stocking costs, and has eventually improved the bottom line. Stanford Medical has saved nearly $17 million (McKinsey & Company and CAPS Research 2000).

In selecting the best POM software provider, a company should consider several general requirements. These general requirements include an intuitive and friendly user interface, electronic forms, e-mail notification, robust reporting, integration to backend systems, system performance and reliability, security, and support for extensible markup language (XML) and service-oriented architecture (SOA).

Extensible markup language (XML) has rapidly emerged as a means of exchanging information between applications and has become the standard for information exchange. The success of XML is based on several characteristics:

- XML is an extension of HTML, the most popular "language" for formatting and displaying information on the Internet.
- XML is based on ASCII text, the lowest common denominator among programs similar to HTML.
- XML and HTML are cross-platform languages.
- XML is extensible.

Using SOA

Service-oriented architecture (SOA) has been a "hot topic" in the technology industry for more than 4 years because of its ability to simplify integration by the use of standards that allow a common method of communication and remove dependence on a software application integration capability that is required when firms manage their own business processes. SOA is designed to enable firms to combine modular, reusable business components or functions to reduce the costs and complexity of integration. SOA provides a platform that enables individual services to be linked together in a scalable, flexible, and secure fashion. SOA is also the architectural foundation for Web services (standardized mechanisms for integrating Web applications based on SOA).

The benefits of SOA implementations can be quantified in three major categories—faster deployment, easier integration, and faster customization and updates. However, companies should try to balance the initial cost of developing

SOA applications against the expected savings from the deployment, integration, testing, and maintenance phases (Mougayar 2005).

The SOA concept in the context of a composite application challenges the rigidity found in existing technology. SOA is based on having loosely coupled functions (known as business services) rather than complex and tightly integrated functions. Legacy systems can also be exposed to these business services, which will give them new life in world of SOA. Companies no longer must buy entire software applications. Instead, they can buy only the individual functions that they needed. Companies receive services from vendors not because they have tightly integrated systems and are "locked in" (e.g., using one software vendor to provide all applications in order to avoid a significant integration effort between the applications), but because the vendors provide the best value for the services. This type of advancement will result in breakthrough increases in competitiveness and will increase the value of conducting business with any vendor.

An example of Web services completing a task would be when a company develops a workflow process for POM that uses a software provider's application. All order requests, advanced shipping notices (ASN), and receipt notifications would be based on standard application modules. However, at the "Shipment Status Tracking" step, the company would choose to connect directly to a transportation carrier's website, which uses another application in leveraging (or reading) the tracking number given to the ASN by a supplier. Web services enables the carrier to simply expose all the tracking tasks and actions as a Web service. Next, a POM application can invoke the workflow server as a Web service, obtain the status of a shipment, and then display this information on a POM application user interface (UI). This step is seamless for a user.

Change related to SOA has become noticeable across the software industry. Large enterprise resource planning (ERP) vendors are building SOA-based platforms. Supply chain application providers are using the SOA approach to improve integration capabilities because as providers they are highly dependant on integration with applications within the enterprise and with business partners. Some providers have even begun to develop composite applications that they can use for their own development purposes (Fotanella 2005). (The use of SOA will be detailed in Part II of this book.)

Is It the Right Time for RFID?

Radio frequency identification (RFID) offers a major technology breakthrough by providing accurate and real-time information efficiently concerning the movement of product supply. Adoption of RFID technology and its standards can replace inconsistent data with accurate and timely data. RFID is considered to be the next generation of barcoding. A major drawback of barcoding has been that the scanner must establish "light-of-sight" (visual contact) with the barcode to be able to successfully read it. In RFID, scanning of tags can be accomplished in a totally automatic manner as packages, pallets, and products pass by a RFID scanner.

An ASN can automatically and instantly be generated when a tagged pallet is dispatched from a supplier's site. Throughout transit from the supplier to the buyer, the shipment can be tagged in RFID-enabled trucks. The buyer, supplier, and carrier can track the status and location of the order at each point and compare it to the ASN. In addition to improving real-time visibility in the supply chain, this high level of tracking can help determine the reason for and the responsibility for a shipment error.

When the buyer receives the tagged and tracked item, a receipt notice is automatically recorded, indicating arrival of the shipment at the buyer's site, which can trigger payment and allow the supplier to receive payment for the shipment more quickly, reducing working capital for the supplier. Tracking pallets or items can also reduce the number of claims and claims-processing costs, which is a benefit that is based on the current level of inaccuracies in invoices, receipts, and shipping records and the resulting time and effort that are spent reconciling and resolving these discrepancies.

RFID is in the early stages of development and therefore must address several challenges such as reliability and cost. A RFID tag must be 100% reliable. Otherwise, a retailer, for example, might inadvertently give away free items because all tags are not being read. RFID scanners must also have an ability to filter out unwanted "reads" within its range. Another challenge is related to the price of RFID tags, which forces some companies to think twice before investing in RFID or to limit the use of RFID to pallets rather than individual products because the benefits of using RFID will not offset the cost of RFID tags.

Three different levels of tracking are available—item, case, and pallet. If the magnitude of net income realized from item-level tracking (or even case-level tracking) is not high, starting with pallet-level tracking and postponing item- or case-level tracking until tags and readers become lower priced and the benefits offset the cost is recommended. Another option is to track only selected items such as high-value items, in which the potential benefits from tracking are high. (The benefits of RFID will be detailed in Part II of this book.)

Change Management Challenges and Solutions

Mastering Change Management

A major obstacle during process redesign (e.g., a drastic improvement) is the absence of effective change management, which includes a lack of ongoing commitment, an unrealistic scope, and overall resistance to change especially when the users, organizations, or business units think they are "victims" of change rather than initiators of change. The "We've always done it this way, so why do we need to change now?" mindset is a leading reason for the failure of many process transformations. Firms often underestimate their need for change management, which results in reduced acceptance of many new technology initiatives. Unless dealt with swiftly, lack of acceptance of change in an organization can cause widespread damage to a transformation effort. The importance of having a commitment from top management also cannot be overemphasized.

Another obstacle to success in an initiative is having confusing and/or inconsistent communications from senior managers or a lack of follow-through once an initiative begins. Senior management, including the CEO, must have confidence in the importance of a change initiative to achieve a competitive advantage and should communicate that internally to the organization and externally to suppliers.

Another major challenge concerns the existing levels of analytical thinking and the understanding of technology in employees. Some employees are just not inclined to analytical thinking. Others may lack the technical education or skills required to operate in a new mode. If this situation exists, the results will be discomfort for the employees and disappointment and irritation for the managers. Typically, new skills are needed to support processes that span across suppliers and business partners. Traditionally, organizations have expertise in optimizing their own internal process, but have little experience in how to extend their expertise to suppliers and customers. Some companies fear that sharing too much information will harm their businesses. Other companies may lack the framework that is required to share the benefits of acting with supply chain partners as if they were a single unit.

Mastering change management is essential—a must—because change is a constant theme when companies explore new ways to streamline and improve the POM process. POM users are typically concerned about job security and how managers will evaluate their contributions. Supply chain managers and program champions should drive user adoption of a new process and system compliance through the use of significant change management efforts and ongoing education of end users. Executives in the firm should also highly market a new or modified POM process. Upper management support to help drive process compliance and ensure sufficient funding and resources is essential—another must.

Effective Measurement Management

Many companies also fail to define the comprehensive, global, and agreed-upon metrics (measures) that are necessary to provide a complete picture of an issue and to allow making a "right" decision. For example, maximizing transportation loads by leveraging the maximum number of full truck loads (FTL) to reduce the unit transportation cost actually causes higher inventory costs and a more obsolete inventory. Therefore considering the unit transportation cost as a metric without considering inventory turnover and inventory obsolescence cost metrics will not provide an accurate picture. Inventory obsolescence measures can be very important for short shelf-life items that are related to aging (e.g., products in the consumer goods industry) or technological changes (e.g., products in the high-tech industry). Metrics misalignment is thought to be the main source of disconnect and inefficiency in supply chain interactions. In many cases, obtaining agreement on the definitions of metrics from a buyer and a supplier is difficult because each party looks at the same metrics from a different perspective.

Melnyk, Stewart, and Swink (2004) identified another aspect of the metrics challenge: "Metrics as discussed by managers differs from the topic of measurement as typically discussed by academics. This is primarily a byproduct of different priorities between these groups." An academic is typically focused on addressing specific research questions. The time required to develop and collect the measures is of less importance than the validity of the results. Conversely, managers can live with a "good" measure to facilitate obtaining useful information quickly and consistently.

Established metrics must also exist within a well-maintained measurement management system. A measurement management system must include best practices processes that lead to:

- Defining comprehensive, global, and agreed-upon metrics or measures
- Setting reasonable stretch targets
- Gathering "clean" data
- Communicating timely status reports
- Taking corrective actions when needed

Trade-offs between competing metrics must be made somewhat subjectively by executives and finalized in a comprehensive and repeatable way. Many firms now use internal auditors to validate performance results and benefits. Metrics targets must be reviewed at least monthly and modified based on business need changes. The measurement management system should be backed up and supported with enough resources to maintain data input streams, data integrity, and data validity.

By using modern technology, a measurement management system is able to collect data for all important activities and events in the supply chain, support preemptive actions, and then move from reactive measurements to proactive and even to preemptive measurements. Intelligent business process analysis software mines the data to build routine and on-the-fly (on-demand) metrics. The software can also provide the capability of rolling up and disaggregating metrics by commodity, business unit, region, supplier, time line, etc. Having a user interface or a dashboard also facilitates management understanding of the metrics and, therefore, drawing correct conclusions.

Many firms implement balanced scorecards—a comprehensive set of metrics—at the executive level. Yet there is need to propagate the use of a balanced scorecard at functional unit levels such as at the purchasing and supply levels of the organization. These functional unit-level metrics should be aligned vertically with corporate goals and aligned horizontally with the goals of other functional units and processes and also tied closely to performance-based incentives. Owners of performance measures across the firm should be identified at all levels.

Changing competitive dynamics places heavy pressure on conventional metrics and forces many firms to look for new metrics to capture the dynamics and complexity of their supply chains. Therefore, executives must define metrics that accurately reflect supply chain performance and its contribution to company competitiveness. When Robert S. Kaplan and David P. Norton first presented the balanced scorecard in 1992, they made their case clear—firms must go beyond financial measures and start incorporating operating performance measures that are used at all levels of the supply chain in addition to the financial ones.

Sabri and Rehman (2004) emphasize the need to capture all operational metrics because improvement in one area can be at the expense of another. They recommend summarizing benefits in six key areas—revenue increase, cost reduction, process lead-time reduction, asset reduction, customer benefits, and supplier benefits.

The concept of a balanced scorecard and other best practices guidelines should be adapted to the POM process with measurement categories that include:

- Cost
- Inventory
- Quality
- Availability (including on-time delivery)
- Buyer performance
- Supplier performance

The 2005 *Supply Management Performance Benchmarking Report* (CAPS) noted that on-time delivery is the highest performance measure that is regularly used to rate supplier performance (94.44 %), but only 48.27% of suppliers are measured by this performance measure (CAPS 2005). POM metrics must be connected to and aligned with other strategic metrics of the firm. The most important common denominator that ties all areas of a firm together is financial measures, including ROI (return on investment), ROA (return on assets), EVA (economic value added), etc.

Having an innovative approach to justify implementation is essential to obtain and sustain support from upper management—another must. Before beginning a process improvement initiative, compute the ROI. Determining the ROI is a critical exercise, which is required to justify an investment of resources and technology. Monitoring ROI is also crucial thereafter to maintain support and to ensure that financial objectives are achieved as a result of the process improvement initiative. ROI can also be used for benchmarking purposes. An established performance measurement system (PMS) that captures all of the related metrics is a prerequisite for computing ROI for a POM process improvement or any other process because PMS provides the metrics history data, which helps to determine the estimated benefits that are needed for a ROI calculation. (ROI will be discussed in Part III.)

Although it is clear that investments in leading technology will provide long-term benefits for a firm, IT strategies should be integrated with the firm's strategies to capture maximum benefits before asking for a "go ahead" from upper management. Yet the benefits created by a process improvement should be more than merely offsetting the cost of implementing a new technology. If the benefits are not acceptable, explore using a lower-cost technology or maintaining an existing process and system.

Support for Postimplementation and Rollout

Lacking the ability to effectively and efficiently support and maintain a new solution is the biggest challenge for postimplementation. (*Note*: A solution is a combination of a new process and technology.) There must be a clear and documented process plan to roll-out the solution throughout the enterprise, which includes user acceptance testing, training, dealing with performance issues when they arise, and maintaining an effective Help Desk.

Effective and appropriate training and continuous refresher sessions are crucial to maintain or increase the level of discipline required in the user community to follow a process and then to use the system as designed. Training can take many forms such as Web-based courses, coaching, or small sessions at facility sites. Another avenue of training is for a manager of the process area to continue to look for additional ways to implement best practices in the process and to stay up to date with new technology.

BIC companies typically invest in their employees by providing training and development programs. For example, United Technologies offers functional supply management training, which includes a two-course online graduate-level certificate program through a partnership with Arizona State University (ASU). *Understanding Supply Chain Networks* is a 6-month program paid for by United Technologies through its Employee Scholar Program. By completing this program, employees can earn six transferable credits and learn leading-edge supply chain practices (Johnson 2005).

As part of rollout and maintenance, having a formal system through which suppliers can provide regular feedback is important. An example would be to establish a council that meets on a regular basis to discuss relevant issues and supplier-buyer relationships. The council should be made up of representatives of management from both buyers and suppliers. Another example would be to conduct confidential surveys that are completed by each supplier.

Providing incentives for suppliers to effectively improve their performance and to participate in process transformation programs effectively is also a critical activity. For example, recognize the best performers by adding them to a "best supplier" list and publicize this list in industry-related magazines, go "public" with supplier contracts, or reward suppliers with additional business. Having an effective POM process can create a win-win environment for suppliers and buyers by removing non-value added activities and streamlining the process. Yet unless a new process offers tangible efficiencies to a supplier's cost structure or unless it opens new avenues of an increased revenue stream, a supplier will be less likely to participate effectively.

RECIPE FOR SUCCESS

A typical PO process includes five main steps that interact and sometimes overlap. Although the PO process varies from industry to industry and even from firm to firm, almost all businesses follow the same five steps (with variations that are related to detail):

- A replenishment trigger or a PO is initiated.
- The trigger or PO is communicated to suppliers.
- The supplier ships the material.
- The material is received by the buyer.
- A settlement is triggered.

These five steps are also common to most supply chains and are a fair representation of POM scope.

Additionally a lack of standardization (a common process) in communicating and collaborating on procurement plans, in resolving exceptions, in gathering and analyzing performance data, and in manually intervening will present a major challenge for an existing process.

Communicating with all suppliers through the most appropriate channel usually translates into better service and stronger business relationships. Increasing the speed and accuracy of communicated business information can shorten procurement time for raw materials and parts, reduce data entry errors, and eliminate the high cost and wasted time that is associated with manual order processing, which boosts productivity and improves response time.

Firms that have not deployed POM using Internet technology, especially mid- and small-sized firms, have an opportunity to take advantage of this technology without experiencing as much "pain" as the early pioneers did and to learn from the past mistakes of others. The lessons learned from the early pioneers are a huge source of guidance for firms that are deploying Internet technology for the first time.

Managers should handle change carefully and intelligently, include the related costs as a component of the transformation program, and allow enough time in the project plan for transformation. Suppliers must be also involved early in a POM improvement initiative and play an active role in process refinement and change management efforts.

Any transformation program or process improvement initiative should encompass three specific phases—initial enablement, which is followed by implementation and then by ongoing support and maintenance. An effective transformation plan must support these three phases and address all of the challenges that surround change management by:

- Selecting the right software provider
- Having proper training
- Maintaining upper management buy-in
- Managing by metrics
- Having rollout and maintenance strategies

Therefore, a recipe for success in a POM transformation program must have the following ingredients—best practices processes (the process element), enabling technologies (the software/application element), and effective change management (the people element) as illustrated in Figure 1.5.

SUMMARY

This chapter has provided an executive summary of POM challenges and solutions, in which POM fits into the "big picture," how POM can contribute to LASC, typical benefits that can be achieved from implementing best practices and Internet technologies, and recipe for success for POM process improvement.

Chapter 2 will focus on POM at the operational level by describing different types of replenishment philosophies and programs and by highlighting the interaction points with other supply chain processes that need to be streamlined to improve supply chain efficiency.

REFERENCES

CAPS. *Supply Management Performance Benchmarking Report.* Tempe, AZ: CAPS: Center for Strategic Supply Research; 2005 November, pp. 1–11.

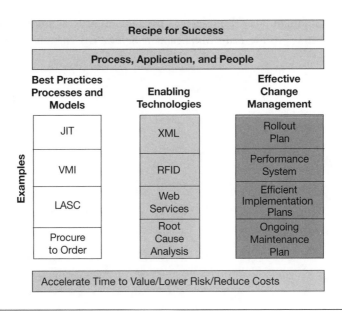

Figure 1.5. POM Transformation Program: Recipe for Success.

CAPS Research and McKinsey & Company. 2002. *E-Commerce Exchanges: Making Informed Decisions. Applying Best Practices.* Tempe, AZ: CAPS Research; 2002, pp. 1–40.

Carter, P.L., Monczka R.M., and Mosconi, T. *Strategic Performance Measurement for Purchasing and Supply.* Tempe, AZ: CAPS Research; 2005, pp. 1–54.

Fotanella, J. *The Service-Oriented Architecture in the Supply Chain Benchmark Report: What Supply Chain Managers Need to Know.* Boston: Aberdeen Group; 2005 September, pp. 1–32.

Johnson, P.F. *Supply Organizational Structure.* Tempe, AZ: CAPS Research; 2003 August, pp. 1–11.

Mayor, T. The supple supply chain. *CIO Magazine*; 2004 August 15. Available at: <http://www.cio.com/archive/081504/supply.html>.

McKinsey & Company and CAPS Research. *Coming into Focus: Using the Lens of Economic Value to Clarify the Impact of B2B e-Marketplaces.* Tempe, AZ: CAPS Research; 2000, pp. 1–21.

Melnyk, S.A., Stewart, D.M., and Swink, M. Metrics and performance measurement in operations management: dealing with the metrics maze. *Journal of Operations Management.* 2004; 22: 209–217.

Mougayar, W. *The SOA in IT Benchmark Report: What CIOs Should Know about How SOA Is Changing IT.* Boston: Aberdeen Group; 2005 December, pp. 1–35.

Sabri, E. and Rehman, A. ROI model for procurement order management process. In *Proceedings of the Lean Management Solutions Conference*, Los Angeles; 2004.

POM AT THE OPERATIONAL LEVEL

REPLENISHMENT PHILOSOPHIES

Two well-known types of replenishment philosophies are *push*-driven replenishment and *pull*-driven replenishment. Push-driven philosophy is primarily forecast driven, whereas pull-driven philosophy is demand driven. Several factors will be considered before a firm decides to adopt the philosophy that best serves their business (Table 2.1). Yet both of these philosophies may exist at the same time in the same firm or supply chain. For example, an automotive firm may use a pull-driven philosophy with suppliers, but continue to apply a push-driven philosophy with dealers. An automotive firm might use a pull-driven philosophy with Tier 1 suppliers, while Tier 1 suppliers use a push-driven philosophy with Tier 2 suppliers. In this case, the pull-push decoupling point would be between Tier 1 and Tier 2.

In any business environment, the further upstream the pull-push decoupling point is from the end customer (the consumer), the greater the adherence to lean principles will be because this situation maximizes the length of the pull-driven part of the supply chain. The pull-push decoupling point varies across industries and even across various supply chains (products) in the same firm.

Most firms produce both high-volume products with a stable demand and low-volume products with an unpredictable demand. Therefore, it is appropriate to adopt a push-driven replenishment philosophy when supply requirements or demand is reasonably well known. Yet it is also appropriate to adopt a push-driven replenishment philosophy when purchasing is the dominant force in determining

Table 2.1. Comparison between Pull-Driven and Push-Driven Replenishment Philosophies

Factors	Pull-Driven Replenishment Philosophy	Push-Driven Replenishment Philosophy
Inventory	A liability; should be eliminated whenever possible	An asset; needed to protect the supply chain against demand variability and supply uncertainty
PO Quantity	Satisfies immediate demand only; minimum lot size desired, determined from EOQ formula	Large lot size, determined by economies of scale or EOQ formula
Order Processing (Setup)	Makes reducing the total cost of ordering insignificant in small lot sizes; considered to be non-value added activity that needs automation	Reducing order processing time not a high priority
Suppliers	Tight relationship based on trust and win-win environment	Big supplier-base and multiple sources to reduce risk of shortage and reduce price
Lead Times	Short lead times to reduce the need for safety stocks; suppliers facilities or their warehouses are located nearby	Long lead times (norm); price first priority regardless of location of suppliers because additional inventories are maintained
Forecasts	Not important in short term; needed for long term to set the correct resource capacity	Very important to determine how much inventory to build and where to keep it
Replenishment Review Policy	Continuous	Periodic
Benefits	If customers demand smaller and more frequent shipments, making the same changes in the supply will be more economical More flexible	Inventory acts as a buffer for uncertainty More responsive because supply is from inventory
Challenges	Shifts costs and inventory onto suppliers upstream when not well managed More vulnerable to changes downstream or upstream of the supply chain	Assets tied up tight-up Obsolete stock

Table 2.1. Comparison between Pull-Driven and Push-Driven Replenishment Philosophies (continued)

Factors	Pull-Driven Replenishment Philosophy	Push-Driven Replenishment Philosophy
Related Strategies for Buyers	Procure-to-order	Forward buying
Related Strategies for Suppliers	Build-to-order, mass customization	Build-to-stock
Replenishment Programs	JIT, sequence-driven, VMI	Schedule-driven, discrete order

replenishment quantities in the supply chain. A pull-driven replenishment philosophy is recommended for fluctuating and unpredictable demand because it is a supply philosophy in which the supply chain is synchronized to control variability and satisfy customer requirements. Supply variability is also addressed by keeping lead times short, particularly when suppliers are located near a buyer's site of operations. Demand variability can also be controlled by more-frequent, smaller purchase orders (POs), but in turn order costs will increase. When using a pull-driven philosophy, the following practices are recommended to mitigate the risk of increasing costs:

- Automate PO generation and communication to reduce order processing costs.
- Counter full-truck-load (FTL) economies by using third-party logistics (3PL) and truckloads with assorted materials.
- Counter volume discount economies by implementing capacity reservations, e.g., a buyer can reserve a total fixed quantity of a product or material for a given period of time and then have it shipped in smaller increments over that period based on the buyer's needs, as long as quantity of the accumulated orders is equal to the reserved quantity.
- Counter item shortages by sharing capacity and supply information in real time with suppliers.
- Counter forecast inaccuracy by improving forecasting techniques or providing point-of-sale (POS) data, e.g., as in a vendor-managed inventory (VMI) program in the retail industry.

PO order quantities are small in a pull-driven philosophy, which means inventories are kept low. Yet to successfully adopt a pull-driven philosophy and achieve target performance, order processing costs must be kept low and a high level of trust and cooperation must be maintained between a buyer and business partners.

Replenishment Review Policies

When deciding to generate replenishment triggers, several options are available. One option would be to wait for a stock-out condition before replenishing. Another would be to replenish only when an immediate demand arises and to keep a zero inventory of raw material. However, these two options are valid only when supply lead times are shorter than the "need" times. In today's business environment, this situation is rare. Therefore, buyers replenish inventories in advance of needing inventory. Two different inventory monitoring policies can be applied to achieve this condition—continuous review and periodic review.

Continuous Review

When using a continuous review policy, inventory is counted continuously and replenishment is triggered (or a PO is placed) whenever the count falls below a predefined reorder point (ROP). ROP is the quantity to which an inventory may drop before replenishment is triggered. The purchased quantity is typically equal to an economic order quantity (EOQ).

The basic EOQ formula is developed from the total cost equation, which involves procurement costs and inventory carrying costs. Procurement costs include the cost of placing, processing, and receiving an order. Inventory carrying costs include the costs of carrying inventory in advance of consuming it, e.g., the cost of space, handling, lost opportunities to use capital that is tied up in the inventory, capital, inventory risks that are associated with shrinkage (theft), damage, and obsolescence, and inventory service costs that are associated with insurance and taxes. The challenge to a firm is that procurement costs and inventory carrying costs work against each either. For example, increasing PO quantities will reduce procurement costs because fewer POs will need to be placed, but it will increase inventory carrying costs. The basic EOQ formula, which was originally introduced by Ford Harris in 1913, tries to find a "sweet spot," or an optimal quantity, at which the total cost (a summation of these two costs of procurement and inventory) is minimized.

The basic EOQ formula is expressed as total cost = procurement cost + carrying cost (Ballou 2004):

$$TC = DS/Q + ICQ/2$$

where,

TC = Total annual relevant inventory cost, dollars
Q = Order size to replenish inventory, units
D = Item annual demand occurring at a certain and constant rate over time, units per year
S = Procurement cost, dollars per order
C = Item value carried in inventory, dollars per unit
I = Carrying cost as a percent of item value, percent per year

The primary drawback of the continuous review policy is the need to maintain accurate inventory at all times. This drawback can be addressed in several ways. One is using a two-bin system in a Just-in-Time (JIT) replenishment program. When one bin is emptied, it is returned to a supplier to be refilled. This empty reusable bin is considered to be the replenishment trigger. Another way is to leverage the point of sale (POS), which is tied to cash register sales transactions as is done in the retail industry. Still another way is to use barcode scanning or RFID tags (radio frequency identification tags) on items that need to be replenished based on sales of these items or the use of them. If a computerized inventory control system is implemented, periodic manual auditing is needed to verify and adjust the computer counts.

Periodic Review

When using a periodic review policy, inventory levels of an item are audited at predetermined intervals. The quantity to be placed on a PO is the difference between a maximum quantity (M) and the on-hand inventory at the time of the review. Typically the review interval is determined by dividing the EOQ by annual demand.

The periodic review policy is similar to the continuous review policy, but the difference is that POs will wait until the next replenishment triggering interval rather than being placed instantaneously. Therefore purchased quantities will be higher to compensate for the delay in triggering replenishment. Larger purchased quantities translate into larger inventory levels being on hand, which makes the periodic review policy less efficient when compared to the continuous review policy. That said, the periodic review policy is preferred in some situations, such as when a manual bookkeeping inventory process is used (counting inventory levels periodically is easier) or when a large number of items must be jointly ordered from the same supplier to achieve significant transportation and administrative cost savings or to qualify for price-quantity discounts.

Extending EOQ

The replenishment quantities calculated in the EOQ basic formula are intended to provide enough on-hand stock to satisfy inventory requirements during the supply lead time, which has been determined by using average lead time and demand numbers. Accounting for the uncertainties of supply lead time and demand can extend the reality of the EOQ formula and result in the addition of "safety" stock. In this case, the average inventory level of an item will be the total of the regular stock plus the safety stock. Average regular stock equals the EOQ quantity divided by 2. A safety stock inventory rises exponentially with the item fill rate (i.e., the target level of item availability).

The EOQ formula becomes complicated if an incentive for purchasing inventory in advance of need (forward buying) is a consideration. To compensate, most buyers use the basic EOQ formula and then increase a quantity if the quantity is close to qualifying for a price break.

Item Fill Rate versus Order Fill Rate

Use of an *item fill rate* is an appropriate measure if a buyer has a single item in each PO. Yet rarely is this the case. Typically a buyer places an order for multiline items to reduce transaction processing costs. In this scenario, an *order fill rate* is a more appropriate measure because an order fill rate can be estimated by calculating the product of (multiplying) the item fill rates for all line items on the order. For example, if an order has three line items for three different items with an item fill rate of 90% for each, the order fill rate will be 72.9% ($0.9 \times 0.9 \times 0.9$), which makes achieving a high fill rate or a high "perfect order" percentage more difficult for suppliers. (*Note*: A perfect order is achieved by on-time delivery and a complete shipment.)

Some companies choose an easy method to increase their order fill rate—they increase inventory levels, but doing so is a costly choice. A more effective way to address the challenge of needing a higher inventory level to achieve a high percentage of perfect orders is to reduce variability, which results in a reduction of safety stock. Another method is to standardize and simplify the order process to reduce procurement costs to a minimum, which will reduce the EOQ quantities and cause frequent deliveries to be more cost effective and to reduce regular stock levels.

Enabled Strategies

Procure to order. Procure to order is a popular pull-driven strategy for high-value items that a purchasing firm cannot afford to keep in inventory (e.g., a service provider in the telecommunication industry).

Forward buying. Forward buying is a popular push-driven strategy used by buyers when anticipatory buying for future demand requirements is desired, e.g., buyers attempting to hedge on future price increases for commodities such as copper, silver, and fuel. Another example of a forward buying strategy is the need to have certain products in-house just before the beginning of a season so that the highest margin may be achieved (such as in the apparel and retail industries).

Build to order. In a build-to-order strategy, suppliers do not produce a product until they have received a confirmed order. This strategy is considered to be on-order production of standard products because the products have a predefined bill of material (BOM).

Engineer to order. Mass customization (or engineer to order) is on-order production of customized products in which a BOM is not fully defined before an order is placed. As a result, product configuration can be tailored as needed to respond to current production conditions and unique customer requirements.

Build to stock. In a build-to-stock strategy, suppliers make products in advance of demand and hold them in stock (in their inventories) to satisfy demand from their inventories as orders come in.

Assemble to order. In an assemble-to-order strategy (also known as an intermediate strategy), products are partially built or raw materials are made available in anticipation of demand, but final assembly or delivery of raw materials is postponed until an order is received.

Some suppliers use a mix of these strategies, depending on the characteristics and maturity of the products. For example, using a build-to-stock strategy is safe for mature products, but very risky for new products. Additionally, a product mix might vary across industries. As a result, a build-to-stock strategy is used for consumer products, an assemble-to-order strategy is used for personal computers, a build-to-order strategy is used for defense projects, and mass customization is used for sporting equipment.

REPLENISHMENT PROGRAMS

Schedule-Driven Replenishment

In schedule-driven replenishment, a schedule for ordered material is released by a buyer with a mutually agreed upon (and reasonable) supplier lead time. (*Note*: The lead time agreement must be determined during creation of the blanket purchase order [BPO] or during contract negotiation as one of the replenishment program parameters [Figure 2.1].) Typically, a buyer communicates a schedule via fax, e-mail, electronic data interchange (EDI), or a website. In the event that the buyer requires material within an agreed-upon supplier lead time, a potential new schedule will be sent to the supplier for review and confirmation. If a written, phone, or e-mail response is not sent to the buyer by the supplier by the next business day after receipt of the schedule, the buyer may assume that delivery will be made as scheduled. *Comment*: Best-in-class (BIC) companies always wait for a supplier to respond. BIC companies emphasize the need for a quick response from their suppliers during contract negotiation and consider response time to be a part of a supplier's scorecard measures.

Depending on the type of business and its system capabilities, the material planning process will be reviewed either on a weekly or a daily basis. With each review, an EDC report (expedite, defer, cancel) is typically generated. An ECD report is used to communicate the status of all open (unfilled orders) schedules as reflected by the material planning system. An ECD highlights schedules that need to be expedited to meet new customer requirements, schedules that need to be

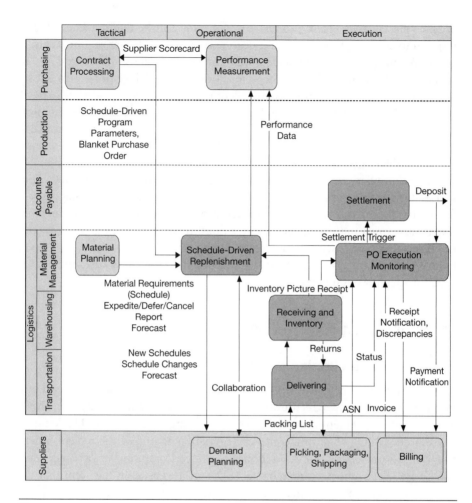

Figure 2.1. A Best Practices POM Process and Related Interactions in a Schedule-Driven Replenishment Program.

postponed or deliveries that do not need to be expedited because of a change in customer demand, and schedules that need to be canceled because demand no longer exists.

Material planners review the EDC report to obtain the status of all open schedules or POs that have not yet been received. The EDC report should also consider shipments that are in-transit and adjust expected delivery dates on the POs accordingly. (*Note*: Few systems are able to do this.)

Material planners may choose to not act on all EDC messages, either because of lack of time or because inaccuracies in inventory often result in inaccurate EDC messages. In this case, material planners will use their judgment to select EDC messages that need immediate action and then communicate with suppliers accordingly. Any deviation from a scheduled delivery or a requested date change will be entered manually in the material planning system.

Some buyer organizations communicate the EDC report to suppliers via e-mail in an Excel® format. Suppliers are then expected to provide the status for all open orders, respond to all EDC messages, and confirm that all orders due in the current week have been shipped or will arrive as required. A response to EDC messages is expected within 2 business days. Otherwise, failure to respond will indicate acceptance of the changes. Material forecast schedules are also generated by the material planning system and made available to suppliers for use in a supplier's demand planning system (see Figure 2.1). These forecast schedules are typically communicated to the supplier through fax, e-mail, or EDI 830 (an electronic version of a paper PO). *Comment*: BIC companies have automated this process, including replenishment triggering, and have enabled real-time collaboration between material planners and suppliers to eliminate waste and provide quick response to demand changes.

The primary drawback of schedule-driven replenishment is that it focuses mainly on economies of scale and price when generating an optimal purchase quantity. As a result, companies are driven to handle and store bulk quantities of raw materials, which can tie up significant capital, in addition to using assets and labor. By using schedule-driven replenishment, companies will often have suppliers with long lead times, which will limit their flexibility for any additional material requirements. Another drawback is dependency on highly accurate forecasting.

The schedule-driven replenishment program has now begun to rely heavily on Internet technologies for distribution of supply and demand information, which allows buyers and suppliers to coordinate their inventory decisions and streamline the flow of material across the supply chain. Relying on Internet technologies requires investment in new technologies and extensive change management efforts to convince business partners to share highly detailed information about their operations.

Internet technologies can improve the POM process at the operational level (the replenishment process) between suppliers and retailers. As an example, Ace Hardware, a $2.8 billion hardware retailer, has experimented with joint forecasting for stock replenishment with Manco, a supplier of tape, glue, and adhesive. Using Web-based software, Manco is permitted to have access to the database of Ace Hardware. Ace Hardware also provides its forecast for items to Manco through a Web browser. Ace Hardware and Manco can view their respective screens in real time and exchange electronic messages before reaching a forecast consensus. As a result, Manco has an opportunity to change a forecast before the forecast is given to their production planning system. Forecast accuracy is reviewed on monthly basis. In the past, forecast accuracy has been 80%, but now has improved to over 90% (Ballou 2004).

As another example, Cisco has embarked on a very ambitious project to create an electronic hub (e-hub) linking multiple tiers of suppliers via the Internet. The e-hub is intended to coordinate supply and demand planning across the supply chain using intelligent planning software. The e-hub will help identify potential supply and demand problems early, give adequate warning to the appropriate parties, and permit prompt resolution, all via the Internet. Grocery manufacturers such as Campbell Soup and Procter and Gamble and retailers such as Hannaford Brothers and H.E. Butt have also found that synchronized replenishment programs improve their inventory turns (Lee and Whang 2001).

Discrete Order Replenishment

A discrete order replenishment program is sometimes referred to by other names or acronyms such as "single PO" and "spot buy." Discrete order replenishment is appropriate for perishable and one-time-demand (or infrequent demand) material. Examples of perishable materials include fruits and vegetables, newspapers, and some pharmaceutical items that have short life cycles. Examples of infrequent or one-time-demand materials include fashion clothing, posters for political campaigns, and subassembly items for a defense project. Infrequent-demand items or one-time-demand items have a risk of obsolescence. Therefore the EOQ should consider the marginal loss that will result from not using this material. The discrete order replenishment program is also used when a supply source or the terms of an order need to vary from the norm. A purchasing department would typically manage discrete order replenishment POs. (*Note*: A material management department plays no role in a discrete order replenishment program.)

A BPO is not a prerequisite in the discrete order replenishment program (Figure 2.2). The price and shipping terms are communicated to suppliers on the PO. (*Note*: The case study in Chapter 3 will provide an example of discrete order replenishment.)

When using EDI, a buyer will send an EDI 850 to communicate a PO. A supplier will send an EDI 855 to acknowledge a PO. When an EDI supplier is ready to make a shipment, an EDI 856 will be sent as an ASN (advanced shipping notice).

VMI Replenishment

A vendor-managed inventory (VMI) replenishment program allows a supplier, in collaboration with a buyer, to manage and restock inventory items which are physically located at a buyer's facility (until these items are pulled from inventory for production). The VMI program is a mechanism by which a supplier creates POs based on demand information sent by a buyer. In VMI, a supplier delivers

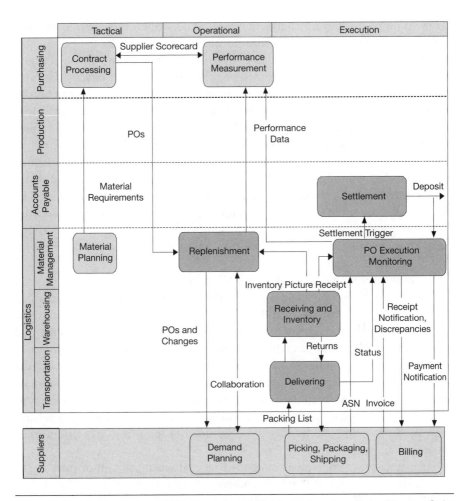

Figure 2.2. A Best Practices POM Process and Related Interactions in a Discrete Order Replenishment Program.

material ordered based on a view of the inventory consumption rate from a queue location in order to maintain a certain queue level of inventory. No pull-driven signal or PO is sent by a buyer to the supplier. Therefore, VMI is a reverse replenishment program in which a supplier creates a PO in addition to performing order fulfillment. The supplier is responsible for maintaining a certain level of safety stock for the buyer. In the retail industry, the buyer is even freed of forecasting responsibility and communicates only POS data.

After the supplier creates the PO based on the demand, the on-hand inventory picture, and safety stock levels, the PO cycle continues when the supplier sends an ASN just before shipping the product to the buyer's warehouse. Soon after shipping the product, the supplier sends an invoice to the buyer. After receiving the product, the buyer matches the invoiced quantity to the received quantity and then pays the supplier if there is no discrepancy. Typically the buyer takes ownership on delivery by the supplier. In some situations, suppliers retain both ownership and control over inventories of their products at a buyer's site. This arrangement is called "consignment." Consignment has proven to be an effective method to sell products that the buyer might not be willing to carry in inventory (e.g., in the retail industry). Obviously, the consignment arrangement is not a preferred one for the supplier because receiving payment takes longer.

Another variation of consignment is shipping material to a buyer's plant or warehouse and entering it into the buyer's ERP (enterprise resource planning) system at zero value. The supplier retains ownership, and the buyer has visibility, but the buyer does not assume ownership of the inventory. Once material from the inventory is pulled from the VMI stocking area for consumption, a receiving transaction is performed, ownership is transferred to the buyer, and payment for the subprocess is triggered.

The replenishment method in a VMI program is based on the min-max inventory control method and has historically been implemented and maintained using a manual process. (*Note*: In this book, the VMI method is considered to be an electronic or Internet version of the min-max method.) The min-max method is a variant of the continuous replenishment review policy with one difference— the replenishment quantity is the difference between the max inventory and the on-hand quantity when the inventory reaches the reorder point (min inventory). So, the replenishment quantity is not necessarily equal to the EOQ as in the continuous replenishment review policy because the amount by which the on-hand quantity drops below the reorder point is added to the EOQ. Max inventory is equal to ROP (min inventory) plus EOQ.

In a VMI program, replenishment is triggered when the sum of stock at the buyer's site, the in-transit material, and confirmed future shipments falls below the ROP. The ROP is determined by the safety stock values and average consumption over the replenishment lead time.

The min-max method is appropriate for "lumpy" demand, which is a condition often associated with slow-moving items (but is not necessarily limited to them). Lumpy demand can be identified when the standard deviation of demand over a period of time is greater than the average demand (Ballou 2004).

VMI improves visibility across the supply chain, increases material planning efficiency, reduces inventory, and improves stock availability. VMI is being widely used in the retail industry and for consumer-packaged goods, in which the end customer's demand for products is relatively stable and has short-term fluctuations in demand and supply. VMI has also been used in some industries for high-volume, small-size, or low-dollar-value items and for items that can be easily managed by suppliers.

Buyer Benefits of VMI

- Reduces inventory: a supplier reviews the inventory picture on a more-frequent basis, which reduces the safety stock levels
- Reduces shortages: a supplier takes responsibility for item availability and keeps track of inventory movement better when compared to a buyer who interacts with hundreds and sometimes thousands of suppliers
- Reduces stock-outs, which usually translates into increased sales
- Reduces inventory management activities such as daily monitoring, planning, and order processing

Supplier Benefits of VMI

- Reduces safety stocks at a supplier due to improved visibility
- Reduces PO discrepancy and errors: a supplier sees the potential need for an item before it occurs
- Strengthens partnerships and collaborations with buyers

Challenges and Limitations of VMI

- Incomplete and untimely visibility due to lack of effective system integration
- Inaccurate data about warehouse inventory balances from a buyer
- Inventory costs offloaded to a supplier if inventory not well managed
- Resistance and skepticism from employees

Overcoming the Limitations of VMI

- A buyer must stay engaged until the VMI program reaches its full potential.
- Capture supplier delivery performance, including stock-outs and performance against min-max target levels of inventory.
- In addition to providing projected consumption information, provide the current inventory of each VMI part with a supplier on a real-time basis, including both supplier-owned and buyer-owned counts at all stocking areas.
- Adopt an automated data transport method to exchange data on consumption confirmations, ASNs, inventory status, and forecasts.

Two Popular Variations of VMI

The type of VMI program used differs from buyer to buyer and from industry to industry, but two major variations are popular—inventory-driven VMI, which is used primarily by manufacturing companies and their suppliers (Figure 2.3), and

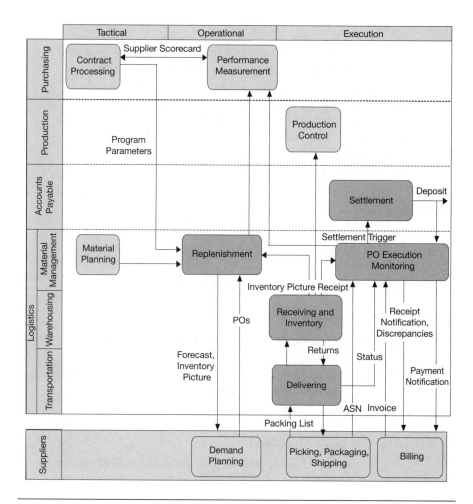

Figure 2.3. A Best Practices POM Process and Related Interactions in a VMI Replenishment Program: the Inventory-Driven Variation.

consumption-driven VMI, which is used by retailers and their suppliers (Figure 2.4). The differences between these two variations are based on the nature of a particular business and tend to promote the adoption of certain best practices in these sectors.

A consumption-driven VMI replenishment program is driven by usage or by POS rather than by inventory levels, which makes consumption-driven VMI replenishment more accurate than inventory-driven VMI replenishment. Typically retailers will assign forecasting responsibility to suppliers after providing visibility to their POS data. In inventory-driven VMI replenishment, manufacturers retain control over forecasting in most cases because multiple suppliers

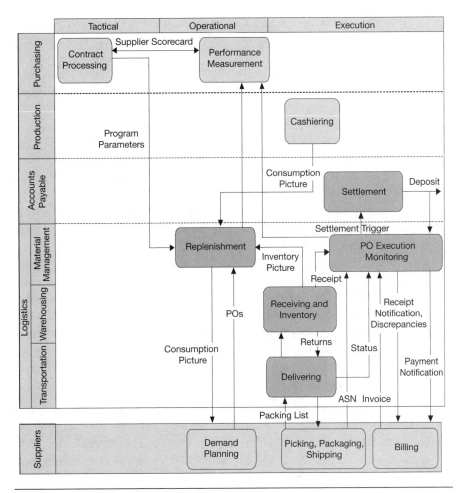

Figure 2.4. A Best Practices POM Process and Related Interactions in a VMI Replenishment Program: the Consumption-Driven Variation.

are often involved in making product delivery possible. Consumption-driven VMI replenishment is the preferred variation if the inventory at a buyer's site is inaccurate.

JIT Replenishment

The essence of the Just-in-Time (JIT) program is that a supplier, warehouse, or manufacturer will only deliver items as they are needed so that there is no excess inventory. Items required for final assemblies are pulled from a nearby supply storage area in small batches as they are needed. The main objective of JIT is to reduce or eliminate shortages and reduce inventory.

A most-popular method used for implementing the JIT replenishment program is by using Kanban (an acronym for Kan-card, Ban-signal; also KanBan). Historically, Kanban has been an internal manufacturing technique used to improve the efficiency of material movement. Kanban was originally developed at Toyota in the 1950s to manage material flow on assembly lines. Kanban is one of the more-visible tools that support a lean manufacturing environment.

Using Kanban limits the amount of work-in-process inventory by acting as an "authorization" for replenishment. Because Kanban is a supply chain process in which orders flow from one process to another, components are *pulled* to the production line, in contrast to the traditional forecast-oriented method in which parts are *pushed* to the production line. Parts or raw materials are delivered in containers such as bins, racks, or carts. Scanning of a barcode on an empty bin will trigger a replenishment request. If RFID tags are used, an empty bin returning to its shelf location will trigger replenishment.

The number of Kanbans in the replenishment loop between buyers and suppliers determines the amount of inventory being held in the supply chain as a buffer, so it is critical that the number of Kanbans is accurate. If the number of Kanbans is too low, too little inventory will be available to replenish the needs of the buyer's consuming warehouse or facility. Conversely, if the number of Kanbans is too high, the supply chain will have more inventory than is needed.

Leveraging Internet Technologies in a JIT Program

A JIT replenishment program that is enabled by Internet technologies can calculate optimal Kanban levels (the number of Kanbans and the quantity per Kanban) based on actual demand and lead times, allow rapid detection of exceptions, and flag significant changes in demand. A JIT replenishment program provides suppliers with visibility of a factory's true production schedule and consumption. If the JIT materials or other items are included in the planning review, and the corresponding demand forecast (procurement proposals) is created to provide a preview of future consumption (Figure 2.5), an Internet application can communicate demand forecast information to suppliers in real time. A JIT program enabled with Internet technologies provides other important inventory control benefits, including full automation, which reduces work and increases accuracy, and real-time replenishment communication to suppliers, which reduces planning and the PO cycle.

Using Internet technologies in a JIT program allows a buyer to "empty" Kanban containers directly over the Internet. The supplier has a clear overview of an item's stock level throughout the replenishment loop and can determine the quantities of the item that must be delivered. This type of replenishment communication replaces sending a Kanban card or some other type of order form to a

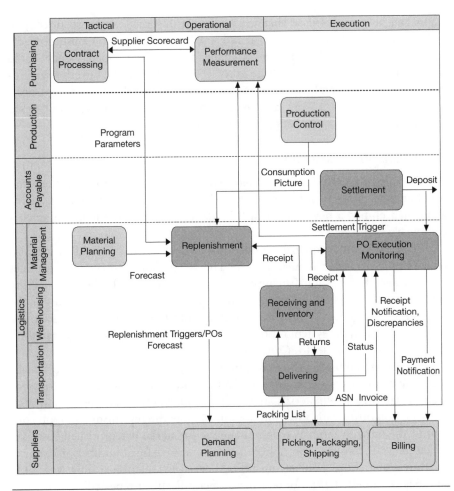

Figure 2.5. A Best Practices POM Process and Related Interactions in a JIT Replenishment Program.

supplier or returning empty containers to a supplier if delivered containers are a trigger for replenishment.

The supplier can also set the status of Kanbans to deliver to "In Process" directly over the Internet either manually by changing the flag from "Open" to "In Process" or by simply generating an ASN in the Internet application. In this way, buyers can know which Kanbans are to arrive with the next delivery.

Once the items or material are received by the buyer, and a receipt notification is sent out, the status of the Kanbans can be changed to "In Stock." In this way, buyers can confirm delivery quantities at any time of day for suppliers located all over the world. Once these Kanbans are consumed by the buyer, the status can be configured to change to either "Consumed" or to go directly to "Open" based on the business's need and supplier lead time. In "Consumed" status, an additional trigger is needed to change the status to "Open," which would indicate to a supplier that it is time to replenish. A user in the buyer's organization can also trigger replenishment manually by changing the status or replenishment can be triggered by a time-based event. When determining a time-based event, consider the required supplier lead time.

JIT Replenishment Variations

The one-bin (card) Kanban system. The one-bin Kanban system actually has two Kanbans in a replenishment loop. When a container to be replenished is about half empty, a new Kanban will be delivered before the first container is completely empty.

Tracking Kanban quantity. Individual quantities in the Kanban are also tracked in the one-bin Kanban system. The system stores the actual quantities received and the individual quantities withdrawn. When the Kanban quantity reaches zero, the one-bin Kanban system *automatically* sets the status of the Kanban to "Consumed." This process differs from the classic JIT replenishment program in which the system is not informed of the quantity in the Kanban until the status is *manually* set to "Consumed."

JIT replenishment without communicating forecast. Only the replenishment Kanban triggers are sent to suppliers for the materials included in this program variation. These materials are not planned for in the planning review.

Exact quantity. This variation does not follow the replenishment loop concept of the one-bin Kanban system. Requested material is replenished based on actual material consumption rather than from a predefined number of Kanbans or from a predefined Kanban quantity. Material is replenished only when it is specifically requested. It is not replenished periodically or repeatedly.

Key Points to Consider in JIT

The JIT program requires a strong partnership between a buyer and a supplier. During transition to a JIT delivery program, a buyer will work with a supplier(s) to make significant changes—from receiving large shipments of materials to receiving small shipments of materials, from placing monthly or weekly orders to placing multiple orders daily, and from unloading received orders in a central receiving facility to unloading received orders directly to the shop floor. Many buyers who adopt JIT will also try to implement the same type of JIT program on the outbound side of their operation, which is when they deliver finished goods to customers.

General Motors has implemented JIT delivery replenishment in one of its manufacturing plants. A receiving cross-dock was constructed near the assembly building to unpack the materials arriving from suppliers prior to moving these materials to an assembly line. A supplier's shipping location had to be no farther away than 300 miles, and the number of suppliers was reduced from thousands to hundreds. For example, one supplier was selected to be the sole provider of paint. In return this supplier was required to maintain an inventory near the assembly line. To increase the level of trust with the supplier, GM would provide the schedule of future automobile production to the paint supplier (Ballou 2004).

In the JIT replenishment program, a firm will carry materials in inventory for only a few hours of production, which will not accommodate delivery delays at the receiving dock. In JIT replenishment, if the transaction is by EDI, shipments often arrive at a firm before the corresponding ASN is received, which makes receiving shipments into the firm's system difficult and time consuming. The firm must enter shipment information manually instead of entering it (repopulating) from an ASN (due to late arrival of the corresponding ASN). A solution to this issue would be to improve ASN communication by enabling real-time integration between a supplier's and buyer's systems. Another effective alternative would be to include data-rich shipment details on the actual pallets by using RFID tags.

Buyers are often reluctant to implement JIT with suppliers because inventory variability may be reduced, but it cannot be eliminated. JIT replenishment with no inventory buffers also makes supply chains very fragile. Any slight interruption in the flow of materials could shut down an entire supply chain. Yet, obstacles such as these can be overcome by having visibility and collaboration between buyers and suppliers, which helps control variability.

Suppliers are also reluctant to join collaborative-type programs because of concerns that buyers will push inventory costs over to them. According to Hochman (2006), "A recent AMR Research study found that organizations were five times more likely to push inventory cost to their suppliers than they were to coinvest in demand pull. These companies are saving direct costs, but leaking profits to lost velocity."

Using the JIT replenishment program is not the answer for all industries. For example, JIT replenishment is not relevant for the process industry (e.g., gas, oil, and chemicals). Using JIT replenishment is also not the answer for supply chains that have low-volume products, new products, and uncertain-demand products.

Sequence-Driven Replenishment

Sequence-driven replenishment originated as a variation of the JIT replenishment program, which was introduced by automotive manufacturers and their suppliers in the early 1990s. Depending on the manufacturer and the industry, a sequence-driven replenishment program may be referred to by using other terms or acronyms such as ILVS (in-line vehicle sequencing) and JIS (Just in Sequence). In a sequence-driven program, suppliers not only deliver parts to buyers just in time, but they also deliver parts in an appropriate sequence to meet assembly requirements. Compared to JIT programs, sequence-driven replenishment programs require more sophisticated techniques to ensure that subassemblies and parts are loaded in the proper sequence for shipment.

In a vehicle production plant, the essence of a sequence-driven replenishment program is that as vehicle production is scheduled at a plant, the required parts and subassembly items from suppliers are sequenced-delivered and brought to an assembly line just in time to meet assembly requirements, which have been requested by the end customer. Although items in a JIT replenishment program are not referenced to the finished product and are not delivered in a sequence, in a sequence-driven replenishment program, suppliers ship items so that they are delivered in a particular sequence that is required by an assembly process and that is referenced to a specific end customer's finished product order.

Demand-based delivery requirements for finished products are referenced (pegged) against POs to provide traceability in a sequence-driven replenishment program. In some industries such as the chemical and pharmaceutical industries, POs are pegged to customer orders so that quality issues may be tracked.

For a sequence-driven replenishment program to be successful, a supplier's lead time should be short, e.g., between 2 and 5 hours, because the exact subassembly options and the required sequence of delivery for each required item may not be known until this time frame. A supplier's lead time includes sequencing, packing, loading, transit, unloading, moving, and the final subassembly of options, if any.

In a sequence-driven replenishment program, a buyer's forecast is communicated to Tier 1 suppliers to reduce the amount of uncertainty and to allow suppliers to smooth out demand on their facilities and to allocate their productive capacity to avoid buildup of excess inventories. Often suppliers are provided with additional information in order to support a buyer's program and better understand a buyer's needs, e.g., finished product demand (customer orders), in addition to the forecast for parts.

The real-time consumption picture (final assembly progress) is also communicated to suppliers in a sequence-driven replenishment program (Figure 2.6). By receiving feedback about what is actually happening at the buyer's assembly line, the supplier will be able to adjust their production line accordingly. Feedback information may also be used as a settlement trigger. For example, every product, such as a machine or vehicle, that passes the final stage on an assembly line will create a record of receipt for the related parts and subassemblies and will consequently generate a request to the buyer to trigger payment to the supplier.

Generally a sequence-driven program maximizes the buyer's floor space by minimizing the in-house space required for inventory, decreases the time a consumer (or end customer) waits for a new product, optimizes production efficiency,

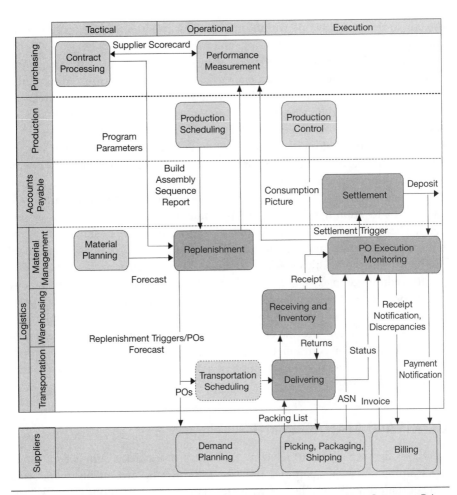

Figure 2.6. A Best Practices POM Process and Related Interactions in a Sequence-Driven Replenishment Program.

and reduces inventory levels being carried by the buyer and the supplier. For a supplier, a major benefit provided by build-in-sequence is maximized utilization of floor space because storage of only a minimal amount of finished goods is needed. A sequence-driven program is expected to expand quickly in the automotive industry to include shipping of more parts and subassemblies in sequence.

The Chrysler Group has implemented a sequence-driven program. Ordered parts will be delivered to a plant in same order (sequence) that vehicles are assembled. For example, the Chrysler Group will tell a vehicle seat supplier exactly when a particular seat will be needed by an assembly line as well as when the shipment of seats should be delivered. The seats will arrive on the floor and be delivered directly to the assembly line within minutes. This program eliminates secondary storage, reduces excess transportation, and minimizes inventory (Mayor 2004).

If a supplier does not have sufficient resources to implement a sequence-driven program in-house, the sequencing function will be outsourced to a third party for management. In this practice, the third-party sequencing/warehouse company receives products in batches from the supplier and then picks, packs, or assembles these items in sequence order before the items are shipped to the buyer. Loading of parts for shipping must be in reverse sequence (i.e., LIFO or last-in-first-out). The part needed for the first product or process on the buyer's assembly line will be loaded last so that it will become the first part to be unloaded at the buyer's receiving dock. The third-party sequencing/warehouse company is usually at a location that is within a 30-minute delivery time from the assembly plant. The company will also make more frequent deliveries of shipments to the buyer's assembly line. In a sequence-driven program, the buyer performs the final assembly process and ships the final product to the end customer.

To reduce complexity and provide real-time visibility, Internet technology should be leveraged in a sequence-driven program. The technology that supports a sequence-driven program should be able to communicate alerts to suppliers for conditions such as engineering changes, changes in assembly sequence on a production line, etc. in addition to supporting the entire business process from receipt of the forecast signal to creation of a delivery schedule to delivery confirmation by the supplier.

CONTRACT MANAGEMENT

Decisions that are related to selecting locations from which a supplier ships and determining shipping quantities (lot sizes), the timing of replenishments, and transportation methods affect POM performance. These decisions also affect the price paid, transportation costs, and inventory-carrying costs. Therefore decisions of this type should be negotiated carefully with a supplier(s) during the contract process and should be based on the replenishment program that is required for the contracted items.

Changing a destination location within a buyer's facility should be permitted by a supplier until the time of shipment to provide a buyer with flexibility to select the final destination for the shipment. Some buyers decide to bypass a cross-dock or warehouse location that has been stated on the BPO and ask a supplier or carrier to ship directly to an operations site to expedite receiving materials in case of shortages. Also common is the practice of diverting delivery of in-transit shipments to plant locations other than those that were originally specified on the PO as the destination (or as originally scheduled) to avoid material shortages or inventory buildup. Having this flexibility will increase transportation costs.

During contract negotiation, performance metrics related to execution should also be agreed upon. For example, the on-time-delivery metric could be defined as follows—the supplier will deliver material as requested on the PO (or per subsequent revisions to the PO), the correct and entire quantity will be delivered no later than the PO due date (if the supplier is responsible for transportation), and the shipment will have no defects. Therefore, a shipment with partial quantities, quality concerns, or issues that arise due to a lack of supporting documentation will not be considered to be an on-time-delivery shipment. This metric is sometimes referred to as "perfect order" percentage.

If the buyer is responsible for picking up ordered material from the supplier's site, on-time-delivery performance will be measured based on the ship date, which is the date the material leaves the supplier's dock or is available for pickup. Late shipments will be subject to a premium freight charge at the supplier's expense. If the supplier is responsible for transportation, delivery performance will be measured based on the due date. Suppliers should also be contractually required to proactively notify the buyer of any shipment that will not arrive or ship on time.

The tolerance level for "ship early" and "ship late" windows should also be negotiated during the contract process. Many buyers will allow suppliers to ship early so that suppliers will have an opportunity to optimize transportation. Compared to "ship early" deliveries, "ship late" deliveries are typically not tolerated; therefore, a "ship late" tolerance level is set at 0 (zero) days by many buyers.

Although delivery of defect-free goods is expected from a supplier, a common practice for a buyer and a supplier is to define the process of returning or repairing defective items. Typically an agreement between a buyer and a supplier will include a time period after delivery during which defective items will be replaced at no charge to the buyer.

The payment process, which includes the timing, frequency, and terms of payment, is also part of contract negotiation and is mutually agreed upon beforehand by the buyer and the supplier. For example, payment of an invoice might be calculated from the date that an acceptable invoice which conforms to the PO is received in the buyer's accounts payable department or from the date of receipt of acceptable goods at the buyer's warehouse, whichever is later. Other methods include paying the supplier on a monthly basis by summing up the total amount of all invoices due that month or by paying the supplier when the invoice is due.

Because suppliers typically benefit from economies of scale, suppliers frequently encourage buyers to purchase large quantities by offering lower prices for large-quantity orders. Yet buyers want to have the best possible price, but not to receive delivery of the full amount purchased at one time. Therefore, having a BPO contract with a predetermined total unit quantity (or dollar amount) for a specific item (or set of items) and with a specified time frame allows the buyer to request delivery of the exact item needed and the exact quantity needed throughout the year (or specified time frame). This arrangement is a good formula for both the buyer and the supplier. For the buyer, a lean replenishment philosophy, which strives to eliminate inventory, can be adopted, yet the benefit of volume buying and related discounted prices can also be obtained. For the supplier, better planning is facilitated because future overall purchases by the buyer are known.

During contract negotiations, the best practice for the sourcing manager in a buying organization is to focus on the lowest total cost, not the lowest price. Total cost includes not only the unit cost of materials, but also transportation, handling and storage, and other related cost implications such as obsolescence, spoilage, loss, etc. Understanding the total (true) cost of purchased materials will often change the equation used to make sourcing decisions.

When all of these considerations are carefully thought out, purchasing in different environments will require different relationships and different types of contracts with suppliers, which are not based solely on unit cost and supplier quality. Therefore, during negotiation of a contract agreement or when changing from one replenishment program to another, address policies and procedures such as:

- Define a standard agreement. If possible, apply standard terms across all suppliers. Each partner to the agreement should clearly understand the risks and the rewards of the new replenishment program.
- Discuss how the replenishment program should function. Try to anticipate likely events that could impact the flow of product or information and decide how each party to the agreement should react.
- Define a standardized process for sharing production and forecast information that theoretically should result in maintaining a lower inventory in the supply chain.
- Communicate joint metrics clearly with each partner. A variety of metrics are used. Some common ones include:
  - Fill rate (availability)
  - Quality rate
  - Inventory turns
  - Lead times
  - Forecast accuracy
- Identify a team of executives that represents the buyer and the supplier. This team will actively participate in periodic review meetings to discuss the results of the joint metrics and any process issues.
- Consider the supplier's scorecard at the time of contract renewal (see Figure 2.6).
- Keep contract and price terms up-to-date. Synchronize contract and price terms across different buyer systems.

- Automate creation and maintenance of accurate supplier and buyer performance scorecards.
- Define a process to support a smooth transition from one replenishment program to another.
- Negotiate with suppliers to maintain sufficient inventory levels to support supply and demand variations.

The above procedures and policies can be applied to all replenishment programs. In addition, each replenishment program will have its own specific policies, which should be considered and agreed upon before activating the program. Operational policy decisions that will be required to activate VMI and JIT replenishment programs will now be provided.

Procedures and Policies for VMI Replenishment

- Select the parts and the appropriate supplier to be placed in the VMI program.
- Negotiate contract issues typically associated with VMI:
  - Material liability (particularly which party will be responsible for obsolete inventory)
  - Freight liability
  - Ownership liability (i.e., the time when the title to goods actually transfers from supplier to buyer and when a VMI shipment is considered for payment, e.g., at the time of receipt or when consumed)
  - Min-max inventory levels that the supplier is to support
  - Expected response time
- Location of VMI stocks (e.g., at the buyer's plant or at a third-party warehouse)
- Mechanism to pull inventory from the VMI stock area
- How the entire VMI program cycle is supported in the replenishment system

Procedures and Policies for JIT Replenishment

- Set the replenishment quantity using the classic ROP method of inventory control.
- Calculate the optimal number of Kanbans in the replenishment loop based on actual demand and lead times.
- Develop a system to trigger replenishment.
- Negotiate with the supplier to reduce lead time.
- Determine the personnel who will need training.

Full truckloads (FTLs) are seldom used in JIT replenishment programs. Therefore logistics managers at the supplier need to become accustomed to shipping smaller lots (or quantities) of material when switching to a JIT environment. Using third party logistics (3PL) companies (to share and integrate loads) and freight forwarders and consolidators (for international and cross-border shipments) are two methods that allow smaller lots to be shipped at the same cost per unit as larger loads and reduce the costs associated with storing and handling bulk shipments.

MATERIAL PLANNING

A material planning process determines the net requirements for purchase proposals of raw material and other items by calculating the difference between total material requirements and the quantities of materials on hand. Some of these purchase proposals will then be translated into POs if they fall within the supplier's lead time. (*Note*: This type of purchase proposal is primarily for items that are in schedule-driven or single-order replenishment programs.) The remainder of the purchase proposals will be communicated to suppliers as forecasts.

Material planning applications that are based on advanced planning and scheduling (APS) logic are very helpful in determining the most effective way to execute production schedules with respect to material plan constraints. APS applications identify material shortages, capacity overloads, and bottlenecks before production is affected. They enable a manufacturer to change a plan, to adjust the capacity, or to expedite material to fulfill the plan.

Forecasts for raw material and other items are generated by the material planning process and are made available at least once a week. Forecasts are typically presented to a supplier in an Excel® format via e-mail or are made available via a website. Forecasts are used by a supplier to help predict future material requirements and to understand the in-house capacity requirements of a buyer. (*Note*: All forecasts are subject to change and are wholly dependent on customer demand.)

Certain finished products require items that have long lead times in the supply chain. Therefore a buyer is forced to place POs with suppliers well in advance of the receipt of an end customer's order (i.e., demand for the product). In this situation, an alternative would be to have different states (conditions to be met) in the forecast to address this situation. For example, the forecast can have a "material authorization" state to allow a supplier to place orders with their suppliers (Tier 2). In this case, the buyer will be responsible for the cost of material even if a forecast does not translate into a PO. Another state would be to authorize a supplier to start production based on a forecast that has a required due date that is close. The forecast is therefore more certain to become a firm PO. Once an end customer order is received, a forecast will be converted into a PO.

Based on the replenishment program being used, additional forecast states might be provided as a requested forecast schedule progresses until it becomes a PO or the supplier is authorized to ship (triggered schedule). The life cycle of a sequence-driven forecast schedule is considered to be the most comprehensive (complex) compared to other replenishment programs:

- Planning: A long-term forecast is developed by the material planning process.
- Material purchasing authorization: The forecast state is an authorization for a supplier to purchase the material needed. This authorization considers Tier 1 supplier lead time plus Tier 2 supplier lead time. Supplier lead time is the production and/or processing lead time plus transit time between a supplier's facility and a buyer's facility. Sequence lead time is included in processing lead time.
- Commitment: The forecast state is an authorization for a supplier to start fabricating an item. It considers only Tier 1 supplier lead time, which could range from 1 to 4 months.
- Frozen schedule: A buyer's production/assembly schedule is firm (no changes anticipated) and will have minimal variation during the next 5 to 20 days. In this state, a forecast is typically converted into POs and pegged to a customer order, but a supplier is not yet authorized to ship.
- Shift schedule: POs related to the next shift's production schedule are highlighted and put into a different state, which allows a supplier to be prepared to react.
- Triggered: A supplier will be authorized to ship materials. A supplier's sequenced lead time includes sequencing time, packing time, loading time, transit time, unloading time, and moving time. Authorization to ship will consider a supplier's sequenced lead time. In many cases, a supplier's sequenced lead time is within a shift's scheduled lead time (2 to 5 hours).

TRANSPORTATION SCHEDULING

Transportation scheduling focuses on the routing and scheduling of transportation equipment to optimize vehicle and driver utilization while still meeting customer service requirements (Bowersox and Closs 1996). When considering available alternatives, a favored delivery service (i.e., a combination of carrier, route, and transportation mode) will be the one that provides the lowest cost, but also meets the customer's requirements.

The first objective of transportation scheduling is to minimize transportation costs by reducing the mileage required to deliver a product and to build optimal loads by reducing the number of occurrences of partial loads as well as loads that leave full but come back empty. The second objective is to communicate a validated/detailed transportation plan to carriers, which requires several types of data:

- Demand requirements, which include customer pickup and delivery requirements
- Operational constraints, such as the maximum available number of trucks, truck capacity, and weight restrictions, driver constraints, and operating costs
- Carrier and hub selection data (e.g., carriers can be in categories such as common carriers, contract carriers, private carriers, and agents)
- Routing network, which captures all possible routes and transportation modes (e.g., air, rail, truck, water, and pipe)

Over a long distance, air transportation is generally fast and has a fair degree of relative variability (Ballou 2004). Air transportation is usually chosen for very high-value or time-sensitive products. In some cases, air transportation is also used for very small-sized products. Rail is commonly used for low-value and large-size products, including many raw materials. Trucks are used for moderate-value and time-sensitive products and to deliver products to an end customer who cannot be reached directly by other modes of transportation. Water is primarily used for international shipments, whereas pipe is limited to oil, natural gas, and petroleum products. Pipe is very slow, but reliable.

Transportation scheduling and service selection can either be a buyer's responsibility (see Figure 2.6), a supplier's responsibility, or be controlled by a 3PL provider (if the transportation function is outsourced). Transportation scheduling and service selection might be also a combination of all three options based on different products and business units. Therefore the transportation scheduling and service selection function is shown as a dotted-line box in Figure 2.6. BIC companies consider service selection to be a joint decision between a buyer and a supplier.

The best practices process of transportation scheduling should be able to achieve the following:

- Reduce transportation costs and improve customer service by finding the best route that a load should follow through the use of a network of roads, rail lines, water, or air
- Support different variations of routing problems such as multiple origin and destination points

- Incorporate all transportation restrictions and special extensions, such as maximum legal total driving time, lunch breaks for drivers, stops, and time windows for pickups and deliveries
- Coordinate transportation resources across different business units and support a common database for all transportation data
- Encourage companies to ship in large quantities (freight consolidation) when possible (e.g., when the customer delivery time window is not violated), by consolidating small shipments into large ones to achieve lower transportation cost per unit of weight

Freight consolidation can be achieved through use of demand consolidation in which demand for an item across multiple time buckets (specific time intervals) is consolidated into one shipment. For example, if a buyer has a daily demand for 10 pieces, and the time window for early receipt is 3 days, a supplier can ship 30 pieces in the first shipment if they are available. Another method is load consolidation in which less-than-a-load shipments are consolidated into one load. Hub consolidation is still another option which allows the transportation of full loads over long distances and the transportation of less-than-full loads over short distances.

SUMMARY

If best practices to improve the POM process at the operational level are implemented as discussed in this chapter, the loop between contract negotiation, material planning, transportation scheduling, and PO execution can be closed to facilitate a lean and agile supply chain,

Chapter 3 will now discuss the PO at the execution level. Chapter 3 includes a case study from a large telecommunication company and describes the needed technology capabilities to support best practices in the POM process.

REFERENCES

Ballou, H. *Business Logistics/Supply Chain Management, Fifth Edition.* Upper Saddle River, NJ: Prentice Hall; 2004.

Bowersox, D. and Closs, D. *Logistical Management: Integrated Supply Chain Process.* McGraw-Hill; 1996.

Hochman, S. *The Lean Supply Chain.* Boston: AMR Research; 2006 June 8. Available at: <http://www.amrresearch.com/Content/View.asp?pmillid= 19510>.

Lee, H. and Whang S. *E-Business and Supply Chain Integration.* Stanford, CA: Stanford Global Supply Chain Management Forum at Stanford University; 2001 November, pp. 1–20.

Mayor, T. The supple supply chain. *CIO Magazine;* 2004 August. Available at: <http://www.cio.com/archive/081504/supply.html>.

3

POM AT THE
EXECUTION LEVEL

PO EXECUTION

The main objective of a purchase order management (POM) best practices process is to streamline direct material replenishment (see Chapter 2) and purchase order (PO) execution between a buyer and a supplier by electronic collaboration. The PO process includes several key steps (Figure 3.1). Material replenishment is included in Steps 1 through 3. (See Chapter 2 for a complete discussion of these steps.) Steps 4 through 10 involve PO execution, which is the subject of this chapter (Figure 3.2):

Step 1. Replenishment signals are triggered to suppliers based on consumption information, an inventory "picture," or electronic data interchange (EDI) messages.

Step 2. POs or schedules are issued and communicated to suppliers.

Step 3. Suppliers acknowledge and confirm with buyers the availability of items and the delivery of items.

Step 4. Suppliers prepare items for shipping, plan logistics, and contact carriers.

Step 5. Advanced ship notifications (ASNs) are sent to buyers by suppliers.

Step 6. In-transit status notification and exception detection are performed by suppliers.

Step 7. Materials are received by buyers.

Step 8. Returns, if any, are monitored by buyers.

Step 9. Settlements (e.g., invoices and payments) are conducted by buyers.

Step 10. Delivery performance is captured by buyers.

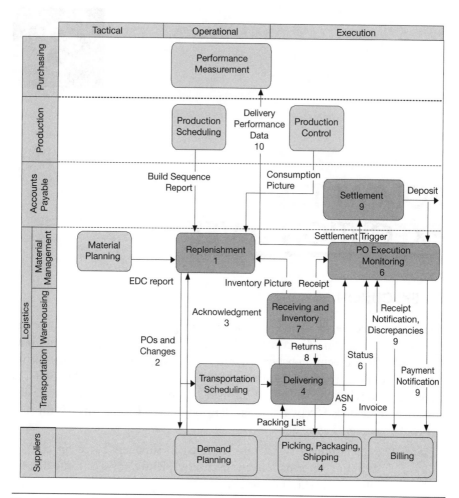

Figure 3.1. Best Practices: POM at Operational and Execution Levels.

PO Format

A PO has at least two levels—header and line. The header level contains supplier information, such as remit to and purchased from information, PO dates, payment terms, buyer information, and other information that is valid for all of the line items on the PO. The line level contains information about the items on the PO, e.g., item description, quantity ordered, unit cost, unit of measure, request date, and promised date. At each level, there are certain required fields that a buyer must fill in before sending out a PO. These fields include delivery schedules, terms of payment, unit of measure, method of shipping, and schedules for any noninventory items. (*Note*: Noninventory items represent items that are not part of

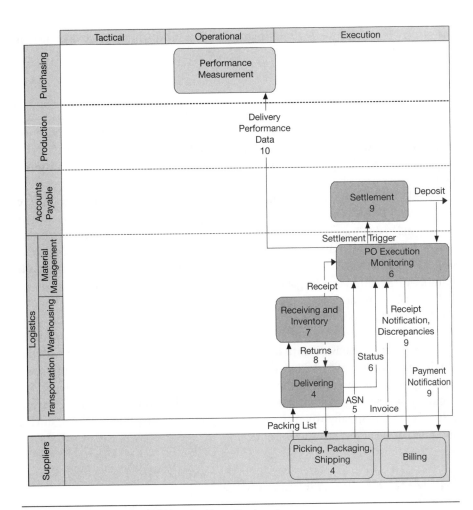

Figure 3.2. Best Practices: POM at the Execution Level.

inventory management or the item master (a catalog of all items) such as services and business expenses.) At each level, optional fields can be used to communicate additional information such as reason codes, postal codes, country, state, FOB (or free on board), and comments. Required and optional fields vary depending on firm and industry.

FOB terms are used to indicate the point in the delivery of merchandise at which ownership of the goods transfers from the supplier to the buyer. Typically a buyer takes title to the goods and becomes responsible for any freight charges incurred after the FOB point. Several alternatives are available in FOB pricing. The most popular ones are the FOB factory policy, in which the price is quoted at the factory level, and the FOB destination policy, in which the price is quoted at the destination level.

BPO

A blanket purchase order (BPO) is a shortcut method for ordering items that a supplier will deliver to a buyer over a period of time. A BPO permits a buyer to take advantage of volume discounts without having to commit to a specific time frame for delivery of goods. A BPO permits a supplier to achieve better planning by having better visibility of future demand.

A BPO is typically not used in a discrete order replenishment program (see Chapter 2) in which the need for a strong engagement with a supplier has not yet been established; however, a BPO is heavily used in other replenishment programs in which long-term relationships are required. A BPO contains the same information as a standard discrete PO. Other information may include the maximum number of POs that can be generated, the maximum dollar amount that will be allowed, and contract information.

When a standard PO is generated from a BPO, the amount and quantities that are selected to generate a standard PO will be deducted from the open amounts and quantities on the BPO until no remaining open quantities are left or until the maximum number of specified POs have been met. When no remaining open quantity remains on a BPO, the BPO status changes to "closed." Some buyers decide to not specify a quantity or dollar amount limit on a BPO. In this case, a BPO is closed manually when there is no pegged (specified) demand and after a supplier has been given sufficient notice.

SHIPMENT DELIVERY PREPARATION

The process of picking/pulling, packing, rating, palletizing, loading, shipping, and documenting an item is known as shipment delivery preparation. Shipment delivery preparation also includes solving problems associated with last-minute changes and expedited shipments, goods that suddenly become damaged or are missing, and carrier's equipment/traffic problems. The owner of (or the entity who is responsible for) each of these activities varies from business to business. At times, a supplier is responsible for picking, packing, and shipping, but a buyer's private carrier is responsible for the remainder of the activities as shown in Figure 3.2. In other cases, a third-party logistics provider is responsible for all of these activities. However, if a supplier has its own delivery fleet, the supplier will most likely be responsible for delivery from the supplier's location to a buyer's receiving site.

Shipment delivery preparation is tightly integrated with transportation scheduling to execute an optimal load plan that will be generated during transportation scheduling and to eliminate guesswork and approximations because actual item dimensions and weight are used for palletizing and container loading.

In tight integration of the transportation scheduling process, freight loads are prepared and sent to carriers for confirmation of service and rates. Once a carrier is selected, an advanced shipment notice (ASN) can automatically be generated and sent to a buyer because all needed information is available at this stage. If a supplier needs to enter additional information or to review information before a shipment is sent out, the transportation scheduling system should support this step.

ASN

A supplier is expected to send an advanced shipment notice (ASN) immediately after material has been shipped. Therefore an ASN is generated and transmitted when a truck leaves the shipping dock. Generation and transmission of an ASN can be achieved online by a supplier by simply sending electronic information about a shipment. An ASN is typically sent by a supplier when an actual shipment is made based on an open PO. Key attributes of an ASN include:

- Shipment identification number (SID)
- Bill of lading
- Packing slip number
- Shipment time, reflecting the supplier's time zone
- Cumulative year-to-date shipped quantity (for a BPO)
- Gross weight
- Net weight
- Number and type of containers
- Total packages
- Transportation method
- Transport carrier ID
- Tracking number
- Estimated departure date
- Estimated arrival date
- Shipping days (if this area is filled in, "estimated arrival date" can be calculated)
- Line item number
- Part number
- Quantity shipped

An ASN has a vital role in providing status information that allows a buyer to view which shipments are in process (en route) and to perform better planning. Generally ASN information is created at the time a shipment is being prepared, just prior to sealing and shipping a package. Sending the ASN is the last step prior to a transportation carrier picking up the shipment for delivery to a buyer's site or warehouse.

The PO number and other specific identification information should appear clearly on all documents, e.g., shipping notices, bills of lading, packing lists, and other papers, and on each package, box, bundle, or other type container. All goods are to be packaged and adequately packed to ensure arrival at the destination in an undamaged condition. All international shipments must be boxed and otherwise protected to prevent damage in transit and to meet all export shipping requirements (if required).

If a supplier is responsible for delivery, the supplier assumes risk for the equity in the materials being supplied under the terms of the PO or contract. Insurance is typically in place in an amount that is at least equal to the value of the materials. Unless otherwise instructed, a supplier who is responsible for delivery usually prepays all transportation and related shipping charges and itemizes these charges on the invoice or on the ASN (e.g., if an ASN is used to trigger payment). In the absence of specific routing instructions, the default route for shipments is to be made "best way."

Unless otherwise agreed to in writing, a supplier should not be allowed to make material commitments or production arrangements in excess of the amount ordered or in advance of the time necessary to meet a buyer's delivery schedule. Many buyers specify explicitly in the contract that goods shipped to them in advance of a schedule or in advance of a PO may be returned at the supplier's expense or payment of invoices may be withheld until the required delivery date, unless authorization is granted by the buyer for an advanced delivery. The same applies to partial shipments of goods for which no partial shipment is specified in the PO or contract. These materials may be returned to the shipper at the supplier's expense or payment of invoices may be withheld until the order is complete, unless specific authorization has been granted for partial delivery.

Although suppliers are not authorized to ship materials without a valid schedule or a PO, some suppliers may still do so at times for many reasons. This situation is a major trouble point in existing POM processes because tracing and matching the shipment will be very difficult. This troublesome issue may be addressed by allowing a supplier to propose a new schedule or to obtain a new PO. Approval of a new schedule or new PO by a buyer will be considered to be an authorization for a supplier to ship materials.

A buyer's internal system is used to store and validate the ASN information sent by a supplier. Depending on the source of the error, if for any reason there is an error in validation, the supplier and the buyer are to receive notification informing them of the error, typically by e-mail. A supplier can resubmit an ASN and other rounds of validation may take place until there are no errors.

If a subprocess is automated and a supplier uses an Internet application to generate an ASN, the best practices would be to validate the ASN before sending it to a buyer. A supplier could fix any mismatch immediately, which will allow a buyer to receive a valid and "clean" ASN quickly. Some items typically checked include:

- Valid PO (i.e., a PO is in the system)
- Valid part (the part number on the ASN line item is also on the PO in the system)
- Valid quantity (the quantity on the ASN line item is also the quantity on the PO in the system) (*Note*: If undershipments are allowed by the buyer, a PO may be submitted for payment, but an e-mail must be sent by the suppler or an alert must be generated on the supplier's website indicating that the quantity is an undershipment.)
- The tracking number and bill of lading number fields

Many times, e.g., in an international shipment, a buyer will require additional status notifications about in-transit shipments, particularly when shipments go through several stops or modes of transportation. A carrier should be able to provide this type of notification to a buyer, either directly or indirectly through a supplier. Some suppliers also ask a carrier for proof of delivery (POD) from a buyer as a prerequisite for payment of delivery services, which makes status visibility mandatory to complete an order-to-cash cycle. (*Note*: Many technologies such as RFID have recently evolved to support status communication and visibility, which will be discussed in Part II.)

RECEIPTS

After a PO is issued and goods or services are delivered, a receipt will be recorded. One or more receipts may be recorded for each PO. Therefore a receipt must have a header and at least one receipt line record. Typically payments are processed by comparing the receipt records with the PO and then with the invoice, i.e., there is a three-way match. The accounts payable function will not authorize payment unless a complete quantity has been received or a partial shipment/receipt is allowed. (*Note*: Partial receipts and multiple invoices are common.)

Before processing receipts, the quantities received, the units of measure on the receipts, and associated receipt weights and volumes for all items are typically checked based on the original PO. Receiving generally occurs in a specific warehouse. Generating a receipt includes the following steps:

- Select an item that has been received from an existing PO for inclusion on the receipt document. Typically the system can only receive shipments for valid POs. (*Note*: Opening a closed PO or schedule can be handled in a system as an exception that only an authorized person can resolve.)

- Alternatively, prepopulate the receipt with items on the PO automatically. The user can then manually enter the count of items received.
- A third option is to prepopulate the receipt with items and quantities on the PO automatically. The user can then override a received quantity if needed.
- Compare/match the quantities on the receipt to the quantities on the associated PO. If an item is received and is not on the associated PO, that item must be added to the PO before the item can be documented as "received." Otherwise the item must be sent back to the supplier, with the supplier paying for return freight.
- Register/post the receipt, which includes printing the receipt and posting the invoice information.

Matching a receipt to a PO can be done based on predefined tolerance codes. The purpose of tolerance codes is to define the degree to which the quantity of items, the cost of items, and the delivery date may deviate from the PO when receiving goods or processing invoices. For each tolerance code, the following can be determined:

- The amount (or percentage) that the total purchased amounts, unit costs, or received amounts cannot exceed or fall below
- The minimum receivable quantity percentage needed to automatically close a receipt line during receiving
- The maximum number of days earlier than or later than the PO due date in which the shipment may be received
- The action to take if a transaction does not meet the defined tolerance criteria during the matching process

RETURNS

At times items are damaged during shipment. At times items are incorrectly shipped or a buyer incorrectly orders items. Poor handling of returns can cause dissatisfaction for a supplier and a buyer. Additionally, costs associated with returned items can decrease profit margins. Therefore, this subprocess must be automated and managed in a timely manner. Coordinated management of item returns and shipping of replacement products or repaired products can help address these issues. By capturing returns information, an organization (buyer, supplier, or carrier) may also perform root cause analysis to determine trends or common reasons for why products are being returned and then be better prepared to take corrective actions.

If items are rejected, the buyer will communicate this rejection to the supplier. The location of the items determines the type of action that is required by the supplier. Parts rejected by an incoming inspection process will need to be replaced on the existing PO. A debit memo with a unique identifier (ID) must be created to track the return of the goods to the supplier. If the PO is closed, the system will have to automatically reopen the order and the PO line to allow the return and to show that the replacement items must be considered to be due immediately. In this case, the buyer's accounts payable function should be able to exclude the defective quantities when the supplier is paid based on the invoice. Once the replacement items are received by the buyer, another invoice will be expected to be paid.

Parts that are rejected during an assembly or fabrication process, for example, and for which an accurate PO number cannot be determined (traced) will require replacement by either the next open PO or a new PO. The method used, the actual quantity, and the timing of delivery for any replacement part will be determined and communicated to the supplier. All replacements will also default to a premium freight shipping method. Additionally, a debit memo must be created to track the return of the goods to the supplier. Entering the bill of lading number and a reason for the return is recommended when a buyer is returning items.

If a buyer determines that the rejected parts can be repaired onsite and that the timing of the repairs meets the buyer's production requirements, all arrangements for the repair activity and any subsequent charges is typically coordinated through the buyer's purchasing department. However, if the buyer decides that there is no immediate need for replacement, e.g., because of sufficient existing inventory, the defective items will be returned to the supplier for credit. In some situations, the supplier will ask the buyer to scrap the rejected items and to not return them to save the cost of return transportation, particularly for low-value items.

Best-in-class (BIC) POM solutions should allow the defining of each item in the item master table as being "returnable" or "not returnable." (*Note*: A solution is a combination of a process and enabling technology.) A BIC solution should also allow for return of goods for credit or replacement, to allow differentiating between repairable and nonrepairable return items, and to support scrapping or repair onsite. A BIC solution should also have the capability to backtrack to the original PO or invoice and record a reason code for returns, in addition to integration with an accounts payable function to create debit memos for returned items. This allows the organization to ensure that processing of return or credit memos can be directly linked to a previous purchase, which helps avoid situations in which a buyer returns a product to the wrong supplier; to have data available that provides an ability to perform analysis of potential problem areas; and to achieve efficient and timely management of returns.

The process of shipping a replacement item by the supplier while the buyer is returning the original item should also be supported by the solution. Invoicing the buyer for the replacement product if the buyer has paid the total invoice should not be necessary. If the items to be returned have not been received by the supplier within the specified lead time, a BIC solution should allow the supplier to create an invoice for the replacement items, which ensures that the buyer will be charged for the replacement items if the buyer does not return the original items. A return summary report should be generated on demand or on a regular basis and should contain the following information:

- Supplier's name
- Returned from
- Return date
- Return type
- Return status
- Return number
- Return line number
- Item quantity returned
- Unit of measure
- Unit cost
- Reason

In summary, reverse logistics (or returns) are generally underemphasized. On average, almost 20% of all goods are returned. Inefficient management of returns can inflate inventory levels and erode profits. Firms should automate processing of returns upon receipt (including inspection and disposition), speed up the process to reduce risk of obsolescence, and track reverse logistics and net asset recovery to improve effectiveness.

SETTLEMENT

Step 9, the settlement step, is a mechanism by which the user/buyer verifies receipt of goods or services, the supplier bills (or invoices) for the delivery of goods or services, and the buyer's accounting system issues a check to the supplier or deposits money in the supplier's account. The settlement step also includes a match between the PO and the receipt (a two-way match) or a match between the PO, the receipt, and the invoice (a three-way match). Payments are made based on approved invoices.

The buyer's accounts payable function is typically responsible for the overall settlement subprocess (see Figure 3.1), which includes invoice reconciliation and payment. (*Note*: Unlike other subprocesses or functions in POM, the settlement subprocess has remained a manual process, in which Internet technologies have not been successfully leveraged to result in transformation.) The importance of the settlement subprocess stems from its ability to facilitate payment to the supply base, manage cash flow, earn early payment discounts, avoid duplicate payments or late penalties, avoid fraud by tracking compliance to audit controls (e.g., as in the Sarbanes-Oxley Act), and to enforce budget and contract conformity. The best practices for the accounts payable function and the related Internet technology will provide the settlement subprocess with an underlying platform that enables buying organizations to allow the enterprise to consistently and efficiently receive, validate, approve, and pay suppliers' invoices.

The use of electronic integration, messaging, reconciliation, and reporting solutions in the accounts payable process could reduce transaction costs by 63 to 67%. Yet only 3% of accounts payable processes report having a high-level of automation (Pikulik 2005b). Key challenges to transformation of the settlement subprocess include (Pikulik 2005a):

- Executives being unaware of the vital importance of settlement in cash management, collecting discounts/rebates, conducting spend analysis, reporting compliance information, and maintaining strong supplier relationships
- Managers typically being in a reactive mode: Managers "chase paper" and repeat transactional tasks instead of focusing on resolving root issues.
- The reconciliation and dispute resolution step expanding across several functions and entities such as purchasing, accounts payable, suppliers, and material planning department, but having no sole responsibility or performance metric owner for this step
- The accounts payable department inheriting supplier problems and distrust and being the last department to receive budget funds for business process improvement, automation, or data management

BIC e-Settlement

A BIC e-settlement solution is achieved by streamlining and automating the settlement subprocess, which simplifies billing management, eliminates manual handling, and removes direct paper invoices. Users can simply send an e-mail with an invoice attached, typically in a .PDF format, and gain access to invoices online for viewing. An e-settlement solution contains the following five major steps or elements:

- Settlement trigger receipt: includes receiving a paper invoice, an electronic invoice receipt in EDI, .xml, .csv, or some other file format, or the receipt signal, e.g., such as in the ERS settlement program
- Approval and verification: includes approval processing workflows, rule-based routings and approval hierarchies, invoice format and content verification, and exception flags resulting from discrepancies or delays

- Validation and reconciliation: includes matching of price, terms, quantities, discounts, and service level and contract compliance; supports reconciliation with real-time dispute resolution workflows
- Payment: includes selection of the most appropriate payment method, e.g., check, wire, etc., in addition to optimizing taxation, discounts, rebates, and international trade financing
- Reporting and analysis: includes the importance of assisting executives in assessing the operational performance of the settlement subprocess by evaluating payment cycle times, compliance rates, contract performance, payment penalties, and other factors (*Note*: BIC solutions provide role-based dashboards for these types of performance measures.)

BIC e-settlement solutions should also be able to support the automated generation of reports required by the Sarbanes-Oxley Act and by industry, tax, and other reporting requirements. BIC e-settlement solutions should also support e-mail alerts, escalations, and process triggers based on predefined milestones (e.g., payments) and thresholds (e.g., volume, termination dates), in addition to supporting performance-based analysis of contract terms (Pikulik 2005b).

Each of the five elements can be coordinated independently, depending on the organization, the process, transactions, or supplier constraints. Therefore, companies can outsource one or more of these elements for economic reasons without affecting the performance. Yet the settlement subprocess depends on several touch points (i.e., integration points with other related subprocesses) that should be considered carefully when outsourcing. Touch points can include purchasing integration, budget and contracts integration, bank integration, and supplier data.

According to Pikulik (2005b), several success stories describe substantial benefits that have been realized from implementing best practices invoice reconciliation and payment frameworks:

- Invoice processing cost reductions of 30 to 60%
- Processing cycle time reductions of 65%
- Head count reductions of 25 to 40%
- Increases in on-time payments earning discounts of up to 500%

ERS

Evaluated receipts settlement (ERS) is a settlement program used by purchasing professionals to eliminate the manual cost of processing and reconciling supplier invoices. ERS coordinates shipment receipts and supplier payments without using invoices. By using ERS, a receiving department can scan a barcode or read an

RFID tag associated with an arriving shipment to electronically verify the existence of a PO. Payment can then be authorized for the exact quantity received, based on the price on the PO or contract, with no need for an invoice from the supplier.

In a conventional account payables process, a three-way exact match must exist between an existing PO, the invoice, and the receipt. Otherwise, an invoice discrepancy will be created, which must be resolved by a purchasing discrepancy analyst. Spending time on non-value added activities prevents purchasing personnel from concentrating on strategic procurement issues. Discrepancies, which may occur for many reasons, can be grouped into two categories—price mismatches and quantity mismatches.

Price mismatches occur when the price on the supplier's invoice does not match the price on the buyer's PO. Often the supplier must be called to determine the contracted price. (*Note*: Before moving to ERS, a process should be established to ensure that prices in the buyer's system are kept up-to-date.) Quantity mismatches occur when quantities on the invoice differ from quantities on the PO. A quantity discrepancy must be resolved by recounting the received quantity or by double-checking the quantity on the invoice. (*Note*: ERS should be accompanied by an accurate type of receiving barcode or an RFID system when replacing a manual process of inputting a received quantity.)

Traditionally, manual invoice processing has created mismatches between the paper invoice and the PO that range from 20 to 30%. Purchasing professionals have been forced to delay strategic tasks in order to resolve these accounts payable discrepancies. Non-value added activities of this type have convinced procurement organizations of the need to consider adopting ERS to replace manual processes (Ruzicka 2000).

ERS reduces processing costs by repositioning discrepancy analysts, by reducing input errors by having less human intervention, and by streamlining the reconciliation process by the elimination of non-value added steps in paper invoice processing, which includes opening of supplier mail, manual data entry, and manual three-way matching of invoices, receipts, and POs. ERS enables a supplier to be paid sooner because of a lower discrepancy rate, which results in improvements in the supplier's relationship with the buyer.

Some companies that have adopted lean supply chains are now applying the same philosophy to the settlement subprocess. Once a shipment of material from a supplier arrives at the buyer's site, scanning a barcode or an RFID tag automatically triggers an electronic deposit in the supplier's bank account. Having no invoices and making instant payments will reduce costs to the buyer and the supplier and facilitate faster cash flow up the supply chain.

CASE STUDY: A LARGE U.S. TELECOMMUNICATION COMPANY

Overview

This telecommunication company is one of the world's leading providers of communications services. The procurement/logistics manager is responsible for a procurement group that has about 100 employees, with $700 million to spend, and it has 300 suppliers. The suppliers are primarily domestic suppliers. The group is responsible for procurement of materials to sales orders that are from businesses and not from individuals. In an interview with the procurement/logistics manager, the POM processes, challenges, and best practices have been captured.

Procure-to-Order Strategy

Of the company's POs, 80% or more are procure to order (a popular buying strategy for high-value items that is pull-driven), which are derived from sales orders and are considered to be the norm. There is no need for bill of material (BOM) explosion because the sales order lists the required procured products. (*Note*: BOM explosion is the process of generating a list of all the subassemblies, intermediates, parts, and raw materials that are required to produce a parent, or finished, product that provides the quantity of each item that is required to produce the finished product. Then these quantities are multiplied by the total demand for the finished product to determine how much the company will be required to procure from suppliers.)

No configuration or assembly is done inside the company. The sales department simply uses the item master catalog to select items and to check prices. Typically the warehouse will then perform a consolidation of all line items on a sales order before shipment. (*Note*: Less than 20% of the POs at the company are procure to stock (a forward buying strategy).) POs typically include stocks for spare parts needed for maintenance, stocks for incoming promotions, and stocks for long-lead time products.

Contract Parameters

All POs are discrete (i.e., they are for one-time-demand or infrequent-demand items) and are to be placed with preferred suppliers that have a valid up-to-date contract. Exceptions to the policy of having a valid contract with a supplier before executing a PO are minimal. The root cause of exceptions is always to be investigated. A contract with a supplier has one price and a fixed discount rate. The fixed discount rate considers the annual buying history of the company. The company once maintained different price ranges depending on purchasing volume, but no longer does so. The company makes no commitment about the total amount that will be spent with a supplier. The company has 30 days from the date of issuing a PO to pay a supplier even if the material and the invoice were received earlier.

The company is typically responsible for transportation through its own transportation division. The PO contains shipping data, a ship-to location, and a price. The ship-to location is automatically assigned to a warehouse that is closest to the customer. In some cases, particularly when the lead time is short, the ship-to location will be the end customer's site. This situation is known as "direct ship" and is determined at the time the sales order is generated.

PO Execution

Depending on a supplier's capabilities, discrete POs (or spot orders) may be communicated by:

- EDI 850: POs are sent by a buyer via EDI 850 (an electronic version of a paper PO) to a value added network (VAN) service every 2 hours. POs will then be extracted from the EDI VAN based on the supplier's extraction frequency.
- Fax: All POs are printed out the next business day by the buyer and then faxed to any supplier that cannot receive EDI signals. For POs that are urgent and must be fulfilled quickly, the buyer can override the "next day print" flag and ask the system to printout the PO immediately so it may be faxed the same day.
- Manual entry: The PO may be manually entered on the website of a supplier. (*Note*: This supplier also accepts faxes, but manually entering a PO in the supplier's system will require more time and delay fulfillment by the supplier.)

An EDI-enabled supplier sends an EDI 855 to the buyer as an acknowledgment of receipt of the PO. If the supplier requests a different ship date, the buyer might cancel the PO and find a different source. When an EDI-enabled supplier is ready to ship, the supplier will send an EDI 856 as an ASN. The company allows receiving partial shipments and a backorder is generated. Once shipped, the supplier issues an invoice and sends it to the buyer either by EDI, fax, or mail.

Receiving a shipment in a warehouse is accomplished by entering the PO number in the buyer's system and verifying that all of the line items on the PO have been received. Items that are not received are removed (or excluded) from the receipt screen before posting receipt of the shipment. (*Note*: Only in big warehouse facilities is barcode technology used for receiving shipments.)

Three-way matching is performed once an invoice is received. Three-way matching compares the price on the PO, the quantity on the PO, and whether or not the shipment has been received as invoiced. A procurement match error (PME) is issued if there is no match. The supplier will not paid unless the PME is resolved. Although a PME resides in the accounts payable system, the purchasing department is responsible for resolving a PME, not the accounts payable department. A PME may be the result of several things, e.g., a discrepancy in a unit of measure (UOM), obsolete prices, or materials that are not yet received due to a long lead time. PMEs are now part of the company's performance scorecard for buyers to encourage them to resolve errors as quickly as possible. PME scorecards for suppliers have a target of "less than 2%" within the first 30 days and "less than 1%" for over 90 days.

Once this PME measurement was added to the company's scorecard and frequent updating of the price list was implemented, a significant reduction in PME percent has been observed at the company, which has translated into the company having greater satisfaction and trust with suppliers. (*Comment*: The authors recommend following the actions of this company to accelerate the cash flow cycle in the supply chain.)

The company has also achieved success by supporting end-to-end integration and by having greater visibility of complex solutions. Complex solutions can include hardware such as equipment, software, and services. Another challenge that has been addressed in this integration is procurement of a warranty on behalf of the customers from vendors for their products. A warranty may be different, e.g., it may depend on a time period (5 or 10 years) or the type of support provided (24/7).

Challenges in the Company's Existing POM Process

Lack of visibility. The average in-transit time for all suppliers is 4 to 5 days. Having a lack of visibility for in-transit shipments is a challenge, particularly when dealing with non-EDI-enabled suppliers. Because suppliers rarely proactively address problems as they arise, the company's buyers must regularly follow up manually on each open PO to obtain its status. Another potential challenge is if major suppliers outsource their manufacturing to facilities that are outside of the United States. Because international shipments require additional time in customs, having adequate lead time and visibility are therefore more critical.

Delivery destination. At times the destination location for a delivery is an end customer's site and not the company's warehouse, an arrangement known as "direct ship." The challenge with delivery to an end customer's site is the receiving process. Confirming the delivery process is an entirely manual process in which the end customer or the company's technician will confirm receiving the delivery and fax the packing list included with the delivery to the company's warehouse so that the information can be manually entered into the receiving system.

Inability to maintain supplier and carrier performance. The performance metrics of suppliers and carriers is maintained by two separate systems at the company. The inability to maintain supplier and carrier performance effectively is therefore a challenge. One system captures quality issues (e.g., missing items and damaged parts), either from the manufacturer or during transportation, and another system monitors returns. Contributing to this inability to maintain supplier and carrier performance is a lack of internal resources to capture and maintain suppliers' performance data.

Multiple POM systems. Having multiple systems for the POM process is a challenge. At times parallel systems are used for the same POM component (subprocess).

Settlement process. Challenges that are related to the settlement process are the inability to track the full return cycle from the buyer to the supplier and a lack of visibility of payments for the supplier.

Solutions

Major strategic initiatives have been undertaken at the company in the area of supply management to address these challenges and to better align supply management with corporate strategic goals. Implementing a SRM solution to reduce costs and provide visibility by moving from multiple systems to a single system is one of the initiatives. Other initiatives are reducing the supplier base by using distributors for large-volume/low-dollar-value items and replacing the large number of small suppliers with a small number of big distributors. (Compared to big distributors, small suppliers are typically not able to use EDI.)

Performance Metrics

Supplier and carrier performance metrics are captured and monitored by the sourcing group and not by the procurement/logistics group. Most of the metrics are qualitative and are based on surveys and onsite visits. Internal metrics for the procurement/logistics group are published monthly and captured daily. These internal metrics are divided into two categories—group and individual:

Group performance metrics. Characteristics of group performance metrics include:

- Item availability
- No movement for 6 months (The dollar amount of inventory with no consumption for 6 months or more should not exceed a certain limit.)
- Days of supply (Target level is less than 19 days of inventory.)
- Inventory plan attainment
- Survey results for level of satisfaction (Target is 75% for outstanding performance and 90% for the combination of outstanding + good.)

- "Junk" dollars (or obsolete inventory) (Junk inventory should not exceed a certain dollar amount.)

Individual performance metrics. Characteristics of individual performance metrics include:

- Item availability
- On-time delivery (on-time receiving) (Delivery/receiving is calculated by comparing the actual date a shipment was received and the required date for shipment delivery. The required date for a shipment is controlled only by the sales organization. In the sales department, the end customer delivery date = the needed date for the supplier's delivery + the transit time between warehouse and the customer's site. On-time delivery is an indication of the buyer's capability to manage the PO process so that the end customer is satisfied.)
- Number of received but not invoiced items
- Database accuracy (Targeted database accuracy is 100%, which is 0 tolerance. Database accuracy consists of completion of returns, which should be completed within 60 days, and PO generation time, which should not exceed 48 hours.)
- Promised date (The target for a promised date is 98% achieved. The procurement group should update the status of the PO manually every week.)
- Training (The target for training is a minimum of 12 hours per year.)

Additionally aggregated "days of supply" and "line item availability" metrics are being used by top-level executives in the company to determine the value contributed by POM to the competitive and financial performance of the company.

POM REQUIREMENTS

To implement POM process best practices, the POM solution should be able to support several requirements, which may be categorized into eight groups:
- Delivery and process compliance metrics
- Flexible architecture
- Friendly user interface
- Open interfaces
- Exception-driven workflows
- Effective tracking
- Configurable data retention policy
- Intelligent business rules

Each group has a set of related requirements.

Delivery and Process Compliance Metrics

The POM solution should be able to capture and communicate a supplier's delivery performance in addition to measuring process compliance. A supplier falling below a delivery performance target should be subject to corrective action requests to address the shortfall. Continued failure to meet performance targets may result in more severe measures and may impact future business from the company.

Repetitive failure to have on-time delivery or on-time shipping may result in charges for direct losses for the buyer. Delivery metrics are necessary to prevent these consequences earlier in the game by providing a "heads up" using the performance trend. Delivery metrics allow the buyer to provide performance feedback to all suppliers and to recognize suppliers who continually meet or exceed the buyer's standards. All suppliers are also strongly encouraged to monitor and analyze their own metrics.

Compliance metrics are vital for the success of a POM process transformation. Capturing metrics, such as the number of instances when shipments were made without sending an ASN, will have a major impact on enforcing the process of sending an ASN at the time of shipment to provide visibility for the buyer for the incoming material and in-transit shipments.

The solution should also provide a key performance indicators (KPI) dashboard to monitor the process and to permit taking corrective action when needed. KPIs are critical-to-success metrics that senior management will use as a gauge to measure the health of the business.

Flexible Architecture

The POM solution should have a software architecture that is both extensible and flexible to meet the company's specific requirements, rather than to force the company to reengineer its processes to fit the software. If specific business requirements make customization unavoidable, extensions to the open, documented application programming interface (API) set should be quickly and easily made.

The POM solution should also be able to receive transaction signals via EDI and XML. Processing EDI transactions such as EDI 850 (BPO/PO), EDI 860 (a PO change), EDI 855 (a PO acknowledgment), EDI 865 (a PO change acknowledgment), EDI 830 (a forecast), EDI 856 (an ASN), and EDI 820 (an invoice) should be supported. Transaction signals will be screened for errors and exceptions will be logged along with detailed error messages about what went wrong while the clean data was successfully imported. The users should be able to view and fix errors online using robust error handling capabilities.

Friendly User Interface

Regardless of whether a user is experienced or not, the user interface (UI) should provide convenient viewing of summary information and the status of orders and shipment details as well as the capability to enter information quickly and easily. The POM solution should bring the information to the users in all forms, rather than requiring them to navigate around in the system to find information. An intuitive and friendly UI typically reduces training costs and increases acceptability.

The solution should also easily generate reports based on the needs of users and provide the capability for users to download them. For example, the "Expected Delivery" report, which displays information about items for open POs, is important for the receiving department because it permits identification of items that are expected to be received based on promised delivery dates.

Open Interface

The interface with warehouse and logistics systems can streamline the entire logistics process, including picking, packing, shipping, and final delivery while optimizing warehouse processes. Therefore, integration with carriers' websites (e.g., UPS, FedEx, etc.) to retrieve shipment tracking information should be supported by the solution. Integration also needs to be tied closely to the material planning solution to permit reacting faster to fluctuations in demand and supply and to provide a "what if" capability. In addition to the ability to coordinate planning recommendations with the actual execution picture, the solution should be able to import POs and changes from other systems.

Exception-Driven Workflow

Eliminating the requirement for users to view every activity in the supply chain while looking for potential problems, which is provided by exception-driven workflows, is a huge shift toward a lean and agile supply chain (LASC). The solution should tell the user when, and sometimes even how, to react. Other related requirements include:

- Alerts, notifications, and event management
- Alert resolution workflows for managing alerts and exceptions to bring them to closure
- Electronic collaboration between business-to-business trading partners

Important alerts that could be of interest to a user are related to backorder POs. An alert could produce a list of POs currently on backorder. Another alert could be for past-due POs. This alert would identify and display items that are late or have not been received based on the promised date of delivery. The user may want to expedite shipment of some of these items.

Effective Tracking

Effective tracking is the ability to track changes made to POs effectively, i.e., by providing an audit trail of changes, deletions, or additions made for analysis and discrepancy resolution. Providing the ability to sort reports by PO status to produce more meaningful and informative reports is also useful. This requirement includes the ability to electronically match receipts and invoices to POs and maintain calendars of shippers, receivers, and customers. For example, when matching invoices to POs, the solution should compare quantities and costs associated with invoices and POs. The matching process should verify unit costs, extended amounts, and the total amount of the PO according to tolerance codes assigned at both the PO header level and the line level.

Configurable Data Retention Policy

Historical and transactional storage of PO and execution data allows more insight into year-to-year comparisons, trends, and analysis. Establishing a data retention policy is necessary to avoid deleting required data. Performing a backup of data before a purge is also necessary for long-term analysis.

A purge process is required to eliminate unwanted records, which will save disk space and allow the system to efficiently perform inquiries and process data. The solution should support configurable purge selection criteria. For example, when purging POs, the system might be configured to purge all change orders associated with these POs. An open BPO with no attached PO would not purged even if it meets the age criteria. A closed BPO with no attached PO would be purged only if the PO meets the configured age criteria. Having configurable aging criteria (which might range from 6 months to 5 years) should be supported by a solution. Based on business needs and the database/memory size, the company wants to have an ability to change the aging criteria on an as-needed basis.

Intelligent Business Rules

From a business standpoint, eliminating non-value added activities in the process to help users manage the PO cycle more efficiently is critical. Therefore, the solution should support certain business rules to achieve this objective. Examples related to PO business rules include: automatically default tax codes and tax groups to POs and control the override ability; close the PO line after the first receipt is posted (if this is a business requirement); and default the unit price of an item during PO entry from the BPO. For noninventory items such as services, the unit price default information is derived from a common source (e.g., a database table) maintained in the system. Other examples that are related to shipment execution rules include:

- Create tolerances for over- and undershipments by item, buyer, supplier, and buyer site.
- Close order lines automatically if items are shipped within an undershipment tolerance.
- Allow shipments within an overshipment tolerance and pay for either shipped or ordered quantity.
- Allow authorized users to override an overship exception (or flag) for selective shipments that have a good reason for exceeding their tolerance.

SUMMARY

Chapter 3 has provided a comprehensive description of the life cycle of a PO at the execution level. It has also provided an explanation of how the steps (subprocesses) in the life cycle of a PO can be integrated seamlessly to eliminate non-value added activities and provide real-time visibility. The chapter concludes with a description of the POM technology requirements that are needed to support process best practices that have been described in the chapter and in Chapter 2, which will serve as an introduction to the Part II of the book. Part II will focus on enabling technology for POM.

REFERENCES

Pikulik, J. *Invoice Reconciliation and Payment Benchmark Series: Accounts Payable Success Stories.* Boston: Aberdeen Group; 2005a June, pp. 1–44.

Pikulik, J. *E-Invoicing Solution Selection Report: Leading an Accounts Payable Extreme Makeover.* Boston: Aberdeen Group; 2005b December, pp. 1–40.

Ruzicka, M. *Invoiceless Procurement: Streamlining the Receiving and Billing Processes.* Tempe, AZ: CAPS Research; 2000 June, pp. 7–10.

PART II:
ENABLING TECHNOLOGIES

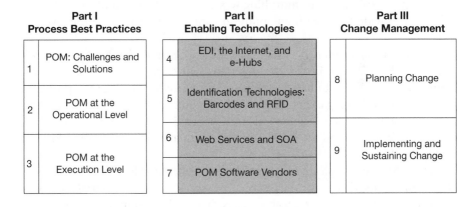

Figure 1. Organization of Part II.

Part I of this book has discussed POM processes. The maturity of POM processes has followed the maturity of communication technology, and any POM component that requires visibility has been positively impacted as technology provided better methods of communication. Telephones provided instant conversation and were a major improvement over postal communication. Yet a shortcoming of telephone communication was the lack of an ability to archive conversations for history tracking. Facsimile provided an improvement over postal communication and the telephone because it allowed quick delivery of information and a record of the communication. Electronic commerce (e-commerce) mechanisms such as EDI, electronic mail (e-mail), and the Internet provided significant improvements over paper-only and audio-based-only communication.

As communication mechanisms have improved, POM processes have adapted these technologies to improve existing processes. Although POM processes can be executed without technology, technology has significantly speeded up POM processes and reduced the errors that are associated with manual tasks. Technology has also provided insight into processes and trading partners to an extent that firms can now use technology to perform tactical tasks and to develop their sourcing strategies. By using data mining on the vast amount of POM data, companies can also drive out inefficiencies in procurement activities, reduce buffers, and allow for trending their processes to obtain a better grasp of their supply chains.

Part II will discuss existing and forthcoming technology for POM processes (see Figure 1). Chapter 4 will discuss communication technology and how this technology has morphed into several solutions for POM processes. Also discussed in Chapter 4 will be electronic data interchange (EDI), the first technology that allowed computers to "talk" to each other; the Internet, a technology that has been in vogue since the mid-1990s; and Internet hubs (also called exchanges, electronic hubs, or marketplaces). This morphing was a natural extension of Internet technology to provide firms with an ability to conduct POM transactions over the Internet.

Identification technology, which is a key component of the POM process, will be discussed in Chapter 5. With the ability to identify items, trading partners can define and develop automated processes to streamline their POM processes. Identification technologies described are the ubiquitous barcode and the upcoming radio frequency identification (RFID). Chapter 5 will also provide a brief history, the technology, and the standards along with an example of how RFID can enable POM processes.

POM processes typically use several heterogeneous information technology (IT) components. Chapter 6 will describe Web services and SOA (service-oriented architectures), which are new technologies that are beginning to be used as the "glue" to put these heterogeneous components together. Web services and SOA allow firms to quickly develop solutions from their components. The beauty of these technologies is that they allow quick changing of an existing solution in order to adapt to changing business needs. A brief history, the technology, and the standards used in Web services and SOA will be provided in Chapter 6. Some examples will be provided to demonstrate how these technologies may be used.

Chapter 7 is the concluding chapter of Part II. Chapter 7 includes a brief description of software vendors that provide POM solutions. During the dot.com "golden days," software vendors proliferated. Although few vendors survived following the dot.com bust, there are signs of resurgence in that industry. A description of a few software vendors and their products will be provided to demonstrate some capabilities provided by software programs. In addition to the vendors, Chapter 7 will also present guidelines for selecting software providers and implementing a software solution.

EDI, THE INTERNET, AND e-HUBS

INTRODUCTION

Since the advent of computing technology, computers have been used to enable business processes. In early use computers were primarily used for transaction processing. At that time the value added by using computers was in automating repetitive clerical tasks, thereby increasing the efficiency of transaction processing. Initially all automation was internal to an organization. Soon, however, it was recognized that this automation could be extended externally to the organization for major benefits, and workflows began to include external entities as well as internal processes. The next phase in computing technology provided an ability to utilize historical data to perform data analysis, which provided organizations with a capability to understand their past operations and to put into place mechanisms to improve their processes.

Proliferation of the Internet was the next phase in which automation capabilities were further extended to entire workflows instead of merely repetitive tasks. Automation capabilities started with simple workflows between an organization and its consumers that are known as business-to-consumer (B2C) workflows. B2C was followed by connectivity between various internal and external users that provided the ability to extend workflows beyond an organization and into the realm of suppliers and customers, which is known as business-to-business (B2B) workflows. The current status of this phase is connectivity between internal and external information technology (IT) in the form of application-to-application (A2A) workflows. Introduction of the Internet is considered to be a major milestone in the advancement of IT as a business enabler.

The current state of IT meets the key requirements of an efficient supply chain, namely, to have quick information flows upstream and downstream of the organization, which provides supply chain partners with visibility across the supply chain and minimizes disruptions. Each entity in the supply chain is also provided with an ability to perform predictive modeling by utilizing data available in the IT systems. Companies such as IBM are developing on-demand, pervasive, and autonomic computing tools and processes to add further business value within supply chain systems and within other business processes.

Chapter 4 will present a brief history of two key technologies—EDI (electronic data interchange) and the Internet—along with electronic hubs (e-hubs) and exchanges. These technologies have played a major role in improving various business processes such as purchase order management (POM).

EDI

Information sharing requirements in supply chains are complex. Typically business processes are very different between industries as well as between different companies within an industry. Yet these business processes require the exchange of business "objects" (e.g., documents) such as purchase orders (POs), advanced shipment notices (ASNs), etc. between supply chain partners. Before the advent of computers, business documents were exchanged using mechanisms such as postal mail. By using computers, however, the electronic data interchange (EDI) mechanism has been developed so that organizations can use EDI to electronically exchange business documents. EDI was intended to minimize, if not eliminate, manual (human) intervention to make business processes faster, cheaper, and better. Business processes were completed faster because data was exchanged electronically without manual intervention. Business processes were cheaper because costs associated with manual intervention were reduced. Because manual processing of business data introduced errors during data entry and EDI minimized these errors, business processes were better. EDI is now used globally in several areas:

- Finance—credit reports, invoices, and payments
- Materials management—production sequencing, shipment notification, and planning and scheduling
- Transportation—freight invoices, shipper's export declarations, and shipment information
- Purchasing—price catalogs, POs, responses to requests for quotes
- Distribution and warehousing—direct store delivery summary information, promotional announcements, warehouse shipping orders
- Insurance—vehicle damage claims, laboratory reports, healthcare claims

Typically the costs for manual document preparation and processing are about $40 per document, whereas the costs for electronic document preparation and processing are less than $2 per document. Therefore the reduction in document preparation and processing has resulted in many organizations (>80%) using electronic data preparation and communication. For example, the U.S. Department of Defense conducts 90% of its document exchange via EDI.

A brief history of EDI will now be provided, which will be followed by a summary of EDI standards and related organizations, a description of implementing EDI, barriers to EDI implementation (which will continue to be barriers), and a high-level description of how EDI works.

A Brief History of EDI

True EDI as it is now known emerged primarily due to the growth of computerization. Yet the seed for EDI was sown in 1948 during the Berlin Airlift. The problem to be solved then was to simplify the coordination of distribution and transportation of food by utilizing a common shipping manifest in a manual fashion. During the Berlin Airlift, business documents were communicated via postal mail, with telephones acting as a quick confirmation or collaboration tool. All information was communicated in a human-readable form. Differences in the layout of a document were not an issue as long as all of the required data was available. Even with computerization, the need for EDI was not initially explored because only internal repetitive tasks (e.g., month-end accounting) were being automated. The next phase, in which nonrepetitive tasks were automated, also did not warrant a need for EDI. At this time, however, many companies began to identify problems with manual processing in conjunction with automation, e.g., issues with processing speed and an increased potential for errors. Manual processes were adding unnecessary delay in the cycle time required for completing business processes and were introducing errors that resulted from manual data entry. Yet these errors were not detected until much later, long after decisions based on erroneous information had already been made.

As a result, some large organizations began to cooperate with each other to develop processes and systems that would incorporate EDI between the computers at their respective organizations. For example, at one company, a business process would generate electronic documents (e.g., a PO, an ASN, etc.), open an electronic connection with a computer at another company, electronically transmit the document, and then receive a confirmation of receipt of the document. At the other end, the receiving computer at the other company would accept the document, process it, and if necessary transmit a notification. No human intervention was required in this workflow! Connectivity at this time was point-to-point for each document transmitted. Yet as more organizations jumped in, the point-to-point nature of connectivity made data exchange more difficult to manage and maintain. Furthermore, because there was no human intervention, document formats were machine readable and had to be precise. Therefore changing formats would result in incorrect processing.

In 1960s the U.S. transportation industry recognized the issues that were associated with the proliferation of ad hoc document formats and the need for standards in the EDI landscape. In 1968, the Transportation Data Coordination Committee (TDCC) was formed to resolve these issues. The TDCC set forth three ground rules:

- The solution must be independent of the electronic communication mechanism.
- The solution must be independent of the communicating entities' hardware and software components.
- The solution must be responsive to the needs of new and changing business requirements.

The first EDI standards were a result of these TDCC ground rules. The EDI standards were first used by the rail line industry and then were adopted by motor carriers. About the same time, large U.S. companies such as General Motors, Ford, and Chrysler were extending these EDI standards to their own standards for suppliers. At the same time, large suppliers were doing the same thing for their customers. All of these multiple initiatives created considerable confusion in terms of whose EDI standard should be used, what EDI standard should be used, and when a EDI standard should be used. Because the automobile industry was the largest user of EDI, confusion in this industry resulted in formation of the Automotive Industry Action Group (AIAG). A goal of AIAG was to generate EDI standards for the automobile industry. The success of the AIAG encouraged other industries to follow suit, leading to the American National Standards Institute (ANSI), the Uniform Commercial Code (UCC), and the National Wholesale Druggists Association. Although having standards was a major step forward, these EDI standards did not help companies who had business ties across industries. This situation resulted in an ANSI-initiated effort to develop cross-industry EDI standards known as the X12 Business Data Interchange Committee. The results of this effort have not yet produced an exact standard because an EDI document in one industry (or, for that matter, even in a company) still may not be usable in another industry. Additionally, several industries such as telecommunications, electronics, government, chemicals, metals, etc. are not covered by EDI standards.

EDI Standards and Organizations

To ensure that organizations achieve maximum return on their investment in EDI technology (or any technology), establishing appropriate mechanisms to maintain

Table 4.1. Differences between X12 and EDIFACT Communication

ANSI X12	UN/EDIFACT
More messages	Few messages
Small message size	Large message size
Greater number of single data elements	Composite data elements
Multiple begin message headers	Single begin message header

global EDI standards is important. Furthermore, because advances in Internet technology are available as a tool for the electronic exchange of data, determining how these two technologies can coexist is also important. For example, EDI deployments are perfectly capable of addressing the needs for exchanging several types of business documents.

This section will present several standards that are currently in use in industry as well as the organizations that are responsible for managing and maintaining them. There are two primary EDI standards:

- The ANSI Accredited Standards Committee X12 standard (ANSI ASC X12)
- The United Nations Electronic Data Interchange for Administration, Commerce, and Transportation standard (EDIFACT)

The ANSI ASC X12 standard is primarily used in the United States, whereas EDIFACT is primarily used in Europe. Elements in each of the standards result in differences in ANSI ASC X12 and EDIFACT communication (see Table 4.1 for a comparison of ANSI ASC X12 and EDIFACT). Although both standards are in wide use, ANSI ASC X12 is moving toward having one global standard, i.e., the EDIFACT standard.

EDI Implementation

Because EDI uses computer technology to send and receive data without human intervention, any business document sent or received by a company can be exchanged with another company using EDI if both organizations have a computer infrastructure that is set up to accommodate EDI. The EDI infrastructure cannot be set up quickly. The infrastructure must be planned and then thoroughly tested. Several steps are involved in planning and testing and each step takes time. Typical steps in implementing an EDI solution as well as a brief description of the technologies involved include:

Step 1. Determine the volume of transactions and the number of supply chain partners (trading partners), which will help determine which technology should be used and whether the expertise should be built in-house or if it should be outsourced.

Step 2. Obtain translator and mapping documents along with an implementation manual. Trading partners who are already EDI-enabled will have their own implementation manuals that contain mapping details that are specific to each trading partner.

Step 3. Decide on how data will flow from the source to the destination. Two mechanisms are available—direct connect or a value-added network (VAN). The direct connect mechanism connects directly to a business partner's system. Connectivity can be via a dial-up line or a dedicated leased connection. A dial-up line is used when volume is low and there are few trading partners. A dedicated leased connection can be a virtual private network (VPN), a file transfer protocol (FTP) connection, or the Internet. VAN connectivity involves an electronic mail (e-mail) box that provides asynchronous connectivity. A VAN is a secure network link between two or more business partners. A VAN also smoothes out incompatibilities between a business partner's heterogeneous environments and allows business partners to focus on business processes rather than on technology. The sender "deposits" an electronic document (e-document) into the VAN mail box for the receiver. At a predetermined frequency, the receiver will access the mail box and pick up any e-documents that are in the mail box.

Step 4. Software is installed and mappings are configured according to the requirements of the documents being exchanged. Translators and mapping from Step 2 are required to achieve Step 4. Documents generated by the application software at the organization are used in the mapping activity to ensure correct mapping.

Step 5. Before turning on EDI as a document exchange mechanism, the final step is to perform an end-to-end test in both directions—from the business (the customer) to the other business (the supplier) as well as from the supplier to the customer. This step is crucial step to ensure that all mappings are correct. An end-to-end test also involves load testing and testing for abnormal conditions.

All entities that are involved in establishing an EDI must perform all five of these steps. Entities already using EDI and wanting to get their business partners onboard must also become engaged with their trading partners who are preparing to start using EDI. Engagement with business partners is particularly important in the end-to-end testing in Step 5.

Barriers to EDI Acceptance

EDI provides several benefits. Yet acceptance of EDI in businesses is not universal due to several barriers.

Cost. Cost is the biggest barrier for any company considering entering the EDI arena. EDI requires an organization to make a significant initial investment. Large organizations with a large number of documents to communicate and with stable processes (e.g., automobile industries, government agencies, etc.) are more likely to be able to afford EDI, but smaller companies may resist the large initial investment.

Nonstandard standards. Another barrier is having "nonstandard" standards. The format for the same document at one company may not be compatible with the format at another company. Infrastructure components of EDI systems are inflexible and proprietary, which adds to the expenses associated with EDI.

Batch orientation. EDI systems are batch-oriented rather than real time. Batch orientation prevents key workflows from reaching their full potential once they are automated. (*Note*: The next section will detail how EDI functions and the batch nature of EDI will become clear.)

Two networks. For EDI in large organizations, another barrier is the need to have a VAN as well as a VPN. Both VAN and VPN technologies increase the cost as well as add to the complexity of the solution.

Many organizations now consider EDI to be a necessary cost of doing business. Yet these organizations do not consider that EDI adds a significant value or a competitive edge. Based on this perception, several software vendors have started developing tools that allow an organization to transmit EDI via the Internet at a significantly lower cost. These software tools reduce some problems, but raise other issues such as security and guaranteed delivery.

How EDI Works

EDI will be described through a typical business scenario using several steps. The scenario involves a supplier, Acme Corporation, and a customer, Mr. Willie Coyote. Mr. Coyote determines that he needs to purchase a trapping contraption for road runners from Acme Corporation. Because Mr. Coyote needs the contraption rather quickly, he decides to use his corporate software and his newly established EDI connectivity with Acme Corporation. However, because Mr. Coyote's organization is not a large company, he is using the VAN specified by Acme Corporation to place his order. (*Note*: Only one VAN, which is the VAN managed by Acme, is being used.)

Step 1. The PO software at Mr. Coyote's organization generates a PO with details about the order. The EDI software converts the PO into an EDI transaction document known as an EDI 850.

Step 2. The EDI software is configured to transmit all EDI data from Mr. Coyote to the VAN for Acme. The EDI 850 that has just been generated is transmitted at a predetermined time (e.g., 1:00 a.m.) to the VAN to be ready for pickup by Acme.

Step 3. At a predetermined time (e.g., 3:00 a.m.), Acme's EDI processing system examines the VAN mailbox, finds the transaction document, picks up the document, and transmits an acknowledgment transaction back to Mr. Coyote.

Step 4. Acme's translation software converts the EDI 850 into a format that is recognized by its order processing system and transfers the result into a predefined system directory with a predefined name.

Step 5. Acme's order processing solution detects a new file in the directory, picks up the file, checks the validity of data components within the file, and if everything is correct processes the data as a new order. If there are errors, an EDI failure transaction document will be transmitted to Mr. Coyote.

Step 6. Acme then manufactures the contraption according to the PO and after 3 days the order is complete. Acme prepares to ship according to the PO.

Step 7. A shipping clerk at Acme generates an ASN in the Acme shipping system. Once this document is created, the shipping system determines whether the receiver is EDI-enabled or not. If the receiver is not EDI-enabled, the system is configured to print a shipping document. Otherwise the ASN data is transformed into an EDI 856. (In this scenario, the Acme system recognizes that the Mr. Coyote is EDI-enabled, it then transforms the ASN data into EDI 856, and then it transmits the ASN document to the VAN at the predetermined time (e.g., 2:00 a.m.).

Step 8. After the shipment has been transmitted, Acme's accounts receivable system generates an invoice for Mr. Coyote. The invoice is translated into an EDI 810 document and just like the EDI 856, the EDI 810 is transmitted to the VAN.

Step 9. Mr. Coyote's system has been configured to scan the VAN daily at 3:00 a.m. Mr. Coyote's system detects transaction documents waiting for pickup, it picks them up and then transmits an acknowledgment transaction back to Acme.

Step 10. Mr. Coyote's system processes the EDI 856 and EDI 810. Both of these documents are now waiting for the next event, which is receipt of the shipment, before any further processing takes place for the order. Because Mr. Coyote has not enabled electronic payments, the EDI-based workflow for this order will end here.

Other business transactions that utilize EDI follow a similar mechanism. From the above example, it is evident that a significant amount of upfront work must be performed for each of the systems involved in order for these steps to occur in an automatic fashion. All of these steps must be coordinated among business partners to ensure that delays in processing data and in business workflows are kept to a minimum.

THE INTERNET AND THE WWW

Since its advent, EDI has successfully achieved the goal of providing an electronic mechanism for document exchange. However, changing business requirements and a desire to improve supply chain visibility have resulted in the pursuit of alternatives to EDI. Upton and McAfee (1996) described the shortcomings of the then prevalent technologies used in business document communication, e.g., EDI, groupware, and dedicated wide area networks (WANs), for achieving what they referred to as the "real virtual factories." They also discussed how the Internet and information brokering could overcome these shortcomings. With the proliferation of the Internet and related technologies in the 1990s and 2000s, overcoming the shortcoming of early technology and more have been achieved. In fact, collaboration as described by Upton and McAfee (1996) has been extended in other dimensions of supply chains such as collaboration on demand, supply, manufacturing, logistics, etc.

The next section will briefly relate the history of the Internet and the World Wide Web (WWW). It will also discuss some of the concerns users have with techniques and describe how the Internet and the WWW can be used in POM by using electronic hubs (e-hubs) and exchanges.

Infrastructure of the WWW

The Internet is the infrastructure upon which the WWW resides. The infrastructure is made up of network components, computers, and devices capable of performing computing tasks. This infrastructure has been developing over the past four decades into a showcase of collaborative development between government (mostly the U.S. government), academia, and industry. The Internet provides the capability to instantly broadcast, collaborate, and interact with individuals (e.g., colleagues, suppliers, customers, friends, and family) at any time of the day across the world.

The Internet has had a major impact on mankind not only in the use of IT in business processes, but also in various aspects of human endeavors such as leisure, knowledge acquisition, etc. The Internet has also had an important role in making the world "smaller." Using the Internet, a user in any part of the world can connect to information nodes located anywhere else in the world with or without the use of authorization and authentication mechanisms. This ability allows a user to work from a "virtual" office (including a home office), share information with colleagues, or collaborate with business partners. A sizeable number of elderly people are now "Web connected." Availability of high-speed networks in many parts of the world has significantly facilitated using the Internet.

A Brief History of the WWW

The foundation for the Internet was laid in when Leonard Kleinrock presented a proposal for his doctoral dissertation at the Massachusetts Institute of Technology (MIT) and subsequently wrote a paper on information flow in "large communication nets" (Kleinrock 1961). His paper was quickly followed by formation of the Information Processing Techniques Office (IPTO) in 1962, which was funded by the Advanced Research Projects Agency (ARPA) of the U.S. Department of Defense. The charter for IPTO was to conduct research on command and control systems. Also in 1962, Paul Baran, at the RAND Corporation, proposed the first packet switched network for a U.S. Air Force-sponsored project. In the mid 1960s ARPANET was developed, which connected four universities—Stanford University, the University of California at Los Angeles (UCLA), the University of Utah, and the University of California at Santa Barbara (UCSB)—via a 50-Kbps circuit. During the 1960s, development continued with three concurrent and independent efforts: research at MIT, research at the National Physical Laboratory (NPL) in the U.K., and research at the RAND Corporation (a U.S. government agency).

In the 1970s, networking standards such as TCP/IP (transmission control protocol/Internet protocol) and physical media such as Ethernet were developed. The first documented use of the term Internet also occurred in the 1970s (Cerf 1974). A "blockbuster" application of the 1970s—e-mail—provided easy communication between people and became a widely used application. Prior to development of the World Wide Web (WWW), e-mail was the largest network application for over a decade.

The 1980s produced refinements of standards and protocols that had been developed earlier. The U.S. National Science Foundation also constructed a network backbone for universities that facilitated research on network-based collaboration. Early in the 1980s, researchers in Geneva at the European Particle

Research Laboratory (or CERN, Conseil Européan pour la Recherche Nucléaire) had been searching for a solution to manage all the files, documents, and other resources and to share their work with other researchers. A solution would eventually be developed by Tim Berners-Lee as a result of his vision for a World Wide Web project through which links could be made between any nodes on a network (Berners-Lee 1980). The World Wide Web project was first publicized by CERN in 1989 and was released on CERN machines in 1991 (Berners-Lee 1989). Development of local area networks (LANs) and the connection of personal computers to these LANs increased use of the Internet in the 1980s. Yet interfaces were not very user friendly and acceptance was largely limited to only the academic community.

In the years that followed, with the availability of "browsers" such as Mosaic and Netscape®, acceptance outside academia began to grow and terms such as the Internet and the WWW became reasonably well known within the developed world. Another key component that allowed use of the WWW to expand outside academia was an ability to use names instead of numeric addresses to address websites. Domain name services (DNS) functionality has provided this capability and has allowed addressing to be much more user friendly and increased the usability of the WWW. Further explosive growth in Internet and WWW usage occurred with the availability of free browser software, which resulted in the Internet becoming "a prime example of a large-scale, highly engineered, yet highly complex system" (Willinger 2002). Non-proprietary and "open" protocols have also allowed vendors to develop Internet solutions that have added to the growth. Another contributing factor to the growth of Internet usage is that the Internet has no "central control."

Although the Web has seen widespread use in the last decade, only now are large organizations realizing that the Web is a serious business tool (Bowen 2005). Advancements in Internet technology have provided standards-based tools such as Web services, service oriented architecture (SOA), Internet, EDI, etc. that have significant potential for POM and similar B2B initiatives.

Internet Standards and Organizations

Today the Internet is a truly distributed and heterogeneous system without central control and without a person or a group paying for or charging for its use. When considering all of the work that is being done in the field of Internet technology, the realization that no one controls the Internet becomes a rather scary thought. Internet protocols and parameters are defined by various organizations. Organizations voluntarily adhere to these protocols and parameters when developing their products. Although a number of organizations manage only the protocols and parameters essential for proper functioning of the Internet, no boundaries exist outside of these protocols and parameters.

The Internet Society (ISOC, www.isoc.org) is the organization under which several groups develop and manage Internet standards. Groups that fall under the ISOC include:

Internet Architecture Board (IAB, www.iab.org)

Internet Steering Committee (IESG)

Internet Engineering Task Force (IETF, www.ietf.org)

Internet Research Steering Group (IRSG)

Internet Research Task Force (IRTF, www.irtf.org)

Request for Comments Editor (RFC Editor, www.rfc-editor.org)

Internet domain names and the Internet protocol (IP) addresses are managed by the Internet Corporation for Assigned Names and Numbers (ICANN, www.icann.org) and the Internet Assigned Numbers Authority (IANA). WWW standards are developed by the World Wide Web Consortium (W3C, www.w3c.org). Several other organizations such as the Organization for the Advancement of Structured Information Standards (OASIS, www.oasis-open.org) are responsible for tools used within the Internet.

Issues and Concerns

Use of the Internet and the WWW has increased tremendously in the last decade. Currently there are over four billion Internet addresses and approximately 20% of the global population is using the Internet. As customer needs change, additional devices will required, with the Internet being expected to eventually connect over a trillion devices. This expansion will require technology to change. One such change will be in the mechanism used in Internet addresses. The next version of IP, IPv6, is in development and will support 35 trillion subnets with each subnet having 1 million devices each.

A major concern of users is the "churn" in technology. Technology does not—and will not—stabilize, which prevents firms from maximizing their return on technology investments. Other major concerns about the Internet include:

Security. With the ability to access websites from anywhere in the world, the Internet has expanded the term security to include areas beyond the physical security of assets. Every firm must now also plan for the security of its nonphysical assets such as data. Data is made available to employees over the Web, with passwords being the primary mechanism used to prevent unauthorized access. Technologies such as VPN have enhanced security that is beyond merely using passwords, but firms still must be extremely watchful of all access, actual as well as attempts, to their system. Any compromise of security can have a disastrous impact on a firm.

Spam. Unsolicited e-mail is known as spam and those who use it are classified as spammers. The insignificant cost associated with mass mailings via the Internet has made e-mail a preferred tool for spammers. Internet technology, particularly e-mail, has allowed anyone an ability to communicate en masse as long as e-mail addresses are available. Information such as e-mail addresses can be purchased like any other information, which makes them easy to obtain and use. If a user's machine is infected with a mass mailing virus, the user's machine can be accessed, and unknown to the user, the machine can sent out e-mail. Unsolicited e-mail can be identified as being sent by spammers by the filter software used in many firms. Filter software often categorizes large Fortune 500 firms as spammers. For example, when a person within a firm uses an automatic "out of office" response message that is available in their e-mail software, it will respond to spam, which triggers the software and results in additional spam. All e-mail software providers have options that will prevent automatic messages from going out of their domains. Users should use these options to prevent their firm from being classified as a spammer.

Phishing. Phishing is a more recent form of the malicious use of the Internet. In phishing, a customer will receive an e-mail, e.g., apparently from their financial institution. The e-mail indicates that there is a problem with the customer's account and asks that the customer validate account information with the financial institution. The e-mail contains what appears to be a valid link to the financial institution's website, but in fact it is a link to a website that is controlled by the e-mail sender (the phisher). The e-mail sender then captures the user's key financial and personal data and uses it to assume the user's identity. In effect, the senders are "fishing" for personal and financial data.

Viruses. Because of the potential for security "holes" in computer and e-mail systems, Web and e-mail software can cause a user's system to be prone to attacks by pieces of software code known as a virus. Viruses can be benign and cause only a nuisance message to appear or they can be malicious and wipe out a user's disk. Viruses may also contain code for a delayed execution and therefore execute on a specific date. Initial versions of viruses were mostly benign. These viruses were created with no intent by the creator to benefit from the impact of the virus. Yet newer versions of viruses, such as the code for phishing, are intended to derive financial gains from using the malware. (*Note*: Malware is a combination of two words—"malicious" and "software"—to create a word which indicates the intent of the creator of the malware. Malware software is designed to damage or infiltrate a user's computer system, without the knowledge or consent of the user.) For example, malware has been used as a means to blackmail firms. The FBI has discovered four cases in which animal rights activists have blackmailed investment firms to sell stock that the firms held in companies that performed testing using animals (Esposito 2006). Viruses can include worms, Trojan horses, and other types of malware such as adware and spyware. These pieces of software code are embedded in seemingly legitimate software. They are activated and deployed on a host machine when the malware software is executed. Adware is a category of malware that is mostly a nuisance. In adware, software components are installed that track a user's Web habits and then use that information to "pop up" Web windows with advertisements from sites that support the adware. Spyware is similar to adware except that spyware typically sends back information about a user's Web habits (and more recently key logging information) to the owner of the spyware. To ensure that there is no impact from malware, users must ensure that three tasks are performed—routinely backup data; apply software and operating system patches when they become available; and update virus software definition files.

Defunct links. Each Web page typically has several links. However, because Web pages are so dynamic, most websites contain links that are "defunct" and no longer point to a valid Web page, leading to these links being called defunct links. Defunct links are very annoying, particularly when a user thinks a site has been reached that the user has been looking for only to find that the site no longer exists. Content management software identifies defunct links as long as the pages are within the realm of the organization running the software. Once outside the realm of the organization, there are no guarantees.

Digital divide. The term "digital divide" is used by politicians to describe the ability of the rich to access the Internet versus the inability of the poor to do the same. Although this term depicts the socioeconomic divide between societies that has always existed, the divide becomes more pronounced in the widely Web-enabled world of today, more so than when use of telephones became prevalent.

Even with these concerns and other issues, the Internet is "here to stay" for a long time. The Internet may evolve from its current form, but it will remain with us. The ability to access the WWW from mobile devices, the proliferation of mobile applications, and the vast utilization of the Internet in key business processes ensures this.

e-HUBS

Earlier in this chapter, EDI was described as providing an early electronic mechanism to automate business processes. Several processes still successfully use EDI. However, major constraints such as inflexible and proprietary technology, high cost barrier to entry, and point-to-point connectivity have prevented EDI from advancing to the next stage.

The Internet and the WWW have provided the capability to automate business processes, but without most of the constraints of EDI. The second stage of conducting business electronically has involved simple websites offering a few products or services. Yet with the growth of the Internet, the initial offerings focused on selling the technology rather than the business value. The goal of early offerings was to "wow" the user and customer. Therefore, the value added by technology was large, but from a process-improvement perspective, the incremental value added was marginal.

With advancements in the Internet, novel ways of conducting business using what is known as electronic commerce have emerged (also e-Commerce, electric commerce, and EC). e-Commerce is defined as the use of electronic mechanisms to conduct business transactions. In the 1990s, procurement began to utilize technology and Internet-based marketplaces proliferated (also known as electronic hubs and electronic marketplaces, or e-hubs). e-Hubs are merely an extension of the market concept into the Web. Simplistically, sellers put their wares in the market and buyers go to the market seeking things they need. In e-hubs the market is an electronic market that is enabled by the Internet. When a buyer finds what is needed, a finalizing transaction is invoked and a transaction is completed. Extensions of the e-marketplace such as auctions, reverse auctions, clearing houses, catalog procurement, and requisitioning have enhanced the capabilities of these e-hubs beyond a simplistic market concept to a concept that is similar to a portal, which enables a large number of firms to conduct business with each other over the Web. A key goal of such Internet tools was to reduce procurement and supply chain costs. In mid 1990s, during the prime of the "dot.com boom," several initiatives for e-hubs were undertaken, leading to a steady stream of announcements of the availability of such e-hubs.

The rationale behind the e-hub business model is to overcome the overhead associated with complex, expensive, and inefficient conventional procurement processes. Typical PO processing (a subset of POM processes) costs using traditional methods is over $100 per PO. Increases in procurement overhead are attributable to data problems (e.g., incorrect, incomplete, duplicate, late, etc.) and process problems (e.g., manual reconciliation, improper forecasting, incorrect pricing, etc.). Electronic procurement processes are touted to save from 10 to 25% of procurement costs. Aggregation of buyers and sellers in the form of e-hubs adds to these savings.

Issues with e-Hubs

Most e-hubs failed in the dot.com bust or in the early 2000s. The major reason for failure was that business process capabilities were not aligned with the value that participants were expecting from e-hubs. Other issues existed that were barriers to wide acceptance of e-hub technology. Some of these issues, such as governance-related issues, are applicable even today and require careful design:

- The Internet is not constrained by national boundaries, which limits enforceability of contractual agreements between parties conducting business over the e-hub, the e-hub owners, and the governments involved. Additionally, without recognition of national boundaries, defining which entity has jurisdiction over transactions—entities in the host location, entities in the seller's location, or entities in the buyer's location—is difficult if not impossible.

- With consortium e-hubs, the risk of consortium members misusing their market power and violating fair trade regulations is high.

- Privacy regulations, security, and encryption are of concern, e.g., a few years ago, the 128-bit electronic security mechanism for the Internet was unavailable to several countries.

- Intellectual property (IP) rights are an area of concern for e-hub participants. With no global standard for IP protection, participants are hesitant to conduct business via e-hubs.

- Because significant business activities are conducted over e-hubs by global participants, service levels associated with the availability of an e-hub as well as its performance are crucial concerns.

- When firms conduct business via e-hubs, there is a high probability of the existence of implied warranties and conditions. Such unwritten terms and conditions will always cause conflict between the parties involved.

Other issues will be covered as the different types of e-hubs are described later in this section.

The Present and the Future

Buyers and customers were initially connected directly to their suppliers, which resulted in a connectivity network similar to the network shown in Figure 4.1a. This model (relationship) was followed by the addition of a distributor who was responsible for several components of the procurement process, which transformed the connectivity network to that shown in Figure 4.1b. With e-hubs, the model migrated to the relationship shown in Figure 4.1c. e-Hubs aggregated information about buyers and sellers and provided them with access to a wider market base. The difference between the distributor model (b) and the e-hub model (c) was that distributors reacted to demands of their customers, whereas hubs with their aggregation allowed for "discovery" of appropriate suppliers.

After the failure of e-hubs during the dot.com bust, new models were developed. According to Professor Morris Cohen of the University of Pennsylvania's Wharton School, the natural progression from e-hubs (as enablers of business-to-business processes or B2B) will be to peer-to-peer (p2p) portals as shown in Figure 4.1d (summary of an interview; RAND Corporation 2003). p2p portals will allow businesses to connect to supplier resources such as the file-sharing services provided by Napster™. Instead of having a mediator or aggregator, suppliers will be able to access customer needs through p2p portals. The p2p model will give suppliers a wide customer base and provide customers with competitive

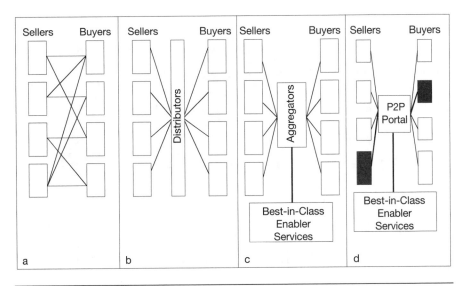

Figure 4.1. Types of Procurement Models. (a) Point-to-point; (b) distributor; (c) aggregator/hub; (d) peer-to-peer.

pricing as well as minimal changeover costs. Such p2p portals are expected to utilize advanced optimization techniques along with powerful algorithms to dynamically link suppliers and customers at the transaction level, e.g., a current status of demand and supply determines the link between the customer and supplier (as shown by the heavy lines and shaded boxes in Figure 4.1d).

The ability to perform business activities on the Web has also made significant advancement. Several survivors of the dot.com bust have evolved their business model to provide supply chain services just to "survive." Yet failures during the dot.com bust have resulted in people being wary of the electronic marketplace as a place to conduct business activities. Therefore future models must account for the reality that commerce consists of a set of complicated business processes and relationships that have been built over a long period of time and with significant investments. Trading partners will not be willing to jump to a new technology or a new way of conducting business. A new way of doing business must ensure them that there is coordination between inter- and intra-firm activities and that trading partners will have the necessary process capability. These characteristics will go a long way toward facilitating conducting business transactions over the Web, making e-hubs successful, and building trust among partners.

e-Hub Categories

The remainder of this section will discuss categories of e-hubs and the advantages and disadvantages of each of the categories. Depending on the owner and

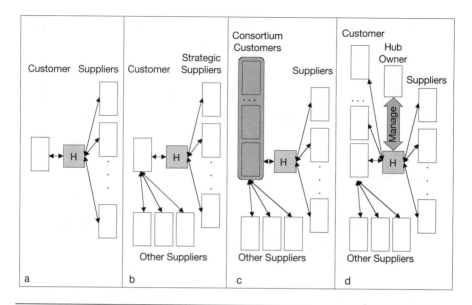

Figure 4.2. Types of Hubs. (a) Private; (b) strategic partnership; (c) consortium; (d) public.

operator of an e-hub, four categories are common (although other characterizations have been used)—private, consortium (sponsored by a specific industry), strategic partnership, and public. Figure 4.2 shows the relationship between customers and suppliers for each of these categories.

Private e-Hub

A private e-hub is managed by the party who yields the greater power within the relationship. Such e-hubs are either purchaser-managed or supplier-managed (mostly they are purchaser-managed). POM also usually falls under these same conventions. In a private e-hub category, the managing entity develops the solution, deploys the related POM software tailored to its specific needs (purchased or developed in-house), and provides necessary security and privacy mechanisms to ensure that participants will not have concerns about their information being shared with anyone other than their trading partner. The owner of the e-hub has full control over who can access the e-hub and creates barriers that prevent competition from entering the e-hub. Such hubs have a one-to-many connectivity—one customer owner and many suppliers (POM) or one supplier owner and many customers (SOM or sales order management). This mechanism works effectively only if the POM (or SOM) processes are core competencies of the owner of the e-hub. If POM is not a core competency, the e-hub owner should consider joining a consortium e-hub.

Parties in e-hubs participate either due to a mandate by the power-wielding owner or due to incentives provided by the owner. For example, IBM has reported saving $1.7 billion by using its private marketplace and having about 25,000 suppliers (Duke-Wooley 2001). Other large companies such as Wal-Mart and Dell also follow this approach. However, because this type of e–hub is tailored to specific needs of its owner, participants may have to develop separate internal processes to conduct business over the private e-hub. Another consideration is that suppliers may not want to give up their investment in technology (e.g., EDI) to join an e-hub because they will be forced to apply multiple standards. Supplier participants must weigh the impact of such different processes on their bottom line when considering whether they should join a private e-hub or not. Often the perception is that a private e-hub will be a method to squeeze margins instead of optimizing the supply chain and that the owner will achieve a disproportionate percent of the value. Yet for a private e-hub to be successful, the owner must work with participants to ensure that these concerns are resolved.

POM via private e-hubs works very well for parts that are industry-specific or parts that require special logistics. Typically private e-hubs are not well suited for indirect parts or for MRO parts (maintenance, repair, operation), which are better suited to a public e-hub. Private e-hubs provide increased efficiencies due to customized workflows and also allow for additional capability through collaboration. With tight control over access, confidentiality and security are increased. Private e-hubs also facilitate keeping the business intelligence associated with POM in-house.

Strategic Partnership e-Hub

A strategic partnership e-hub is a special type of private hub. Participants in a strategic partnership e-hub act as an "extended family," which typically allows for complex collaborative relationships with extensive collaboration. The owning firm creates the e-hub (and the necessary infrastructure and processes) and invites key suppliers to join the e-hub. The relationships between the invited suppliers and the owning firm are irreplaceable in that the parties share proprietary information and product designs and make joint decisions on inventory management, planning, scheduling, and shipping. Integration between the owning firm and invited participants is deep. The Toyota model falls in this category.

Consortium e-Hub

A consortium e-hub is a special type of private hub in which two or more firms join together to create an e-hub for a specific industry. A consortium e-hub can be utilized vertically or horizontally within an industry or across various industries (e.g., for MRO items). Trust is a key component of a consortium e-hub. The most publicized example of such an e-hub is Covisint, which was created by

General Motors, Ford, and Daimler Chrysler specifically for the automotive industry. Covisint handles transactions with a value over $240 billion per year and with participation by over 30,000 suppliers. Covisint also overcomes some of the barriers that the automotive industry has faced with other e-hubs. For example, the automotive industry has long-term relationships with suppliers, something that is not common in public e-hubs. Additionally, the automotive industry uses long-term contracts instead of spot buying and auctions. Existence of a lack of trust and suspicion has played a major role in private e-hubs and has prevented the automotive industry from joining a public e-hub. Covisint has also codified several hundred business practices that are specific to the automotive industry, which allows companies to join the consortium and reduce supply chain costs and inefficiencies without additional staff. By some estimates, e-hubs such as Covisint have the potential to save $1000 per car (Teach 2000).

The chemical industry has also created e-hubs—Chemdex for the life science industry (currently defunct) and ChemConnect (Chemconnect 2006). ChemConnect allows companies to share order, demand, and inventory information in real time. ChemConnect also provides training, supports a variety of data formats, integrates with a company's existing enterprise resource planning (ERP) system, and hosts a solution so that it is immediately available to trading partners without any development. ChemConnect has been very successful with its customers in terms of maintaining the key component of trust in its consortium e-hub.

Other industries that have used consortium e-hubs in conducting POM activities include:

- Oil and gas (Chevron, Shell, etc.)
- Retail (Sears, Carrefour)
- Utility (Cinergy, Duke Energy, PG & E, Consolidated Edison)
- Aerospace and defense (Boeing, Lockheed Martin, BAE Systems, Raytheon)

The consortium approach is not as customized as the private approach, but it still provides significant cost savings primarily from two areas. Foremost is that development, management, and administrative costs are spread across consortium members. Additionally the consortium approach facilitates finding the correct part faster and allows owners and trading partners to maintain lower inventory levels, reduce scrap and rework, better alignment of material with low-cost suppliers, and increased asset and labor utilization.

Because the consortium e-hub is an extension of the private e-hub, issues with the private e-hub also become issues to some extent for the consortium approach. However, because the level of customization is lower, issues associated with customization are reduced. The greater issues with a consortium e-hub are related to price fixing and antitrust regulations. Suppliers are wary of collusion among customers for price fixing and governments are concerned that the consortium will result in an organization that violates antitrust laws.

Public e-Hub

The ownership of a public e-hub is neither customer nor supplier. Ownership is neutral. A third party owns, develops, and manages the e-hub. Buyers and suppliers "join" the hub. A public e-hub is well suited for standardized parts or frequently purchased parts. MRO and indirect parts, commodities having volatile price or demand, and standard products are also good candidates for a public e-hub. A public e-hub adds value for a buyer through automation and improvement of business workflows, by having access to several suppliers (if many join the hub), and by having a focus on price. For suppliers, value added is from access to a large customer base (if available) on the e-hub. Based on the e-hub model, a large number of buyers and sellers will increase liquidity and market transparency so that buyers can find sellers and vice versa. The contracting process is streamlined and standardization for parts and contracts is increased. Suppliers are also encouraged to push the concept upstream so that their suppliers will use it as well. However, due to the nature of the public e-hub, concentration has typically resulted in only a few e-hubs surviving. An example is the merger of Global NetXchange and World Wide Retail, two of the longest survivors in the retail arena. These two exchanges merged in April 2005, setting standards for using information technology in the retail industry (Gross 2005). The merger is also expected to reduce costs to customers through economies of scale.

Public e-hubs operate via several mechanisms. One mechanism is a catalog that is created by content aggregators who create catalogs of products that are available on the Web. Another mechanism is the dynamic exchange model in which buyers and suppliers are matched based on price. The dynamic exchange model is well suited for auctions of less frequently traded items as well as for reverse auctions. Public e-hubs can also be used effectively in procurement methods that require complex requisitions or for project-oriented material and services.

The success of a public e-hub depends on the number of participating buyers and sellers. However, there is no guarantee that participants will join the e-hub because participation is voluntary, not mandatory. Because of this characteristic and the reliance of the public e-hub business model on transaction fees supplemented by value-added service fees, the early public e-hub model could not be sustained. Public e-hubs proliferated in the 1990s and early 2000s, yet they did not succeed at that time for several reasons. In the 1990s and early 2000s, technology was developing and expensive and startup costs for e-hubs were high. Business processes were defined as needed but were not standardized for use with e-hubs, which resulted in a customized hub for each implementation. ROI expectations for the public e-hub model were unrealistic. Firms were also not ready to go "all electronic" and there was misalignment between e-hub providers and their ability to generate value for all participants. Large firms also wanted to get into the arena and decided to form their own private or consortium e-hubs thereby cutting into the public e-hub customers.

Current public e-hubs have used lessons learned from failures and have added several other revenue sources to the business model. In addition to the typical transaction, membership, and advertisement income, current e-hubs also generate profit from markups and catalog fees. e-Hub providers are also providing additional value-added services such as contracts management, invoicing and payment, fulfillment, receipt management, financing, insurance, customs clearance, training, etc. e-Hub providers have chosen to make some of these value-added services a part of their core competency and are developing their business model around them.

SUMMARY

Using e-communication as a part of performing business activities and processes has lead to tremendous progress from EDI to e-hubs. Advancements in the Internet have provided perfect enabling technology that allows one individual to instantly broadcast, collaborate, and interact with other individuals to achieve a personal or business requirement. The technology involved in making the Internet easy to use as well as to provide value has also changed significantly in recent years.

Comment: The biggest concern that the authors have is not how technology change will be managed, but rather how process changes will keep pace with technology changes and become more agile. The evolution of e-hubs is a good example of how jumping to a new technology can cause a lot of "grief," yet a well-thought-out business strategy and a standardized process can result in tremendous benefits. Another concern is how the evolution of process change is managed. We believe that if processes do not keep pace with technology, and technology is used to enable existing processes, the same poor results will continue, but they will occur a lot faster. Process owners and executives will then fault technology for poor results and focus on "working" the technology, when the focus should first have been on processes and then on alignment of technology and the changed processes to meet business needs.

REFERENCES

Berners-Lee, T. *The ENQUIRE System, Short Description.* 1980 October. Geneva: CERN. Available at: <http://www.w3.org/History.html>.

Berners-Lee, T. *Information Management: a Proposal.* 1989 March. Geneva: CERN. Available at: <http://www.w3.org/History.html>.

Bowen, D. A decade on the Internet: enterprise finally wakes up to the power of the web. *Financial Times.* 2005, December 14.

Cerf, V.G., Kahn, R.E. A protocol for packet network intercommunication. *IEEE Trans. Commun.* 1974 May; 22(5):637–648.

Chemconnect. *Supply Chain Solutions.* 2006. Available at: <www.chemconnect.com /supplychain.html>.

Duke-Wooley, R. *B2B Exchanges: Public or Private.* 2001 July. Available at: <www.e-principles.com/B2B.htm>.

Esposito, R. *FBI: Cyber Blackmail by Animal Rights Hackers.* 2006 April 28. Available at: <http://blogs.abcnews.com/theblotter/2006/04/ fbi–cyber–black .html>.

Gross, G. B2B retail hubs join forces. *CIO Magazine;* 2005 June 15.

Kleinrock, L. Proposal for a Ph.D. Thesis: *Information Flow in Large Communication Nets.* 1961 May 31; Part 1: 1–11. Cambridge, MA: MIT. Available at: <http:// www. lk.cs.ucla.edu/LK/Bib/REPORT/PhD/>.

RAND Corporation. *Reshaping the Supply Chains.* 2003. Available at: <http://www. rand.org/scitech/stpi/ourfuture/Manufacturing/sec8–reshaping.html>.

Teach, E. Going virtual: big companies want to put their supply chains on web exchanges, but they'll have to overcome a host of obstacles first. *CFO Magazine;* 2000 May 1.

Upton, D.M., McAfee, A. The real virtual factory. *Harvard Business Review;* 1996 July-August.

Willinger, W., Govindan, R., Jamin, S., Paxson, V., Shenker, S. Scaling phenomena in the Internet: critically examining criticality. *Proc. Natl. Acad. Sci. USA.* 2002 Feb 19; 99: 2573–2580.

5

IDENTIFICATION TECHNOLOGIES: BARCODES AND RFID

INTRODUCTION

Two atomic (or most basic) measurements within any supply chain are the *item* and the *quantity*. Decisions that impact the health of a supply chain are based on the quantities of any item anywhere in the pipeline. Hence knowing "how much" of "what item" is available in the supply chain is extremely important.

Before a quantity can be determined, identifying and sorting items that are alike is important. Physical characteristics are used to distinguish between objects and to identify them (e.g., 10 mm and 20 mm, as a measurement of the diameter of bolts), but objects that are not visible cannot be manually distinguished from other objects (e.g., items inside a carton), therefore some mechanism must be used to identify them. An example of a manual identification process would be to open a carton (or the enclosing entity) and count the items within it that are alike. To facilitate identification and counting processes, industry has improved upon this type of manual identification technique with technologies such as basic labels, barcodes, biometric scanners (e.g., retina scans), radio frequency identification (RFID), etc., which has resulted in widespread use of identification technology in industry.

Realizing that identification technology is an *enabler* of business processes is important. By themselves, identification technologies have no value added for a business. The technologies are merely pieces of paper (such as labels and barcodes) or microchips (RFID), but if incorporated into business processes with the proper hardware and software, the shift to significant value added for a business can be dramatic.

Chapter 5 will discuss two types of identification technologies which are known as automatic identification technologies. Automatic identification technologies—the ubiquitous barcode and the trendy radio frequency identification (RFID)—can be used to enable purchase order management (POM) processes. Use of barcode and RFID identification technologies in supply chain processes (as well as other processes) and novel ways in which RFID technology might be used will also briefly be discussed.

BARCODES

Barcodes have simplified inventory tracking and management. Barcodes are commonly found as labels that are affixed to or built into packages containing items. These labels contain encoded character data in the form of black and white patterns, which are recognized and decoded by special barcode readers. Barcode readers typically shine (direct) a light onto a label and register the intensity of the light that is reflected back. The reflection is then decoded by an electronic circuit and matched against a character set that has been programmed into the reader. After being recognized, the characters generate a unique key that is used for matching against a database to obtain information regarding the object scanned. Figure 5.1 is a schematic representation of the process for generating and decoding barcodes. In a typical consumer goods database, information such as descriptions and unit price are stored in a database for barcode applications. For other applications (e.g., customer loyalty cards), a barcode can retrieve data about the card holder (e.g., name, address, and telephone number). Other pieces of data may include shopping preferences, shopping habits, spending profile, and possibly customer ratings.

A Brief History of Barcodes

The first reference to automatic identification technology dates back to a project in 1932 at the Harvard University Graduate School of Business Administration. Punched cards placed in a catalog were used to pull items from a stock room and transfer them to a checkout counter. At the same time an invoice was produced and inventory was changed to reflect the sale.

The concept of barcodes was first developed by Bernard Silver and Norman Woodland in 1948. A United States patent was issued in 1952 (U.S. Patent 2,612,994). The dark background barcode consisted of four white lines, with the first line acting as the reference line, and allowed for seven classifications. The inventors did indicate that more classifications could be added by increasing the number of lines.

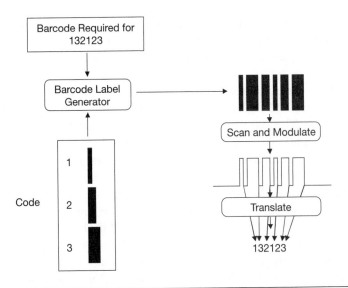

Figure 5.1. Coding and Decoding Barcode Labels.

Barcode technology achieved commercial visibility in 1966 when the U.S. National Association of Food Chains put out a request for information from equipment manufacturers to improve checkout speed. The need for a standard was recognized almost immediately after the first barcode checkout system was put into place in 1967, which resulted in the Uniform Grocery Products Identification Code. This code was quickly followed by adoption of the Universal Product Code symbol set, which is still used in the United States. In addition to using barcodes for consumer products, in 1967 early attempts were made to use automatic identification in the railroad industry, but due to technical reasons the initiative was abandoned. True acceptance of barcodes for industrial applications began in 1981 when the U.S. Department of Defense (DOD) mandated barcodes, specifically the Code 39 symbology, for all DOD material.

Barcode Symbology

Because barcodes contain data, mechanisms must encode and decode this data so that it can be utilized effectively. Furthermore, to ensure that the process is deterministic, a common decoding schema is required. Such schemas are known as symbologies. Over the years, several symbologies have been developed to meet the specific needs of various industries, e.g., library cards based on barcodes utilize a symbology that is different from the symbology used for consumer goods (e.g., on a can of coffee). In addition to defining standards, no duplication is allowed, i.e., no two different items can have the same barcode. The Uniform Code Council,

Inc. (UCC; now known as GS1) was chartered with the responsibility of issuing product numbers and managing the associated specifications for global use. Table 5.1 contains examples of commonly utilized symbologies and sample barcodes for them.

UPC-A barcodes. A typical UPC-A barcode (commonly used in retail applications) consists of 12 digits, which are split across 4 regions. Each region has a specific purpose. The first region contains one digit, which identifies the number system used by the barcode. Potentially ten number systems may be used: regular, pharmaceutical, internal, coupons, etc. The last region also contains one digit, which is used as a check digit to ensure a good scan. Enclosed between the first digit and the last digit are bars that contain manufacturer code and product code. The manufacturer code (also known as the company prefix) is assigned by the UCC and is contained in the first six to nine digits of the barcode. This number is the same for all of the company's products and UCC guarantees that it is unique. The next set of digits contains a product code that uniquely defines a product. These digits are assigned by each company. The company must ensure that these digits are unique within the company (but not necessarily across companies). If a company has more products than can be defined by the product code digits, it must obtain another company prefix from the UCC.

UPC-E barcodes. UPC-E symbology is a compressed form of UPC-A symbology that uses only eight characters. Well-defined rules translate a UPC-A barcode to a UPC-E barcode as well as decode it.

Supplemental barcodes. In addition to the 8 or 12 characters, barcodes may have a supplemental barcode to the right of the main barcode. The supplemental barcode is shorter than the main barcode and consists of two or five digits. This supplemental information is used to encode additional information (e.g., issue number, price) for printed material such as newspapers, books, and periodicals.

2-D barcodes. As use of barcodes has increased, so has the requirement for the amount of data stored within a barcode. Size constraints of commonly used barcodes containing vertical lines (known as linear barcodes) have forced symbology designers to develop two-dimensional (2-D) barcodes. 2-D barcodes contain data in horizontal and vertical dimensions, whereas linear barcodes contain data in only one dimension. 2-D barcodes are relatively new (first commercially used in 1988). As shown in Table 5.1, 2-D barcodes can encode several thousand bytes of alphanumeric or binary data. Each code has a "finder pattern," which is used as a mechanism to center the label with respect to the reader. Due to the added complexity of 2-D barcodes, special readers (e.g., moving-beam laser scanners or charge-couple device scanners) are required, but they operate on the same concept as the linear barcode.

3-D barcodes. A third type of barcode, the three-dimensional barcode (3-D), is also used commercially. However, this barcode is actually a 3-D representation of

Table 5.1. Barcode Symbologies with Examples

Barcode	Type	Character Set	Length (Size + Check)	Applications	Example
EAN-8	Linear	Digits	7 + 1	Worldwide retail	
EAN-13	Linear	Digits	12 + 1	Worldwide retail	
UPC-A	Linear	Digits	11 + 1	USA/Canada retail	
Plessey	Linear	Digits	Variable	Grocery store shelf tags	
Code 39	Linear	Uppercase; digits; Space - . $ / + %	Variable	Wide use across industries	
Code 128	Linear	ASCII + control codes	Variable	Wide use across industries	
Postnet	Bar height encoding	Digits	5, 9, or 11 + 1	USA postal code (ZIP code)	
PDF-417	2-D	ASCII	Variable, to 1850 ASCII or 2725 digits		
DataMatrix	2-D	ASCII	Variable, to 2335 ASCII		
Maxicode	2-D	ASCII	93 ASCII	Parcel destination information for auto-sorting (UPS)	

a linear barcode that has been decoded using special equipment and relying on differences in height rather than contrast in the decoding process. 3-D barcodes are permanently embossed on an item and become a characteristic of the item. 3-D barcodes are typically used when labels will not adhere to a receiving surface or in applications in which barcodes can easily be damaged or rendered unreadable (e.g., due to paint or coatings).

Benefits of Barcodes

Barcodes provide several advantages in the business processes that use them, including increased accuracy, faster data reading, reduced process errors, increased processing efficiency, and reduced operating costs. Typical error rates for manual data entry are about 1 error for every 300 keystrokes (i.e., over 3300 errors per 1 million keystrokes). Barcodes reduce the error rate to between 1 error in 15,000 or 1 error in 36 trillion characters depending upon the barcode type that is used (see Lahiri 2006 for barcode accuracies for different symbologies). Because barcode labels typically contain human-readable characters along with code, a read failure can be easily corrected by using these human-readable characters.

Typical manual data entry of product code and serial number information takes over 20 minutes. With manual barcode scanning, this rate is improved to about 2 minutes. In high-speed applications, strategically placed barcode readers can effectively read barcodes on conveyors running at over 300 feet per minute. However, increasing the scan rate also increases the risk of read failures. Fast, accurate reads result in increased processing efficiency and reduced operating costs.

Customer or regulatory requirements may force an organization into compliance. In addition to meeting the regulatory requirements, compliance provides the organization with an opportunity to leverage changes to improve its processes. In healthcare and regulatory applications, barcodes have played an important role in the reduction of data entry error rates.

Limitations of Barcodes

The intrinsic characteristics of barcodes introduce limitations. Most of these limitations are associated with the readability of barcodes:

Readability. The most common limitation is related to how barcodes are recognized. A line-of-vision scan is required to read a barcode, therefore anything that impacts the optical characteristics of the barcode reader negatively impacts the reading of barcodes. For example, moisture between the reader and the barcode affects readability. Physical damage to barcode labels (e.g., from paint, harsh chemicals, scratches, dirt, and distortion along the principle axis) also causes barcodes to become unreadable. Additionally label printing technology and minimum preciseness requirements for bar widths and contrast can also impact readability.

Barcodes also have drawbacks that are not related to readability:

Fixed labeling. A major drawback is that the barcode on a label cannot be changed. If a change is required, a new barcode label must be affixed over the existing one.

Limited identification. As barcodes are currently used, a potential drawback is that a barcode cannot uniquely identify all items (e.g., barcodes cannot create a serial number for each item). This limitation can be overcome by using dense barcodes, but price will be significantly increased.

Limited security. Barcodes may not be the appropriate technology in security-related applications, e.g., barcode-based identification cards can very easily be duplicated, which defeats the purpose of a secure identification process.

RFID

Simplistically, radio frequency identification (RFID) is an automatic identification technology that uses radio frequency to transmit the identity of an object that contains a RF transmitter. Unlike barcodes, in which scans have to be performed manually, radio frequency transmission in an RFID system allows capturing of identification data without manual scanning. A "reader" recognizes the radio frequency transmission.

A Brief History of RFID

The first application of RFID technology was in the "identify friend or foe" (IFF) system used in World War II. Allied planes were equipped with a transmitter that was activated by a radar signal. Once activated, the transmitter would broadcast a signal that identified a plane as a "friendly" aircraft.

Advances in communications technology in the 1950s and 1960s increased commercial applications of remote identification technology. The earliest commercial application was electronic article surveillance (EAS), which is the use of a single-bit identification tag in antitheft systems. An EAS tag was put on each item. It could be turned "on" or "off." As an item was paid for, the tag would be turned off, which allowed a buyer to take the item out of the store without sounding an alarm. EAS systems are still used commercially today.

In the 1970s additional research in electronic surveillance was done. The Los Alamos National Laboratory lead the way by tracking nuclear material (for the U.S. Department of Energy) and livestock (cows for the U.S. Department of Agriculture). About the same time, other applications using RFID such as building access, electronic toll collection, vehicle tracking, manufacturing floor automation, etc. were being developed.

In the 1980s RFID implementation greatly increased. European countries focused on short-range applications such as toll collection, animal tracking, and industrial applications. The United States focused on access and toll collection applications. Certain industries developed global applications. For example, automobile manufacturers developed antitheft systems using RFID in which a RFID chip was enclosed in the plastic housing of a key. An RFID reader in the steering column could read the RFID chip in the key unit. If the reader did not read the correct (or matching) identification number from the RFID chip (or if it received no identification number), the reader would prevent the car from starting.

In the 1990s RFID technology significantly advanced by offering a wider frequency spectrum for RFID. While the technology was being developed, other organizations were looking for novel methods to commercialize and utilize the technology such as embedding RFID chips in gaming chips, the Mobil Oil Speedpass™ system, snow skiing passes, etc. Although the use of RFID began to experience significant growth, deployment of RFID in applications did not experience a corresponding growth. A lack of standards and the high cost of the various RFID system components were major contributors to the low acceptance rates.

A turning point for RFID occurred in 1999 when the UCC (Uniform Code Council), Gillette, and Proctor & Gamble established an Auto-ID Center (AIC) at the Massachusetts Institute of Technology. The intent of the center was to develop low-cost RFID "tags" (5 U.S. cents) that could be utilized in supply chains. Within the next few years, the AIC gained support from over 100 private corporations (including Wal-Mart, Kimberly Clark, Unilever, and Tesco), the U.S. DOD, and RFID vendors. Executives in these organizations realized the huge potential impact that RFID tags could have on supply chain visibility—knowing the exact location of every item in the supply chain on demand. AIC subsequently developed the electronic product code (EPC) numbering scheme, which complemented the UPC, and two protocols (known as air interfaces) to allow RFID chips to wirelessly communicate with readers (a Gen1 air interface known as Class 0 and Class 1). To ensure that data was communicated securely, AIC also developed a secure network architecture, which allowed Internet-based queries for RFID tag information stored in databases.

In 2003 the AIC technology was licensed to the UCC, which established EPCglobal, a non-profit organization with a goal of commercializing EPC technology. A Gen2 air interface protocol and a network infrastructure known as the EPCglobal Network were subsequently developed. Based on the success of pilot testing, Wal-Mart and the U.S. DOD mandated the use of RFID, first with Gen1 and now with Gen2. However, because the tags are still relatively expensive, current implementation is only at pallet level, not item level.

RFID Standards and Organizations

When several entities want to share data, standards ensure uniform understanding and application. Although over 100 RFID standards exist, most of them are proprietary in nature. Two standards organizations publish and manage the public domain RFID-related standards associated with air interface protocol, data layout, and applications—ECPglobal and the International Organization for Standardization (ISO). Current ISO standards are different than those published by EPCglobal, primarily due to the specific charter for EPCglobal—to develop a simple inexpensive RFID tag and a corresponding simple air interface protocol.

The ISO 18000 series of standards defines the standards for RFID-based item management and automatic identification operating at various frequencies. The ISO 18000 series of standards has seven parts. Each part specifies a standard for a different operating frequency to cover operating frequencies across the globe (ISO 2004):

18000–1: Generic parameters for air interface communications at globally accepted frequencies

18000–2: Parameters for air interface communication below 135 kHz

18000–3: Parameters for air interface communication at 13.56 MHz

18000–4: Parameters for air interface communication at 2.45 GHz

18000–5: Parameters for air interface communication at 5.8 GHz

18000–6: Parameters for air interface communication at 860 to 960 MHz

18000–7: Parameters for air interface communication at 433 MHz

Low-frequency (LF) systems in the sub-135-kHZ range are typically used in security or asset tracking applications in which the tags must be close to the readers to obtain a "read." Typically applications in the mid-frequency range of 13.56 MHz are for communication in which security is not a major concern. Most supply chain applications fall in this category. The ultrahigh-frequency (UHF) systems, 860 to 960 MHz, 2.45 GHz, and 5.8 GHz, provide the longest read range as well as an ability to read at high speed.

EPCglobal began development of standards utilizing the ISO UHF air interface protocols, but soon realized that the ISO protocols were too complex and that implementing the protocols would increase the cost of tags. The ISO protocols were subsequently rejected and a new set of protocols was developed. EPCglobal developed an open set of standards that is based on an ability to read and write on tags. Five classes of tags have been defined by EPCglobal (EPC 2005). A sixth class, Class 0, has been added to accommodate tags with identification that is written during manufacturing. Class 0 tags also require a different protocol than the other classes.

Class 0. Class 0 tags are "read only" tags in which an identification value is written on the tag during tag manufacturing. The protocol used in these tags is different than the one used for other tags, therefore multiprotocol readers are required to read Class 0 tags and tags from other classes. The value in the memory of a Class 0 tag cannot be changed, but it can be read as many times as is required. Because Class 0 tags contain only identification information, they are known as "identity-only" tags. Users must ensure that their software systems can correlate the identification information on the tag to the item.

Class 1. Class 1 tags are simple identifiers and are currently the most prevalent type of RFID tags. Class 1 tags are not necessarily given an identification value during manufacturing. After a Class 1 tag has been manufactured, a value can only be written once to the tag by a user (e.g., at first use in a manufacturing facility for a product, tickets at a theater, etc.). Like Class 0 tags, Class 1 tags can be read as many times as required. Class 1 tags are also known as "write-once-read-many" tags. Because Class 1 tags are often written in the field of use, relating the tag to an item that has the tag is easier. For example, a labeling application can print details of a shipment on a pallet RFID label and at the same time write to the RFID tag memory. The application can then communicate the label information and the RFID tag identification value to a backend system.

Class 2. Class 2 tags are "read-write" tags, which can be written to multiple times during the life of the tag. Typically Class 2 tags contain more memory than is required for identification purposes. Class 2 tags can be written to by a reader, which potentially makes them vulnerable to security threats.

Class 3. Class 3 tags are also "read-write" tags, but they contain built-in sensors that record ambient information such as temperature, pressure, shocks, etc. into the tag memory. Because ambient readings can be taken at any time, Class 3 tags contain a power source.

Class 4. Class 4 tags are more sophisticated than Class 3 tags and are capable of transmitting information that is stored in their memory. Class 4 tags contain a power source.

Class 5. Class 5 tags are an enhanced version of a Class 4 tag and are capable of communicating with other Class 5 tags and other devices.

Class 0 and Class 1 tags are not interoperable nor are they compatible with ISO standards. Class 0 and Class 1 tags cannot be used globally because of differing regulations. Because of these limitations, EPCglobal began working on a second-generation protocol known as Gen2. The goal was to ensure that the Gen2 protocol would be backward-compatible with Class 0 and Class 1 and better aligned with ISO standards. To ensure that this effort was successful, EPCglobal invited vendors that were involved in developing the ISO standards to participate. However, a discrepancy between mandatory versus optional requirements in one field has currently been a barrier to convergence. Even with this issue, the Gen2 standard is actively being adopted by vendors for use in global supply chain solutions.

How an RFID System Works

An RFID system consists of several components: tag, reader, reader antenna, communication infrastructure, and an application portfolio that utilizes RFID technology. Each of these components will be briefly discussed later in the chapter, but a brief discussion of how each of these is used within a RFID system will now be presented.

At a high level, a RFID system operates in the following way. A RFID tag is made up of a microchip that is attached to an antenna. A substrate composed of one of several materials provides the environment onto which the chip-antenna assembly is placed. Optionally a tag may contain a battery that provides power to the tag. A reader containing one or more antennae is used to retrieve data from a RFID tag. The antenna emits RF waves that provide power to nonpowered tags. This power activates the tag, which broadcasts information contained in the tag. The reader receives the tag information and passes it to the target application using a communication infrastructure. Usually three data items are transmitted by readers—tag ID, reader ID, and a time stamp of the read. The target application knows the location of the readers and, based on the information provided by the readers, the target application performs tasks with the data provided.

The following paragraphs will now describe a typical workflow in the manufacturing industry. RFID is used as a supply chain application. The scenario depicts a complete workflow from the packing of an item to the consumption of the item on an assembly line. The intent is to demonstrate one potential application of the RFID technology. Three typical processes in a manufacturing environment—automatic creation of a shipment document (an advanced shipment notice or ASN), receiving, and consumption reporting—are included. A schematic of this process is presented in Figure 5.2.

A manufacturing facility and one of its suppliers have agreed upon a schedule that the supplier will ship against. The supplier manufactures the items requested and, depending upon the type of item, deploys an RFID tag on each item (or on the packages that enclose the items). As the tags are being deployed, the supplier transmits the tag information to its ERP system, making an association between the item and the tag. The ERP system may also capture additional information such as the date and time of manufacture, the batch or lot number, potentially the PO number that the item is fulfilling (in manufacture-to-order situations), etc. In the next step, items are packed into cartons. Each carton also contains an RFID tag. As items are packed into the carton, the RFID reader associates the tag on each item with the carton, which defines the relationship between the items and the carton. The cartons are now ready to be put onto pallets.

The next step puts the cartons onto a pallet and shrink-wraps the pallet to ensure the integrity of the shipment. After the shrink-wrapping process, an RFID

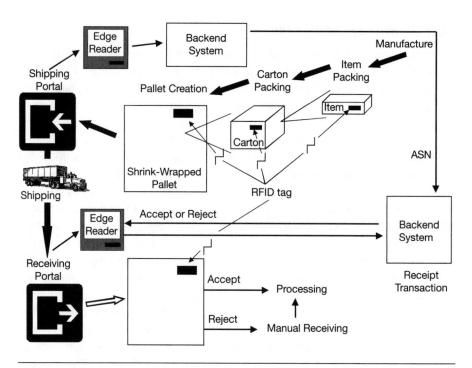

Figure 5.2. Shipping and Receiving Processes using RFID Technology.

tag is deployed on the pallet. During deployment, the RFID reader reads the pallet identification tag and the RFID identification tag of each carton and associates the cartons with the pallet. The pallet is now ready to be shipped.

During the shipping process, strategically located reader portals on the shipping docks will read the outbound movement of a tagged pallet. This event, along with information already residing in the enterprise application, creates a shipment notification (ASN) and records the items as shipped as the pallet goes through the RFID reader portals. At this point, the ASN containing the pallet's RFID tag information can be tied to a specific customer order and sent to the customer, which completes the major steps in the order fulfillment process.

At the other end, after transit, the shipment will be delivered to the customer. Again, strategically located RFID reader portals at the receiving docks will read the RFID tag on the pallet. The ASN containing the pallet RFID tag information transmitted by the supplier is already in the customer's enterprise application software. When the receiving dock reader portals read the inbound pallet RFID tag and transmit the information to the application software, all individual items in the shipment will be automatically received.

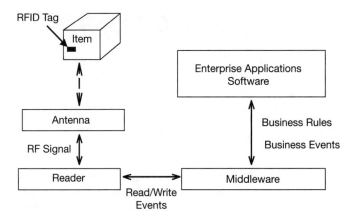

Figure 5.3. RFID System Components.

Because tracking items is important in a supply chain, determining when items are consumed within a manufacturing environment is important. With RIFD-tagged items and readers located along the manufacturing line, consumption can be reported as the items exit the location where they have been used. Consumption reporting can automatically update inventory and the manufacturer (and customers and suppliers if they are integrated) can have a near real-time visibility of raw material and work-in-process levels.

Enterprise applications at each supply chain participant are aware of the location of each reader within its control. As depicted in the above workflow, with reader location, tag ID, and a time stamp of tag reads, the exact location and flow through the supply chain of each tagged item can be determined and a "chain of custody" can be documented.

RFID Technology and Deployment

An RFID solution consists of several components. This section will discuss the most important components—tags and readers, middleware, servers, and application software. Also discussed will be integration of these components as well as components that increase the chances of success of an RFID implementation. Figure 5.3 depicts a schematic of how the component pieces fit together to form a solution.

RFID Tags and Readers

The main elements of RFID technology are RFID tags and readers.

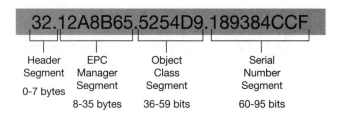

Figure 5.4. Layout for a 96-bit EPC RFID Tag.

Tags. A 96-bit EPC RFID identification tag is shown in Figure 5.4. Tags are placed on the entity to be identified and readers are placed in locations at which the solution requires that the tag information is to be read. An RFID system is classified according to the type of tag used. The three types of tags are passive, semi-active, or active. *Passive* tags do not contain a built-in power source, but instead derive their power from a radio signal sent by an antenna. Passive tags typically contain only identification information. *Semi-active* tags are powered by batteries, but data transmission is achieved via power derived from an antenna. The battery supports communication and enables longer distances, higher speed, and improved readability. *Active* tags are powered by built-in batteries. The battery power is used to communicate with the reader and to perform tasks that the tags are designed to perform. Typically, such tags are "smart" tags that act as data transmitters, even in the absence of readers, and communicate necessary information. Semi-active and active tags have a predetermined life span. Once their power source is depleted, these tags are useless until the battery is replaced. The cost of passive tags is dependent upon frequency, antenna design, packaging, and the memory in the tag. Currently, the cost for passive tags ranges from 20 U.S. cents for high-volume simple tags to 10s of U.S. dollars for tags that are embedded in packing material, which protects them from a harsh environment. Passive tags on a printable label with barcode capability currently cost over 40 U.S. cents. Semi-active and active tags typically run in 10s of U.S. dollars or more, depending upon the same parameters as passive tags as well as battery life, the amount of built-in computing capability, and the functionality provided. Companies may often add redundancy by duplicating tags on items to ensure guaranteed reads.

Readers. Devices that are on the "edge of the network" (from a software perspective) and provide connectivity between tags and backend systems are known as readers. Readers "read" information presented to them by a RFID tag and are capable of powering tags through their antennas. Readers are also capable of writing to writeable tags. Readers can be handheld and mobile or stationary and strategically located in the path of items being tracked. The reader antenna is a key component of a reader and provides the means for a reader to communicate with a tag. The antenna can be located internally or externally to a reader. Multiple external antennae can also be installed onto a reader. Some new readers accommodate up to eight external antennae. Yet readers by themselves do not have much functionality in a stand-alone mode, therefore a mechanism is required to connect them to external devices. An external device allows for extending the overall capability of the system. Such devices are connected to readers via input/output (I/O) ports on the readers. The I/O ports are used to connect readers to computers and networks. Readers can also be connected to other devices. For example, a motion detector can be connected to a reader such that the reader becomes "active" when motion is detected, or a programmable logic controller (PLC) can be connected to a reader, which allows the PLC to control some processes when the reader detects a specific RFID tag.

Price. Readers vary significantly in price depending upon the capabilities provided. Typically external antennae and power and network cable prices are not included in reader pricing, but are determined by the environment into which the readers are installed. Readers that merely read tags and convey the information are relatively inexpensive (under $1000 U.S.). Intelligent readers, on the other hand, are much more expensive (typically over $5000 U.S.). Intelligent readers have significant computing capability and may contain middleware components. Intelligent readers containing middleware communicate wirelessly with middleware servers and perform several local tasks such as validation, commissioning of tags (i.e., associating a tag with an object), and decommissioning of tags (i.e., removing the association between an object and its tag), and vendor- or equipment-specific tasks, etc. In addition to the price for the readers, tags, and cables, the cost of testing tags and readers must be considered.

Middleware

Middleware is a set of software components that provides services to multiple processes residing on one or more machines across a network so that these processes can interact in a predefined manner to achieve a predefined result. In RFID systems, middleware resides between the RFID reader and the enterprise application software systems. Middleware performs two categories of functions— to manage data passing through a system (data management) and to manage systems involved in an application (system management)(MARC 2004).

From a data-management perspective, middleware is a key component because middleware takes raw data from a reader, processes the data, and then transfers the data to an application software system. The characteristics of a RFID deployment make every deployment susceptible to three types of data gaps—geographic (due to reader location), device (due to multiple devices such as a PLC, motion sensor, etc.), and time (due to multiple reads of the same tag, delayed reads, overlapping read fields, etc.). The responsibility of middleware is to overcome this fragmentation and ensure that gaps in data are "filled in." In other words, data management ensures that a true picture of the "what," "where," and "when" of inventory movement within an enterprise is communicated to predefined targets in a timely manner.

Middleware also provides system management capabilities. A typical RFID application consists of several elements that must be managed efficiently—security, devices, and configuration. Middleware provides adequate security for data flowing between the readers and the enterprise application software system. Security between a tag and a reader is the most vulnerable. However, because information communicated between a tag and the reader is typically only identification information, an eavesdropper cannot assign meaning to that information unless other data elements, which can be associated to the identification information, are also available. Device management includes managing the physical devices in the RFID system, including hardware (e.g., detecting and replacing defective devices) and activities such as firmware updates. Configuration management ensures that all entities are configured and calibrated to attain the desired results. As the number of entities increases in RFID deployment, configuration management would also include management of "airtime" to ensure that all readers have adequate time to read within their read zone.

Costs for middleware in an RFID solution can be in the hundreds of thousands of dollars (U.S.). Costs are highly dependent on the complexity of the solution, installation locations, and many other factors. Middleware vendors and subject matter experts are typically involved in an RFID project to ensure that this critical component in the solution provides the desired capability.

Application Software

Application software is the component that contains the business logic and the components that are required to meet business functionality. Application software accomplishes business functionality by accepting data from (or sending data to) middleware components. A number of software vendors such as SAP, Oracle, Manhattan Associates, etc. have been actively upgrading their software to accept and manage RFID data so that it seamlessly integrates with their portfolio.

Deployment

The next crucial component that brings all the above components together to meet the desired business need is deployment. Because several heterogeneous systems are tied together, deployment usually requires resources who are expert systems integrators. Systems integrators use the laws of physics for RFID technology and to determine the correct parameters for RFID tags, readers, and antennas. For example, RFID system integrators analyze the RF spectrum in the target environment to determine the placement of readers, which will ensure that readers are not placed in locations in which RF interference exists and thereby causes reduction in signal strength. Systems integrators also assist in designing the "plumbing" for the system and in ensuring that end-to-end dataflow and workflow are as desired. Systems integrators may also conduct training, a key component of deployment and one that makes any change initiative successful.

Sponsors of an RFID initiative must realize that like any other new technology, deploying RFID technology can be expensive because of the costs of infrastructure components and systems integration. However, choosing to deploy a RFID initiative can provide a payoff that is significant, not just for the deploying organization, but also for upstream and downstream entities.

Because RFID is an *enabling* technology, if the business processes being impacted by RFID are flawed, the results of a RFID implementation will not be as anticipated. The same bad results will occur, but they will occur much faster than before. In addition a tremendous amount of flawed data will have been generated by RFID implementation. Once a RFID implementation has been authorized, the first step to take to make the initiative successful is to validate business processes. If business processes are flawed, process reengineering, including necessary change management, should be included in the implementation. (*Note*: Change management is the subject of Part III.)

Implementing a RFID solution is not easy. RFID implementation does not have "plug-and-play" solutions. Therefore no single strategy will work in all RFID implementations, which causes some implementation efforts to become much more complex. In the remainder of this section, some best practices will be presented to assist achieving a successful RFID implementation.

Certain basic items should be considered before beginning an implementation to achieve success. Project managers must have these basic items on a check list and address each one before proceeding with a RFID implementation. The following are basic items and are presented in no specific order:

- Choose an application that can be enabled via RFID. Associated business processes must also be validated. Keep in mind when selecting an application that although RFID is a mature technology, the widespread use of RFID in supply chains is still immature.
- Make a business case for the application to be enabled via RFID. Justify the project and obtain sponsorship for the solution. Provide the amount of information that is necessary to make executives and stakeholders become excited about the project, but remember that few RFID implementations have claimed return on investment (ROI) as part of a business case (Ferguson 2006).
- Document all steps in all associated *as is* and *to be* processes. The *to be* documentation will generate a baseline for future enhancements. The

documented gaps between the *as is* and *to be* processes will identify the rationale for process change and assist in developing documentation, training plans, test plans, etc.

- Identify risks. Risks are associated with any new technology. Therefore RFID projects are not immune from these risks. Identifying, quantifying, and developing plans to mitigate the risks associated with the new technology will be crucial to the success of any RFID project.

- Ensure excellent project management for the RFID implementation project. Change management is crucial for such projects. The responsibility of the project manager (PM) and sponsor(s) is to ensure proper change management. With new technology, new issues are likely to occur. The PM must give extra effort to managing these new issues.

- Provide timely communication to appropriate personnel about relevant aspects of the project to improve the chance of success.

- Sustain change. The first RFID initiative is one of many such projects an organization will undertake. To ensure that executives, sponsors, and stakeholders remain excited about the initiative, change must be sustained. Therefore documenting and measuring business value must be performed to ensure that buy-in continues.

Several other items could have been included in the above list. Therefore the reader is directed to consult project management books for a discussion of project management-related topics in greater depth.

Specific RFID-related items, if addressed, can increase the chance of having a successful RFID implementation:

- Use an incremental approach. RFID technology standards and capabilities are still evolving as are key components of the solution. Therefore following an incremental approach to deploying RFID solutions is recommended. Architect solutions in such a way that they are scalable and allow for future growth.

- Test the environment before installation. RF interference can prevent successful reading of tags and can significantly reduce read rates, which can negatively impact the success of RFID deployment.

- Develop a RF spectrum management plan and actively execute against this plan periodically to ensure that interference is within a threshold limit at each location.

- Architect the RFID solution so that it will be capable of handling some amount of RF interference. Ensure that unpredictable and/or uncontrollable sources of RF interference have been taken into account.

- Architect the RFID solution to ensure that each read location in the solution is optimized to meet the specific use cases set forth for that location.
- Institutionalize processes associated with changes to the physical environment so that these changes will pass the RF compliance step (to ensure that future seemingly simple environment changes do not cause RF interference and negatively impact the RFID solution).
- Implement solution mechanisms that ensure events and direction are correctly established and transmitted to the RFID system to ensure accurate association of data with direction and events.
- Develop a strategy prior to implementation that defines the appropriate use of various types of RFID readers to avoid a situation during implementation in which installing a stationary RFID reader is impossible.
- Develop a cohesive device management strategy that includes not only the network components, but also RFID devices because a RFID solution will add several devices to a network.
- Build fault tolerance and redundancy into systems to ensure that all tags are read. Build a solution that includes constant automated monitoring of key components so that alarms will be generated when failures occur. Failure alarms avoid a situation in which a tagged pallet has been shipped, only to learn much later that a shipping dock reader failed to read the tag correctly, e.g., because of a missed read or a failed reader.
- Remember the laws of physics. The laws of physics that govern RFID technology should be kept in mind to ensure success of an implementation. In addition to other factors (e.g., RF interference), the solution must consider tag placement and environmental conditions as well (e.g., moisture, temperature, etc.).
- Remember the importance of integration. The effectiveness of systems integration will be a major contributor to the success or failure of deployment. An experienced integrator will be a "best ally" in ensuring that the components in a RFID solution work in concert.
- "Test, test, test, and then test some more." Thoroughly test the solution to ensure that it performs as designed. Plan for periodic checks of the solution as a part of the sustain phase.

Uses of RFID

Because RFID is an *enabling* technology, by itself RFID does not provide much value, but if connected to readers, middleware, and back-end application software and if defined processes exist to use them, immediate value can be seen.

RFID can be used to identify inanimate and living objects. A U.S. company has implanted RFID tags in some employees to test access control to secure environments (Waters 2006). By the very nature of RFID technology, human intervention is not required to read identification information, a characteristic which has led to many uses of RFID. Some uses are commonly observed, yet other novel methods using RFID have been proposed that are still in the early phases of commercial use. Use of RFID can include supply chains, asset tracking, access control, security systems, payment systems, and identification of people and pets. Common uses as well as potential novel uses of RFID will now be presented.

Supply Chain

The key objectives of a supply chain are to provide the right product, in the right quantity, at the right place, to the right people, at the right price, and at the right time. While doing this, every entity in the supply chain must ensure that its personal goal is achieved (e.g., making a predefined profit). Industry has taken several steps in an effort to balance these objectives and still meet its goals. Initiatives such as inventory reduction and Just-in-Time (JIT) manufacturing have helped improve supply chains. RFID can further enhance these initiatives through its unique ability to provide visibility and traceability.

RFID technology has been used to automate pieces of the supply chain that are under the direct control of an organization. Using RFID, internal processes have been reengineered and streamlined, resulting in improved manufacturing efficiencies. Using RFID, organizations have been able to look externally to improve the flow of information and material across their boundaries and to ultimately propagate these improvements to key supply chain partners upstream and downstream of manufacturing. With defined standards and technologies becoming mainstream and robust, organizations are using RFID to seek major improvement in visibility and traceability across supply chain partners. A RFID solution is capable of automatically capturing the "cradle-to-grave" cycle of a tagged item, a crucial component of the supply chain in businesses such as aircraft manufacturing.

Although RFID technology provides significant enhancements to business processes, a key issue associated with using RFID in supply chains at the item level is the price of RFID tags. Based upon current costs of 20 to 40 U.S. cents per tag, every item will not be tagged for some time. Yet the price of a tag will not go down until demand goes up—a "chicken-and-egg" problem.

Asset Tracking

Businesses currently incorporate "shrinkage" into their planning processes (e.g., budgets) to account for lost or stolen assets. RFID technology provides benefits for asset tracking and monitoring and can be used very effectively in any application that requires protecting assets. For example, the healthcare industry is investigating the merits of installing tags on surgical and monitoring equipment to ensure that shrinkage (loss, theft) is minimized, if not eliminated. Similarly, other industries are using RFID technology to their advantage. Items that are lost, stolen, or misplaced due to low usage are typical candidates for the RFID technology. These items may be mid- to high-cost items or items that must be kept in inventory or on hand to be available for crucial tasks. Some manufacturing companies use RFID for returnable containers to eliminate lost containers or to avoid late shipments (inbound and outbound) due to unavailability of containers. Some manufacturers incorporate RFID tags into their tools to prevent pilferage. Other manufacturers use RFID to track parts through a manufacturing line, which has increased throughput, reduced inventory, and reduced defects. Libraries have begun to use RFID to tag their book collections.

Access Control

Many companies currently use RFID technology in access badges to control access to their facilities. Breakdowns are few and less maintenance is required because there is no physical contact between the badge and the reader. RFID badges are also used in medium-level government security areas such as employee parking lots for airport employees. High-security areas incorporate additional security components such as biometric identification. Gated communities have been using similar technology for several years.

Security Systems

RFID technology has been effectively used to secure moveable assets such as automobiles and construction machinery and immovable assets such as manufacturing machinery. A reader is installed in the equipment and a RFID tag is installed in the type of "key" that is used to start the equipment. The equipment will start only if the reader "reads" the correct identification information from the "key," which prevents moveable assets from being moved without the correct "key." RFID reader and key technology can also be used to prevent inadvertent and potentially unsafe startup of machinery.

The nature of a mobile workforce and the wide use of external consulting resources has required organizations to install mechanisms that prevent unauthorized movement of assets that allow access to their critical information assets. RFID technology has been used to prevent assets such as laptop computers from being moved a specific distance or being removed from a specific area.

Payment Systems

An early use of RFID technology was in automated toll payment systems. In an automated toll payment system, a RFID tag that is attached to an automobile is read by a reader in a toll booth. The tag information is transmitted to application software, which debits the toll amount from a customer's account balance. This description is obviously a simplistic rendering of the actual process because it does not include any provisions for error checking or handling abnormal situations.

RFID technology has expanded beyond toll payments to payments at drive-through windows at banks and fast food restaurants. For several years Mobil Oil's Speedpass™ system has allowed customers to pay for purchases by waving their prepaid card containing a RFID tag over a reader. Other potential uses include payment for mass transit, movies, and concerts tickets or any other application that requires issuing tickets and posting charges to a customer's credit account.

Innovative Use of RFID Technology

Identification of animals. RFID tags have been used to tag livestock for some time. The onset of diseases such as mad cow disease and avian bird flu has resulted in initiatives to tag at-risk livestock populations to ensure that infected animals do not get into the food chain or pose threats to mankind. RFID technology has also been used to track endangered species or other species of interest. Researchers tag captured animals using active tags and re-release them into the wild. The RFID tags provide detailed information to researchers who then may use that information to gain understanding of the details of a species' behavior or to provide assistance if necessary. In the past decade, RFID tags have been implanted into pets, which can allow a pet to be reunited with its owner if the pet is lost.

Identification of people. Large theme parks provide bracelets to children that contain active RFID tags to assist in locating a child who becomes lost. By using RFID technology embedded in student identification badges, a school in California recently began an initiative to track students on the school's campus (Lucas 2005). The initiative was abandoned, however, due to privacy concerns raised by parents. A similar initiative began in Japan in 2004. In this case, school authorities determined that the advantages of such a system outweighed the disadvantages.

Monitoring. An RFID technology application is being developed to aid in the monitoring of individuals with Alzheimer's disease, an application which could be extended to monitor individuals with other conditions involving dementia.

Access control. Although the implantation of RFID in humans for the purpose of access control is being investigated (Waters 2006), the authors of this book suggest that a simple access control mechanism that has biometric identification capability may be a more robust solution.

Upcoming Novel Use of RFID Technology

Although several proposed innovative uses of RFID are currently being investigated, documented uses currently in development will be described in the paragraphs that follow.

Records management. With a mandate from the U.S. government, vendors of electronic records management (ERM) tools are in process of commercializing the use of RFID technology for ERM. Although current focus in the healthcare industry is on ERM for patient records, RFID technology can be extended to all records management applications.

Fraud prevention. Because of the rise in counterfeiting of high-priced items and designer goods, use of RFID technology for counterfeit and fraud prevention is experiencing increased activity. Solution providers and manufacturers are actively pursuing RFID technology as a viable option to reduce counterfeiting of designer goods. Use of RFID technology to prevent currency counterfeiting is also under investigation. Embedding small tags into high-denomination paper currency is envisioned to significantly reduce currency counterfeiting. Counterfeiting of high-priced life-saving pharmaceutical drugs has become a major concern around the world. Pharmaceutical companies are aggressively piloting RFID technology to eliminate the introduction of counterfeit drugs into the drug supply chain. A study by the U.S. Food and Drug Administration (FDA) to automate the paper-based chain of custody of prescription drugs has resulted in the "ePedigree" initiative, which will use RFID technology to generate the chain of custody. The target completion date of 2007 for the ePedigree initiative has been extended because the technology and its acceptance did not keep pace with FDA assumptions.

Sensors. A class of applications that is experiencing rapid expansion is the use of RFID technology in wireless sensors. Combined with environmental monitors or motion detectors, wireless sensor systems can use the information gathered from these components to take a certain action such as sounding an alarm (e.g., if the concentration of a hazardous chemical exceeds a preset limit) or shutting down a production line (e.g., if excessive levels of a pathogen are detected on a meat packaging line). The use of wireless sensor technology will continue to have widespread expansion from various initiatives undertaken by the U.S. government's Homeland Security department.

As RFID technology matures and becomes less expensive, several innovative uses of RFID technology will emerge that solve common problems. Companies will increasingly turn to RFID as a potential technology that will allow them to increase their competitive business advantage by enhancing their unique processes and workflows.

Benefits of RFID

Previous sections have described the usefulness of RFID technology. This section will provide advantages and benefits adopters of RFID technology can expect to receive after successful implementation of an RFID project. Benefits can be categorized into two categories—customer-facing and operating costs and efficiency. Customer-facing benefits include accurate shipments and reduced stock-outs. Operating costs and efficiency benefits include reduced operating costs, shrinkage, stock-outs, labor costs, and reduced inventories and improved business processes, resource and asset utilization, productivity, and inventory accuracy.

Customer-facing benefits. When a shipment is made, a RFID reader at the shipping dock generates correct shipping information, which ensures that the associated paperwork is correct. With transmission of the related ASN, the customer will know exactly what was shipped and what is expected to arrive. Discrepancies, if any, would be related to problems in the transportation chain or loading process. With RFID technology facilitating the custody chain, locating items lost in transit will be much simpler. Stock-outs have a significant financial impact in the retail industry. Using RFID technology and proper business process parameters, stock-outs can be minimized. Items shelved incorrectly can be found quickly and made available to customers who have requested them. An unanticipated spike in demand can obviously result in a stock-out, but such occurrences should be minimal.

Operating cost and efficiency benefits. Several components result in reduced operating costs and positively impact customer satisfaction. As described in the sample workflow in Figure 5.2, addition of RFID technology significantly improves business processes associated with shipments and receipts. Because human intervention, if any, is minimal, significant productivity gains result in improved resource and asset utilization. Lack of human intervention also eliminates the potential for errors. The only caveat is the read failure level—if read failures are nonexistent, no data entry-related errors will occur. By using RFID automation, inventory accuracy is increased and stock-outs of raw material and work in process (WIP) are reduced, enabling a reduction in inventory levels. Due to automated identification and tracking, the manual labor required to perform these tasks is also eliminated, which reduces labor costs.

Limitations of RFID

Like any other technology, RFID has certain key limitations and barriers to adoption. For example, significant financial implications and maturity-related limitations of RFID technology are associated with RFID implementation and concerns related to civil liberties have become a barrier to adoption of the technology.

Financial roadblocks. Unless a customer or a regulatory mandate exists, financial roadblocks will impact projects with little or no ROI. Typically RFID implementations have not been able to document a significant ROI (Ferguson 2006), which has resulted in a "wait and see" attitude among potential adopters. In particular, the ROI associated with such projects often becomes a barrier to its acceptance among executives. A company implementing a RFID solution should also expect to have significantly large quantities of data, which will require an upgrade to the existing computing environment. A computing environment upgrade also increases the risk of interfering with existing business processes or causing them to break down, which is a risk that few companies are willing to take.

Technology-related roadblocks. Although RFID technology has matured since the 1940s, the maturity of other components and the processes that are being enabled has not been stellar. The immaturity of RFID technology-related components in systems has resulted in technology-, process-, and acceptance-related limitations. Immature, nascent technology also causes limitations such as RF interference (e.g., reader collision, which is the overlap of signals from one reader with another reader) and an inability of tags to transmit in metal or liquid environments. Additionally the number of tags that are expected to be read, limitations in tag read frequency, and the associated tag read "collisions" (when more than one tag sends a signal at the same time, which can confuse a reader) have not encouraged potential adopters of RFID technology. Lack of global standards also prevents widespread global use. In a global economy, limited global use hinders worldwide acceptance. Worldwide acceptance is expected to improve as a result of the EPCglobal's Gen2 initiative. The Gen2 initiative provides vendors with a standard against which they can begin to develop their hardware and software tools.

Privacy-related roadblocks. Significant discussion has centered on the widespread use of RFID technology and invasion of privacy (i.e., concerns about "big brother" type activities). The time when a tag is commissioned or decommissioned has also been a sticking point with civil liberties and privacy organizations in some parts of the world, although in other parts of the world this concern is not particularly important. *Comment:* Although the authors believe that privacy-related concerns are more related to education issues than to privacy concerns, the volatile issue of privacy is a serious limitation of RFID technology for some adopters and they will not accept it.

TO BARCODE OR TO RFID?

This chapter has presented the "basics" of barcodes and RFID and has described how they add value to supply chain workflows. Because RFID technology costs over 100 times more than barcodes, determining when using RFID is appropriate (rather than using barcodes) is important. To assist making a decision, this section will present some "rules of thumb," which are based on the characteristics of RFID technology.

RFID is recommended when the following are true:

- The environment poses challenges that prevent line-of-sight reads. Because RFID uses RF, not optical reads, RFID is better suited in this situation.

- A longer read range is required. Optical reads limit the distance in which a successful read can be achieved, whereas the distance for RF can be significantly longer depending on the solution hardware used.

- Data must be written back onto a tag. Barcodes are printed once. They cannot be written over. RFID provides the ability of multiple writes as long as the tags are read-write tags.

- A large amount of data is required to be on the tag. Barcodes are limited to slightly over 3000 bytes. RFID is capable of handling significantly larger amounts of data.

- Longer tag life is required. Barcodes are typically paper labels that can become damaged with little effort. RFID tags are typically inside packaging and therefore are much more robust.

- Tags must be placed on items in a harsh or environmentally hostile environment. Barcodes can become covered by paint, dirt, oil, etc., rendering them unreadable. Currently the only restrictions for RFID tags are in environments in which metal or liquid will be between the tag and the reader. Both types of tags are negatively impacted by moisture. Moisture results in optical interference for barcodes and RF absorption for RFID tags.

- Reusable tags are required. Once applied barcodes are difficult to remove from one target and reapply on another target. RFID tags can be reused, depending on the type of packaging and tag type being used.

- Security must be included in the tag. Due to their line-of-sight nature, barcodes must be visible and are thus insecure. RFID tags can be built with security embedded into a chip, which would require the reader and the tag to provide the security data necessary to communicate with another device.

- Simultaneous, multiple-tag reads are required. Only one barcode can be scanned at a time because barcodes must pass over a scanner. With proper anti-collision techniques, RFID readers can read multiple tags.

- Intelligence must be incorporated into the tag. Only identification data can be placed onto a barcode. Because of an ability to embed computing capability within a RFID tag, intelligence can be added to the tag.

Barcodes are recommended when the following are true:

- A low-cost application is required. RFID tags are currently over 100 times more expensive than barcodes. For price-sensitive applications in which other benefits are not as crucial, using barcodes is the best solution.
- Target material is a concern. RFID tags currently cannot be deployed on a target in which the possibility exists that metal or liquid can be between the tag and the reader or in which metal or liquid can cause RF interference. Barcodes do not have this restriction as long as a line-of-sight read is available.
- RF communication frequency is an issue. Barcodes are based on optical reads not RF. Because of the lack of global standards, a single RF is not available for RFID. Several countries have a common RF range that is already committed to special purposes, which makes these frequencies unavailable for RFID.
- There are privacy concerns with the use of tags. Barcodes have no privacy concerns and are therefore best suited to such applications.
- Application requires low mechanical resistance. Barcodes are typically paper-based and therefore present low mechanical resistance to application on a target surface. RFID tags present high mechanical resistance and are not well suited for such applications.
- Application requires a mature technology. RFID is still developing. Users who require a mature and tried application are currently best served by using barcodes.

SUMMARY

Currently some applications are well suited for barcodes, yet others are better suited for RFID tags. The economics of the application should be used to help determine the appropriate technology. (*Comment*: When considering the current limitations of RFID, however, the authors do not envision that RFID will replace barcodes in the near future. Although barcode and RFID technologies complement each other, as RFID technology matures, use of barcodes will ultimately be reduced but not eliminated in the near future.)

REFERENCES

Electronic Product Code (EPC). EPC Generation 1 Tag Data Standards Version 1.1, Rev.1.27, Standard Specification, 2005 May 10.

Ferguson, R.B. RFID loses reception. *eWeek*, 2006 March 6, 2006, p. 11.

ISO. ISO 18000. 2004. Available at: <http://www.iso.org>.

Lahiri, S. *RFID Sourcebook*. Indianapolis, IN: IBM Press; 2006.

Lucas, G. Students kept under surveillance at school. Some parents angry over radio device. *San Francisco Chronicle*, 2005 February 10.

MARC Global. *An Introduction to RFID in the Supply Chain*. Atlanta: MARC Global Holdings, Inc.; 2004

Waters, R. US group implants electronic tags in workers, London: *Financial Times*, 2006 February 13. Available at: <http://search.ft.com/search Article?query Text=Waters+and+electronic+tags&y=6&javascriptEnabled=true&id=0 60212003622 &x=5>.

6

WEB SERVICES AND SOA

INTRODUCTION

POM processes were discussed in Part I. From those discussions, remember that POM processes involve several steps. Each step in a POM process is typically enabled via a separate software component. A desire by many organizations to achieve best-in-class (BIC) performance resulted in most of them adopting a "best-of-breed" software acquisition strategy to enable POM processes. Each of these best-of-breed software components contained specific unique data structures, interfaces, etc., with most of them typically being proprietary in nature. These constraints made integrating software components very difficult and made basing decisions on a unified view of the enterprise facts impossible. Additionally each organization invested significant time and large sums of money in developing and deploying an existing portfolio of business software systems. Because of time and financial constraints, new system developments often began afresh and developed or deployed software components that were integrated tightly with existing systems. This tight integration created "brittle" systems in which changes were expensive, difficult, and typically suboptimal with respect to required functionality. Therefore components added later in the portfolio would be challenged by major headaches during implementation, especially when integrating with other systems, either existing systems or systems being deployed concurrently. (*Note*: The experience of the authors has been that integration efforts and related costs often account for over 60% of the direct costs for later projects. The authors strongly believe that missed-opportunity costs are significantly higher.)

The software industry has been acutely aware of integration-related problems and has recently developed tools such as Web services and service oriented architecture (SOA) to alleviate these problems. This chapter will first describe problems encountered in software integration and then present a rationale for improved integration mechanisms. Then the SOA paradigm and Web services as a potential implementation of SOA will be described. An explanation will also be provided about how SOA assists overcoming implementation problems.

INTEGRATION PROBLEMS

A major issue associated with the best-of-breed strategy is the "trying to put a square peg in a round hole" syndrome—due to the communication and orchestration limitations of each software component, business workflows must be adapted to the software components. Adding to this issue is the existing application portfolio to which the software components must be connected. The result of the square peg/round hold syndrome is suboptimal workflows, which cause users in a business to be less than pleased with the software solution. Gaps in the solution must then be filled via manual processes, which negates any potentially significant elements of business value, adds variability to processes, and increases the potential for errors.

Another significant issue associated with utilizing a best-of-breed strategy arises from the attempt to "marry" unique business processes in an organization with the standard best practices templates for the industry that have been developed by solution providers. From experience, service providers have a wealth of knowledge about the industry segment that they serve. This knowledge is subsequently used to develop industry-specific solution templates that capture a significant portion of the workflows within the industry. However, organizations believe, often correctly so, that their unique business processes are what distinguishes them from their competition. Although this quantum of uniqueness is much smaller than the overall value added by the business processes, it nonetheless consumes a major part of the effort and funding for any project.

When such significant issues exist, an industry naturally seeks solutions to them. Additionally cut-throat global competition forces organizations to try to respond much more quickly and cost-effectively to rapidly changing market conditions and at significantly lower costs and risks, while also optimizing utilization of the organization's existing assets and portfolio. Other drivers for change include:

- A need for real-time information visibility and accuracy
- A desire to optimize business processes
- A desire to extend connectivity to supply chain partners, while accounting for their computing diversity
- Legislation that requires increased governance

In the current business environment, an organization requires systems that can be quickly deployed to meet unique business needs. Once a system is in place, an organization also requires that the system be quickly reconfigured to adapt to changing business environments. Additionally these requirements should be provided at a low cost and with low risk to the business by maximizing utilization of existing business assets. In other words, the organization wants software systems to provide the agility required to be successful. Adoption of SOA and the use of Web services as mechanisms to achieve SOA are two components of a solution that can achieve these requirements.

THE SERVICE-BASED INTEGRATION PARADIGM

The concept of "low coupling and high cohesion" has existed in the software industry for some time (Ghezzi, Jazayeri, and Mandrioli 1991; Sommerville 1995), yet the software industry has not been able to fully utilize this concept until recently, when several advancements resulted in improvement of the software development process. "Cohesion" describes the characteristics of a module, and "coupling" represents the relationship of one module with other modules.

"High" cohesion indicates that all elements of a module are strongly related and grouped within the module to provide a common goal. Details of the service provided such as how it is provided, what programming language is used, or which database components are used are irrelevant. What is important is that the semantics and the interface of the service are well defined and do not change.

Conversely, "low" coupling refers to the low level of dependency that one module has with other modules. These characteristics and relationships allow modules to be individually analyzed, understood, developed, modified, tested, or reused. Object-oriented technology uses the concepts of coupling and cohesion as part of its founding principals, thereby contributing significantly to reuse of software modules.

In software, services are self-contained, are highly cohesive, have well-defined software components, do not depend upon other services, and provide the desired functionality as and when required. SOA has existed since the maturity of object-oriented technology and the development of standards such as DCOM (distributed component object model) and CORBA (common object request broker architecture), but has only now matured enough to be commercially viable.

The concept of services and SOA is abundantly experienced in everyday life. A familiar example is the telephone system. To use a telephone, one picks up the receiver, waits for a dial tone, dials the desired number, waits for the other party to pick up the telephone, begins a conversation, ends the conversation, and hangs up the receiver. Telephone equipment provides the service of communication.

Because of the mature state of the communication industry and standardization, replacing old telephone equipment with other equipment or newer equipment, replacing a corded telephone with a cordless telephone (or vice versa), etc. is easy and still provides the same service. The entire telephony infrastructure is the architecture that has been built for the purpose of providing the service of communication. Extending the infrastructure by adding switches, exchanges, or providing telephone service to new homes is also easy.

Other common examples of services include lighting service provided by an electricity company and water service provided by a water company. In these examples, light fixtures and faucets are the devices that provide the services, which are based on very well-established architectures for providing these services.

As these service examples were developing and maturing, people observed certain patterns and utilized them to develop standards. For example, when a telephone (or water) connection was required for a new house, the architecture developed facilitated reuse.

SOA can provide the agility that businesses are seeking. Yet because each service represents a different paradigm, organizations seeking to benefit from this agility must invest accordingly so that the existing assets are capable of accommodating an SOA. Accommodation may require developing totally new services or putting existing services within "wrappers" that fit an SOA schema. Once such an investment is made, the services will become a tool in an organization's tool chest, which can be used when appropriate.

WEB SERVICES

In recent years Web services have gained significant visibility in software circles. Large software industry "players" such as IBM, Microsoft, and Sun have published their Web services strategies and actively utilize them. A very simple description of Web services is the access of software services via the Web. The software industry considers standards, technology, and architecture to be components of Web services. Standardization and advancements in Web technology have provided the means of describing and publishing the service interface, discovering available services, connecting a service provider to a service requestor, and providing a service over the Web (hence, Web service). Due to their modular nature, Web services act as data transfer agents and therefore can be sequenced into complicated business processes. This ability enables applications to connect to other applications and to thereby form a meaningful workflow. Web services are becoming a key component in enabling B2B (business-to-business) models.

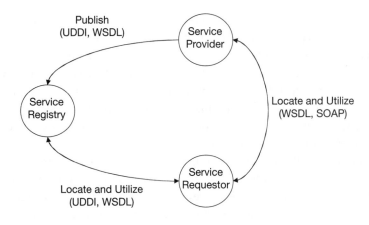

Figure 6.1. Schematic of How Web Services Work.

How Web Services Work

A service provider develops a service and "publishes" it over the Web in a public or a private service registry. To facilitate "discovery" of a service, the service provider will describe the service in a metadata format using a standard known as WSDL (Web services description language). The WSDL for a service includes all of the information that is required for a requestor to locate and access the service, including interface and location. The metadata does not contain details of how the service and a requester communicate. The communication aspect is facilitated by another standard known as SOAP (simple object access protocol).

The service description is published in a service registry, which can be a registry within an organization's environment or a commercially available registry such as those provided by IBM, Microsoft, SAP, etc. To ensure that the service registries are widely available, another standard known as UDDI (universal description, discovery, and integration) is used. UDDI is a Web-based directory in which services can be listed so that they can be found by requestors (e.g., as in a telephone book). At this time, the service and a description of the service are available in a service registry. By using a service registry, a service requestor will look for ("find") a service provider which meets a specific need. Once the service is located, the requestor will "bind" with the provider, obtain the requested service, and then release the service. Figure 6.1 summarizes the operation of Web services.

As an example of Web services, consider the following scenario. A certain Web service provides global import duty rates. This service provider has developed the service and defined it in WSDL. To provide a requested import duty rate, the Web service provider requires three parameters—the source country, the target country, and the value of the goods being imported into the target country in the target country's currency. (*Note*: The conversion of one currency to another is another example of a good candidate for Web services.) The service will then return the import duty applicable for the shipment. This service is published on a public UDDI registry for a fee that is determined by the registry owner. Users of the service must pay the service provider a fee to use the service. This fee can be at a transaction level or it can be a flat periodic rate.

Continuing with the scenario, suppose a supplier wants to determine the customs duty on a shipment to be sent to a customer so that an invoice can be created. (In this case, the supplier is responsible for all costs incurred until the shipment is delivered to the customer.) The supplier's invoice application will send out a query for the amount to be paid as customs duty. The invoice application has been given the required information regarding the value of goods (invoice total), the source country (country from which shipment will be made), and the target country (country to which shipment will be made). A query is then made to public UDDI registries and a service provider is found to be a match. Because a relationship already exists between this provider and the shipper, SOAP is used to honor the request and the amount of customs duty will be returned to the shipper's invoicing application, which completes the Web services transaction. Although this example is simplistic, it reflects the utilization of Web services. Obviously much more is involved in terms of security, privacy, guaranteed servicing, etc. before this example would qualify as an actual commercial application.

Standards for Web Services

The Web services architecture was developed independent of any standard. Yet due to the variety of Web technologies available, putting a structure around this architecture via technology standards became necessary. The standards were developed to provide a common framework for Web services development and usage, thereby increasing its utilization. Each of the technology standards commonly used in Web services, namely, XML, WSDL, SOAP, and UDDI, will now be briefly described.

XML. XML (eXtensible markup language) is the language used to encode each of the standards. XML is a language created by the World Wide Web Consortium (W3C, http://www.w3.org). XML is derived from an older markup language known as SGML (standard generalized markup language). The original goal of XML was to provide a mechanism to publish documents electronically, yet its capabilities have allowed wide use in Web-based and other applications. Representing data in an XML format is the foundation for Web services and SOA.

WSDL. WSDL (Web services description language) is a metadata standard also created by W3C (http://www.w3.org/TR/wsdl). As defined by W3C, a WSDL document contains the definition of services as a set of "network end points" (also called ports), which contains interactions between the requester and the provider (i.e., the operations that the service provides). These operations may contain an input message and a result in the form of an output message. The set of operations defined in the Web service contains all possible interactions between the requester and the service. In other words, WSDL describes the messages, the types of messages, and the operations that are provided by the service. The WSDL description of a service does not contain any information about how the service and the requestor communicate. The communication aspect is determined by the SOAP standard from W3C. The W3C website provides technical details about WSDL.

SOAP. SOAP (simple object access protocol) is a standard for exchanging information between distributed applications. SOAP uses XML to specify the request and response over HTTP. Interoperability is achieved by encoding WSDL information within SOAP. By using WSDL and SOAP, Web services can be described and used.

Nothing at this point has allowed a Web service to be discoverable by requesters, which is a functionality of UDDI.

UDDI. The UDDI specification (universal description, discovery, and integration) was published by OASIS (the Organization for the Advancement of Structured Information Standards), which had the goal of bridging the gap between publishing and using Web services. OASIS is a non-profit, international consortium that uses public standards to create non-proprietary, interoperable specifications. The UDDI registry contains all elements necessary to publish and locate a Web service. In addition, the UDDI registry entry for a service may contain additional metadata regarding payment mechanism, security parameters, discovery keywords, service parameters, etc., thereby providing a complete self-contained package for a Web service.

These standards provide the tools necessary to publish a Web service (via WSDL and UDDI), to locate a service in a registry (via WSDL and UDDI), and to bind to the service (via WSDL and SOAP). All are represented in XML.

SOA

The information technology (IT) department has long been considered to be a "necessary evil" within many firms. Not until the early days of the Internet did this perception begin to change. Unfortunately, executives and users in a large number of firms still have an out-dated mindset concerning IT. Although the concerns of some executives and users have been valid, the way IT was "done in the old days" has reinforced their concerns and a negative perception still prevails in industry, but that is changing.

Application Development Challenges Prior to the SOA Era

Applications were developed as large monolithic systems, with little or no knowledge about the future needs of the organization. Applications were built to achieve a specific set of business functionalities. When a new set of functionalities was required, developing the new application required "starting from scratch" (similar to the time when automobiles were designed in a "start-from-scratch" manner). Yet at this time building a new set of applications from scratch was easy because no constraints from existing systems were considered. This environment resulted in firms managing a set of discrete coexisting applications rather than having well-integrated solutions. Even if applications were integrated, the integration was often "brittle" to the extent that any type of maintenance would potentially "break" the solution. Applications deployed made tying them together with existing applications (to obtain a complete picture of the state of the organization) very difficult.

Discrete application development added to the woes of end users. Quite often end users were forced to accept a suboptimal solution due to integration and technology limitations. The turnaround time to fulfill support or service requests was often unreasonably long. The root cause of many problems was IT process and technology immaturity. As IT advanced, some of the problems were addressed, but a desire to be "first to market" with "bleeding edge" technology introduced instability. IT advances such as object-oriented technology (OO) and its associated reuse ability led some business users and IT groups to believe that they had found the "silver bullet." Due to a lack of best practices and governances for the new technology, this was not the case. Furthermore, reuse at this time was focused on and marketed as a technology that reduced developmental and maintenance costs, but not business-related elements. Yet it is the business-related elements that have a greater impact on the bottom line.

For example, in many large organizations, a typical IT budget would be about 2% of revenue. Therefore for a large $25-billion manufacturing organization, the IT budget would be about $500 million. If IT-based reuse saved the organization 2%, the savings would be about $10 million. Yet line-of-business expenses such as supply chain costs are about 70% of revenue. Therefore for this organization, the supply chain costs would be about $18 billion. A 2% savings in supply chain processes would result in about a $350 million savings. (*Note*: Savings of this significance result in many organizations seriously considering deploying SOA—and these savings do not take into account the impact of being an agile and responsive organization.)

With deployment of OO technology, components proliferated, but because of the state of current deployment, the components could not be easily used. Significant information about a component is required to successfully utilize it. For example, in most existing solutions, the location of the component, detailed knowledge about the interface and invocation, etc. must be manually obtained to effectively use a component. Because components can be located anywhere within the Web, the potential addressable space is large and discovering the correct component becomes difficult. Due to possible inconsistencies in components, attempts to make applications interoperable with other applications also caused problems when "putting it all together."

Application Development Evolution with SOA

In recent years, the success of Web services, the maturing of IT processes and best practices, and improved governance has further increased interest in utilizing Web services to meet business needs. Greater focus has also been given to the use of SOA as a mechanism to develop solutions that will truly meet the needs of business.

Earlier in this chapter SOA was identified as a design principle that presents an architectural framework for developing software-based business solutions. SOA is therefore the mechanism that illustrates how to create a business system(s) from components (i.e., parts). SOA is a concept that has been refined through decades of experience in manufacturing environments.

A common misconception is that Web services are required to achieve SOA, but Web services are merely one way in which SOA can be achieved. Other mechanisms such as Java RMI (remote method invocation) can be used to achieve SOA. Keep in mind that SOA is a design principle that can be achieved using multiple technologies, with Web services being the most common technology. An SOA is an architecture that is made up of components and interconnections that stress interoperability and location transparency. Web services and SOA provide the components necessary to design and build systems using heterogeneous software components that can be accessed via the Web.

SOA overcomes problems encountered in traditional software systems. Although the focus of OO technology is on packaging data with operations, the central focus of SOA is completing a task or business function that is closer to business users. Underlying processes, best practices, and governance have also enough maturity to support the concept of reuse through SOA. Although some component boundary elements cannot be reused directly, the effort that is required to "specialize" these components to meet a business requirement is small. SOA provides the mechanisms to incrementally "reel in" existing applications toward a goal of a "single truth," not just for the organization, but also for its customers, suppliers, and other trading partners. SOA also presents a different paradigm to use IT in business processes—SOA is an event-driven paradigm rather than a traditional process- and control flow-driven paradigm. An event-driven paradigm is necessary for modeling processes that respond to business events (e.g., triggering the creation of a PO when the quantity of an item falls below the minimum level required in inventory).

The brittle integration that has proliferated in industry can be reduced by the use of SOA. By using appropriate mechanisms such as "wrappers" for preexisting components, these preexisting components can be usable in SOA. All aspects of integration are also based on the terms of "contracts" between services (components) and consumers, which prevents ad hoc integration, a common contributor to integration issues. The issue of business processes being suboptimized is considerably reduced in SOA. The application development process is similar to using an interlocking component system that is similar to Lego® blocks, i.e., building with compatible components that "fit." SOA models business processes so that a business is not required to redefine a process to fit technology constraints. SOA is touted to have other benefits as well:

- Improved integration of applications results in accelerating application deployment, thereby reducing deployment costs. Maintenance costs and costs associated with utilizing standardized business processes are reduced. Reusability of a service allows development costs to be spread across multiple invocations of the service, making consumption of the service cheaper and more effective.

- By being able to utilize existing applications, leveraging of legacy investments is possible. Existing applications are tried and true, which reduces risk. Being able to use existing applications as well as leveraging years of intellectual property and development allows an organization to extend the life of its applications. Applications and business processes that are running the business today will continue to add value longer.

- SOA allows for a heterogeneous portfolio in which best-of-breed solutions can be implemented. Formerly, due to integration and technology constraints, best-of-breed solutions resulted in a suboptimized solution. Then organizations typically resorted to utilizing an integrated solution, which might not have been the best choice. Yet with SOA and related orchestration techniques, best-of-breed solutions can now be used, which also allows for interoperability among solutions from various IT vendors.

- Inherent reuse provided by SOA allows an organization to become more agile and to respond to changes faster. SOA promotes assembly of applications from reusable components instead of requiring redevelopment of components.

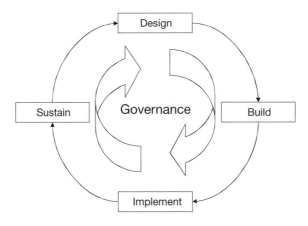

Figure 6.2. The SOA Process.

- Business process management can be automated. Desired functionality can be achieved using SOA via component reuse and orchestration. The gap between organizational processes and industry best
  practices can also be minimized with SOA. Intuitively, organizations
  that can respond to changes in the business environment with agility
  and flexibility will be much more successful than otherwise.
  Organizations that are successful in closing the gap between business
  activities and the technology used to accomplish them will be more
  successful that those who do not close this gap.

How SOA Works

SOA is typically built using services. These services can be newly developed,
wrapped legacy components, or composite services. A service performs a predefined task (e.g., to obtain a unit price from a PO). Because the *what* not the *how*
of a particular service is of prime importance, the underlying technology of the
service is unimportant from a consumer viewpoint. Although a SOA can be built
without them, Web services bring interoperability among heterogeneous technology systems through IT technology standards (e.g., HTTP, XML, WSDL, SOAP,
and UDDI). Therefore most SOA are typically developed using Web services
(hence the perception that Web services are a requirement for SOA).

Development of applications using SOA is a four-step process (Figure 6.2
summarizes the development process). The first step is to develop the solution
design. Business requirements are collected, analyzed, and translated into a design
document that must fit within the enterprise architecture in the design step.
Design is followed by the *build* step. In the build step, existing software assets are

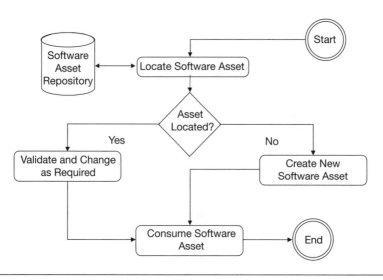

Figure 6.3. Consuming Software Assets by Using SOA.

searched in order to locate a service that can be used. If the search fails, a new service must be developed and added to the service portfolio. (*Note*: Software asset
management is a crucial component of SOA philosophy. Figure 6.3 presents a
potential workflow for managing service assets. Once software assets are known,
the knowledge will add to the orchestration that is required to meet business
requirements.) The build step focuses on meeting functional requirements. The
build step is followed by the *implement* step. The solution that has been built is
deployed within the enterprise infrastructure. The implement step ensures that
the solution will also meet nonfunctional requirements such as scalability,
responsiveness, etc. The final step is *sustain*. In the sustain step, service levels are
defined, maintained, and improved. The sustain step is crucial for ensuring that
the solution is adding value to the business. The sustain step also assists in identifying improvement opportunities for the solution that has been implemented as
well as in identifying other opportunities that the solution may have uncovered.

An SOA initiative should not be under the umbrella of a single project or a
small set of projects. Instead an SOA initiative should be a journey that the organization undertakes and institutionalizes to related processes, best practices, and
check points. An SOA initiative will have impacts across the enterprise computing
infrastructure. Therefore underlying the four steps is *governance*, which is
required to guide the enterprise architecture and to provide control for each individual project.

SUMMARY

Chapter 6 has briefly described two up-and-coming IT concepts that are widely thought to be capable of overcoming several issues that are associated with the ability of IT to meet business requirements. Although the concepts of Web services and SOA can be utilized independently of each other, they are most effective when used together—to provide the "service" in SOA through using Web services. Web services and SOA require enterprise-level support for effective implementation. The concepts of Web services and SOA also "morph" application development from a process flow- or control flow-driven approach to an event-driven approach. An event-driven approach truly models business processes and eliminates the suboptimization that is introduced by attempting to model business events into control flow-based IT processes. The potential for improvement and payoff in business processes such as POM are so significant that executives must keep these technologies on their "radar screen."

REFERENCES

Ghezzi, C., Jazayeri, M., and Mandrioli, D. *Fundamentals of Software Engineering*, Englewood Cliffs, NJ: Prentice Hall; 1991.

Sommerville, I. *Software Engineering*. Reading, MA: Addison-Wesley; 1995.

7

POM SOFTWARE VENDORS

INTRODUCTION

Previous chapters in Part II have covered the IT-related components that enable POM processes. These technology components are the "building blocks" from which solutions for business processes such as POM can be created. Several software vendors have used "building blocks" to create POM solutions. Although these software solutions for POM processes are relatively new, they have begun to mature in the last 2 years.

Chapter 7 will discuss a few of the products that are available in the marketplace. This discussion is not intended to include all of the tools that are available, therefore only a representative sample of the software that is available will be given. Guidelines for software selection are also presented. Because the intent of this chapter is to present only a few of the tools that are available for POM and the functionality they provide, it will not focus on the merits of each tool.

Supply networks that are agile and that respond quickly to changes in demand have been given the name demand-driven supply networks (DDSN) by AMR Research (O'Marah 2004). All DDSN processes are initiated by events occurring in the demand realm. DDSN promotes a customer-centric model as opposed to a factory-centric model. DDSN supports demand-driven replenishment in order to align manufacturing and distribution with demand. Depending on the type of demand, different types of replenishment signals are propagated upstream. The common replenishment models are Just in Time (JIT), sequence driven, vendor managed inventory (VMI), schedule driven, and discrete order based. The high-level processes for all of these replenishment models are the same. The differences in the models are in the mechanisms that are used to trigger the replenishment signals.

Several software vendors, especially the small ones, have focused on replenishment that is related to pull-driven manufacturing. The rationale for this choice is the nature of the supply networks. Supply networks synchronize globally, with local execution and execution that is in a pull-driven system. Applications based on traditional schedules and forecasts are not conducive to pull-driven flow because their batch processing programs can create an unacceptable level of "nervousness" for the real-time execution that is required for pull-driven systems. Some of these software vendors are also enhancing their portfolio beyond pull-driven replenishment. Larger vendors have handled more traditional replenishment programs (such as schedule- and forecast-driven replenishment), but are now incorporating pull-driven programs into their portfolio.

The vendors described in this chapter are SAP, i2 Technologies, Inc., Factory Logic, Inc., Pelion Systems, Inc., and Ultriva Inc. These vendors have been chosen as representative examples of POM software vendors. The choice of these vendors as examples does not promote or recommend any of them. They were only selected as representatives of large and small vendors, with no other criteria used in their selection. All information presented in this chapter has been obtained from the public websites of the vendors. Descriptions of the products are also based on information that is available on these websites. Because Web links are very dynamic, only website addresses for each vendor's home page will be provided.

SAP

SAP (http://www.sap.com) has been in the software business since early 1970s when its focus was primarily on accounting software. In the 1980s, use of its R/2® software grew rapidly in Europe, with some growth in the United States. With the advent of client-server and relational database technology in the 1990s, SAP developed a new generation of software known as R/3® and subsequently incorporated R/3 within several SAP industrial best practices. Wide use of SAP R/3 software resulted in the emergence of a new term in the IT business—enterprise resource planning (ERP)—and mySAP ERP®, a software system that which met several business needs. At the height of the dot.com era, SAP began to focus on linking e-commerce applications with ERP systems, which resulted in their mySAP.com® strategy. In the 2000s, with a focus on business users, SAP developed the mySAP Workplace® enterprise portal and began developmental work on non-ERP applications such as the mySAP Supplier Relationship Management® (SRM) application suite. A key component required for the success of these applications is integration with other systems. To achieve this, SAP has been actively developing and refining its SAP NetWeaver® application. Components of the mySAP SRM application suite appear to be relevant to POM processes.

Most supply chain applications by SAP (including SAP SRM) are built around SAP NetWeaver technology to facilitate integration between various roles and components. Components include back-end non-SAP systems, SAP business applications, and SAP ERP applications. Components also include mechanisms to render data to users in stationary or mobile formats. The stationary format includes laptop-or desktop-based browsers. The mobile format includes PDA or mobile phone-based browsers.

Implementation. A mySAP SRM implementation typically deploys several tools to achieve POM processes. The SAP NetWeaver technology "glues" these tools together to provide seamless integration with non-SAP tools as well. In addition to execution capability, the tools provide the interface required for Web collaboration and the capability to capture execution data, which can then be used to evaluate performance of the POM processes. The tools also enable plan-driven procurement that can synchronize with back-end ERP and financial applications. The tools include:

- SAP Enterprise Portal® is a single location that makes content available to internal and external users. The portal can be personalized at multiple levels, from corporate level to individual user level. The portal consists of several "portlets," which are bundled into business packages. These business packages allow different types of users to perform many business tasks for which they have responsibility. Packages are defined by three user categories—subject matter experts (specialists), managers, and all other users.
- SAP User Management® allows managing internal and external users to meet business requirements. The SAP user management engine provides a single point of administration for all users within the SAP portfolio. Internally an organization will define user identifications (IDs) and roles to authenticate users and authorize their access to SAP applications based on their roles. Suppliers have the capability to manage their users since organizations typically do not have visibility into supplier users and roles. This relieves an organization of the burden of managing change within the supplier's organization and allows the organization to focus on responding to business requirements.
- SAP Inventory Collaboration Hub® (ICH) primarily provides inventory visibility, based on roles, to internal and external participants. When inventory falls below a prespecified minimum level, alerts are generated. These alerts trigger suppliers and customers to react

appropriately. SAP ICH can be integrated with enterprise back-end systems, and the results of actions can be propagated in real time to these systems.

- SAP Enterprise Buyer® is the core of mySAP SRM. Along with SAP Enterprise Portal, SAP Enterprise Buyer allows users to collaborate on workflows that their role is authorized to execute. This component also allows organizations to connect to internal and external electronic hubs (e-hubs).

- SAP Supplier Self-Services®, along with the SAP Enterprise Portal, provides visibility into an organization's procurement information. SAP Supplier Self-Services provides the integration necessary to connect small and medium-sized suppliers with the procurement operations of large organizations.

- SAP R/3 Enterprise® is a functionality that is provided through the ERP version of the SAP toolset. SAP R/3 Enterprise provides information about inventory and procurement orders for all items and suppliers to ensure that the right material required for manufacturing is available at the right place, at the right time, and in the right quantity. Tasks within this component allow for closing of the loop between the plan and execution and ensure that a supply-demand match is made.

- SAP Exchange Infrastructure® provides the mechanisms required to exchange documents between systems, whether the documents are internal to the organization or external to it. SAP Exchange Infrastructure allows integration of business process and heterogeneous systems. These systems may be other SAP components or non-SAP tools. Messaging is used for document exchange and traditional communication mechanisms such as remote function call (RFC) are supported.

- SAP Business Information Warehouse® is a "warehouse" containing data from various SAP systems (e.g., ERP and business applications). Data from non-SAP systems can also be stored in this data warehouse. Users can access predefined, "canned" reports based upon their roles. The SAP Business Information Warehouse also contains the tools that are necessary to generate ad hoc reports. Work group-based workflows driven by events, reports, and alerts from the data warehouse can be designed to meet specific business scenarios.

Capabilities. Based on available documentation, mySAP SRM provides the capability to handle discrete POs, released schedules, and lean replenishment. The documentation does not indicate capabilities for sequence-driven replenishment. The tools in mySap SRM allow for generating requirements within the tool or transferring them from a back-end system. The tools are also broad enough to allow for all execution functions (e.g., creating ASNs and invoices, receipts of shipments, and financial settlements) to be executed within them. These activities can also be conducted in other non-SAP back-end systems. The tools also allow integrating with internal and external catalogs and procuring services. This allows the tools to meet all types of procurement—direct material, indirect material (including MRO), and services. Because the mySAP SRM solution handles indirect material and services (in addition to direct material), it has been implemented in a wide variety of industry segments.

i2 TECHNOLOGIES, INC.

i2 Technologies (http://www.i2.com) was founded in 1988, with the intent of providing software solutions and best practices to eliminate inefficiencies in supply chain-related business processes. Initial offerings focused on optimizing operations that were internal to organizations. Although tools to collaborate with suppliers and customers were made available by i2 in early 1998, these tools were immature and had a limited set of collaboration capabilities. Advancements in Web technology resulted in an i2 focus on tools for entities upstream and downstream of an organization. In 2005, Web technology advancements resulted in the development of the i2 Agile Business Process Platform® (i2 ABPP) as a mechanism to "quickly" integrate various i2 solutions with each other as well as with other enterprise applications. This section will now briefly describe the i2 Collaborative Supply Execution® (i2 CSE) product and the use of ABPP to rapidly deploy this solution.

 i2 CSE. Components of a POM solution using i2 CSE include back-end systems (such as ERP, financial, etc.), the i2 CSE application, other i2 planning solutions in the Supply Chain Management (SCM) processes, and i2 ABPP which acts as the integration element. Rendering data to users in multiple forms (stationary and mobile) is available and is a core component of the i2 CSE solution. The i2 CSE application is a stand-alone product that can be used without other i2 products as long as requirements for different types of material can be provided to i2 CSE from a back-end system. The i2 Performance Manager® (i2 PM) is a valuable addition to i2 CSE because it provides the capability to analyze i2 CSE data to improve a POM process through use of performance scorecards. i2 PM can analyze and present execution data from POM processes in a form that facilitates making strategic sourcing decisions by an organization. i2 ABPP provides components, a business process platform, and a business content library that are required to streamline the development and delivery of the POM solution using i2 CSE. i2 ABPP also facilitates the addition of i2 PM into a POM solution. The core of i2 ABPP provides capability to define business rules and workflow configuration. i2

ABPP data services provide the data models and data processes required to validate, synchronize, stage, and aggregate data. The integration services provided in i2 ABPP allow for bulk data transport for batch processing as well as message- and Web services-based real-time integration. The business content library encapsulates industry best practices processes that can be selected based on the solution's scope. Overall i2 ABPP is a platform that facilitates agile implementation and development of POM processes as well as other supply chain processes. For example, a retailer reduced premium (expedited) freight by 20 to 30% and reduced the annual inventory carrying cost by 2 to 3%. The entire solution was implemented in 10 weeks. A multibillion-dollar consumer-packaged-goods firm achieved $25 million in benefits from implementing the solution, mainly by eliminating stockouts and invoice discrepancies between manufacturers and retailers, and increased the speed-to-shelf time for new products (Sabourin and Srivastava 2006).

A single face. The i2 CSE application provides a "single face" to an organization's suppliers and presents data from multiple back-end systems to enable POM processes. i2 CSE allows the organization and its suppliers to have visibility to the various life stages of an order, including order generation, collaboration, acceptance, shipment, receipt, and invoicing through a Web browser, which allows suppliers that have a varying level of technology sophistication to be involved in POM processes. A role-based user interface is used to invoke various types of POM workflows in a single environment. Best practices workflows are prepackaged in the solution for all replenishment strategies mentioned earlier. i2 also provides a visual tool that allows an organization to customize the user interface and extend prepackaged workflows to meet specific business needs. The i2 CSE solution closes the loop between traditional discrete planning and execution processes through an event- and exception-driven framework.

Collaboration. i2 CSE allows a firm to collaborate with its suppliers on forecasts and execution (long-term, 6 months and beyond; medium-term, 1 to 6 months; and short-term, 0 to 30 days). In long-term and mid-term collaboration, demand forecasts, upstream and downstream requirements, and other planning signals can be shared with multitier suppliers, which allows a firm and its suppliers to jointly resolve mismatches. i2 CSE also allows a firm to work with its suppliers on capacity planning. Short-term execution focuses on order execution elements and lean replenishment. Order fulfillment receives material requisitions from MRP and APS systems and consolidates them into POs. These POs are then tracked throughout their life cycle. i2 CSE has the capability to process and generate execution signals, including shipments, receipts, invoices, acknowledgment, etc. i2 CSE allows document exchange and validation of documents presented to i2 CSE and supports workflows for direct material replenishment, including blanket purchase orders (BPO) and releases, requisitions from planning systems, and orders for material transfer between internal facilities and divisions. On the lean replenishment side, i2 CSE supports vendor managed inventory (VMI) and pull-driven replenishment.

Monitoring. i2 CSE can monitor POM processes, detect exceptions, and launch workflows to facilitate resolution of these exceptions. i2 CSE is an event-based system containing a configurable event detection mechanism, which allows an organization to customize event management workflows. The event chaining capability models a real-life sequence of events to resolve exceptions and contains a complete order and resolution history. The i2 CSE solution has been deployed in several industry segments including automotive, metals, high technology, telecommunication, and industrial. (*Note*: The acquisition of RiverOne, Inc. by i2 is expected to add to i2 CSE capability by extending it to multitier procurement.)

PELION SYSTEMS, INC.

Pelion Systems (http://www.pelionsystems.com) was founded in 1996 as a software and services company for integrating heterogeneous systems, which remained the core business focus until 2000. In 2000 Pelion Systems began development of its tools for Collaborative Flow Manufacturing®. In 2001, consulting, development, and services based on lean manufacturing were added to the portfolio. The current solution provided by Pelion Systems is Manufacturing Process Optimization® (MPO). The MPO solution contains modular software that supports pull-driven manufacturing. MPO consists of several modules—Process Optimizer®, Demand Manager®, Factory Manager®, Supply Manager®, Distribution Manager®, and Performance Manager®. Of these, only Supply Manager contains elements that are related to POM. Performance Manager provides insight into execution based on the data in the MPO modules.

Supply Manager®. Pelion's Supply Manager supports a wide variety of replenishment types. Documentation available indicates "any" replenishment type of trigger will be supported. With Pelion's heavy emphasis on lean manufacturing, Supply Manager has strength in material replenishment that supports lean manufacturing. The MPO software suite provides integration with an organization's back-end systems, including ERP, APS, SRM, and MRP (material replenishment planning). Material requirements are presented by Supply Manager via a Web portal to internal and external suppliers. This Web portal is a single point of contact for visibility to material requirements. The portal also streamlines communication and performance monitoring based on planning and execution data. Alerts generated in Supply Manager are used to highlight events or abnormal conditions. Supply Manager can also communicate various types of electronic signals to different entities. Real-time collaboration about acceptance, rejection, problem resolution, etc. between suppliers and an organization can take place in a Web environment.

The MPO solution has been deployed in several industrial segments, including aerospace and defense, automotive, consumer goods, and high technology.

FACTORY LOGIC, INC.

Factory Logic (http://www.factorylogic.com) was founded in 1998 as a company that provided software solutions based on lean production principles. Focus at Factory Logic is on providing lean manufacturing solutions (i.e., software, consulting, and services) to clients in four segments of industry—automotive, electronics, industrial equipment, and aerospace and defense. The Factory Logic solution is a set of software modules known as Lean Operations Suite®, which provides applications for schedule- and pull-driven material flow. The Lean Operations Suite consists of three modules—Pacemaker Scheduler®, Production Synchronizer®, and Supply Synchronizer®. Together these modules provide multiple control and replenishment signaling strategies so that an individual strategy or a combination of the strategies can be used based on the solution desired.

The modules assist organizations in defining business rules and planning functions to size supply chain parameters and monitor the alignment between production and replenishment. By adjusting lead-time and inventory parameters, the modules allow users to tighten their Kanban replenishment system. A lean production management system can be implemented such that non-pacemaker manufacturing processes are synchronized. Identifying the most at-risk and/or the most expensive parts will allow a user to pay special attention to these parts. Strategies can be implemented using manual signaling or implemented electronically via what the company calls electronic job boards—a Web-based tool that displays replenishment tasks.

The Lean Operations Suite provides integration with an organization's backend systems, including ERP (such as SAP®, QAD®, Oracle®, etc.) and MES (manufacturing execution system). According to the Factory Logic website and the product brochure, the Lean Operations Suite solution builds a solution around the principles of lean manufacturing:

- Demand-driven production planning: key capabilities include replanning for a "pacemaker" operation (such as a final assembly) when significant customer demand occurs or when a supplying cell receives a real-time signal with a recommendation to add or deduct a Kanban from the loop for that cell.
- Pull-driven material flow: key capabilities include calculation of the appropriate number of Kanbans based on demand, lead time, and other parameters and monitoring of Kanban movement status.

- Real-time operations monitoring and alerts: key capabilities include:
  - Workbench: provides event-driven alerts to automatically highlight potential problems within a particular user's domain of control and to provide rapid information that is needed to determine root cause and an appropriate course of action
  - Management by exception: highlights all indicators that are currently or projected to be out of established tolerances
- Tracking and analytics: key capabilities include:
  - RFID material flow: provides automatic real-time tracking of production and shipment activity; provides tracking of Kanban movement through the factory (including receipts and replenishment work centers)
  - Analysis of key metric versus current and calculated planning parameters: provides clear, actionable recommendations, such as where Kanban loop sizes can be immediately reduced without any negative impact on production

ULTRIVA INC.

Ultriva (http://www.ultriva.com) was established in 1999 and was known as eBots Inc at that time. eBots was the first company to develop and implement an independent electronic Kanban system to replace manual, card-based systems. Initially the system was stand-alone, but EDI capability was quickly added to enable integration with back-end applications. EDI capability was followed by Demand Signaling System® (DSS) for non-Kanban facilities. DDS converted MRP schedules and forecasts into JIT signals and communicated them directly to suppliers. Following the success of DSS, eBots released Demand Driven Scheduling® (DDS) and Custom Demand Management® (CDM), which had additional lean manufacturing capabilities. In 2005 the eBots company name was changed to Ultriva. In 2006 Ultriva released the Supplier Replenishment® software.

Ultriva provides POM capabilities through its Supplier Replenishment module. Documentation on the Ultriva website indicates that the Supplier Replenishment software supports all replenishment systems. Supplier Replenishment supports electronic Kanban systems for consumption-based demand and forecasts and production schedules for other types of demand.

A single Web interface provides internal and external access for all types of replenishment systems. This interface gives visibility to demand signals, PO releases, order tracking, receipt management, and inventory transfers. Suppliers and an organization can accept, make changes, and collaborate on requirements.

As a part of execution, Supplier Replenishment generates standard shipping labels with barcodes, which facilitates receiving. Supplier Replenishment provides analytics to track supplier performance on the Web interface. Rules of execution and inventory management can be defined using "wizards" (software that provides a step-by-step interface that simplifies complex tasks in other software systems). Ultriva prebuilds adapters to integrate with ERP and other systems using EDI, XML®, and other mechanisms.

Over time Ultriva has generated a customer base in the automotive, industrial, and electrical manufacturing industries and in the metals industry verticals (industry-specific solutions).

VENDOR SELECTION AND IMPLEMENTATION

Selecting a vendor to provide POM tools is a difficult undertaking, almost as difficult as selecting an ERP vendor. Even more difficult is the deployment of tools and processes to model POM processes. Guidelines for selecting a POM toolset as well as deploying these tools include:

Step 1. **Begin with the end in mind.** Defining the requirements is the first step in POM vendor selection. According to Stephen Covey's second habit, first visualize what the end picture should look like and then actively strive to reach that end picture (Covey 2004). There must be a clear understanding of the business strategy and the vision to ensure alignment. Identify the "must haves" and "nice to haves" for a desired solution. Associate a weight factor with each feature that is labeled as "nice to have" (to use to break a tie between vendors). Set realistic expectations and ensure that the end goal is achievable from functionality, budget, and time perspectives. Many initiatives have failed because of unrealistic expectations.

Step 2. **Gauge process maturity and supplier capabilities.** Determine the maturity of POM processes. Using a framework similar to the one described in Gupta (2006a) can help an organization to gauge the maturity of its POM and other supply chain processes. The organization must also determine the capability of potential vendors. A framework similar to the one presented in Gupta and Hanfield (2006b) can be used to determine vendor capability. Select a vendor that has high capability and a large solution base in areas in which the organization has lower maturity levels. Give special attention to areas in which the organization has a high maturity level and the vendor has high capability. Conflicts can result when mature processes and capable tools collide. Additionally, gauge the scalability of the solution. For large organizations that want to have all of their suppliers in a software-based POM solution, having a user base in the tens of thousands, with hundreds, if not thousands, of concurrent users is not uncommon. Because the solution will typically be a global solution, the internalization capability of the solution will also play a key role in the success of the solution.

Step 3. Stay focused on the end goal. Because vendors typically shift focus from the end goal to the latest features and new technology provided by their products, define a set of rules to ensure a fair and objective selection process and stick to these rules. The rules must be defined and disseminated among vendors early in the selection process. Before becoming deeply involved in the project, obtaining buy-in from all stakeholders is crucial because internally there may not be alignment among all stakeholders.

Step 4. Ensure that the selection team has decision-making authority. Vendors often attempt to bypass the selection team and go directly to top management within the organization to sell their solutions. If vendors are successful with this tactic, selection of a suboptimal solution is often the result. Top management must ensure that any "information sharing" by vendors is directed to the selection team.

Step 5. Insist on a demo and have it on your terms. An agenda for a demo should be developed and controlled by the selection team. A script should be developed that reflects "a day in the life of a procurement professional" and "a day in the life of a supplier" that is based on the solution. Pay special attention to usability and how streamlined the process is because end users will spend a significant amount of time using these tools. Items that appear to be minor inconveniences to the selection team may be unacceptable to the end users. The script should be given to vendors and they should be forced to adhere to it. An external facilitator can be a valuable resource in managing demo sessions. When vendors do not have a particular type of functionality in their products, they tend to resort to using "PowerPoint®-ware" or "vaporware" (a software solution that is marketed as having certain attributes, yet the attributes do not materialize, either because of excessive optimism or sometimes even deception in an attempt to sell an unavailable solution.) The selection team should focus on the available functionality during the demo and be vary of promises of anything else.

Step 6. Negotiate the terms and conditions. Negotiation should include ownership of the solution rather than only the software licenses.

During negotiation, consider the total cost of ownership and include licenses for all third-party software and components. Without third-party software and components, the solution will not work. Many organizations have negotiated for licenses for the core products, but not for the components such as Web servers, which has resulted in cost overruns amounting to tens of thousands of dollars. Also include maintenance and training in negotiations.

Step 7. Make a decision and communicate it to suppliers and stakeholders. To ensure that key stakeholders are kept up-to-date with the selection process, communication with them at predefined milestones, successes, and issues is essential. Once a decision is made, communicate the decision and the reasons why a specific vendor has been selected with stakeholders. Communication with suppliers that were not selected is also essential. Include the reasons why these suppliers were not selected.

Step 8. Select a service provider. System selection is a crucial step in achieving the end goal, but it is only a part of the solution. Complementing system selection is the selection of a service provider to assist in implementation. Implementation constitutes a large portion of the project's cost and time. If execution is flawed, the result will be a solution that may not work as required or a solution that has significant cost and time overruns. Select a service provider that has implemented similar solutions with the tools selected for the solution and that has knowledge of the business.

Step 9. Seek help when needed during implementation. During implementation, an organization often runs into barriers. Typically a barrier is not recognized as something that the organization cannot overcome, which results in wasted time and money. The project manager must identify risks and build mitigating steps into the plan. Also include well-defined criteria in the plan about when to seek additional help if a barrier is encountered.

Step 10. Implementation. The level of success experienced during the implementation phase will determine the level of success that is achieved by implementation of the POM process solution (or for that matter, any implementation). A balance between the solution and cost and time constraints must be maintained. (*Comment*: The authors have seen many solutions that have been deemed ready to "go live," but which were not well received by end users, resulting in a suboptimal utilization of the solution. The authors have also seen implementations that were driven by a date rather than a solution. In an attempt to meet a target date (which may often be unrealistic), testing, training, documentation, and change management are often neglected, which results in a solution that has a short life span or a solution that does not deliver full benefit. POM software business tools are developed using industry best practices. Therefore during implementation, minimize, if not eliminate, customizations. Anything that becomes a candidate for customization must be challenged. Direct efforts toward configuring rather than customizing. (*Note*: Change management and sustaining change will be discussed in Part III.)

SUMMARY

This chapter has provided a sampling of software vendors that provide tools that enable POM processes. Although an organization may already have preferred vendors and best practices for vendor selection, suggestions have been given for selecting vendors. Although the authors do not suggest that preferred vendors or existing best practices for vendor selection be discarded, proven methods have been provided.

Weighing the pros and cons of deploying a software solution for its POM processes is important for an organization. Having a solution that is hosted through vendors or service providers is an alternative that must also be considered. Having a POM solution implemented is a key step (one of many) in an ongoing journey that an organization undertakes in improving its processes and ultimately its bottom line.

REFERENCES

Covey, S.R. *The 7 Habits of Highly Effective People*. New York: Simon & Schuster; 2004.

Gupta, A.P., Handfield, R. Chapel Hill, NC: *A Supply Chain Maturity Model*. Working Paper; 2006a.

Gupta, A.P., Handfield, R. Chapel Hill, NC: Using and Configuring the Supply Chain Maturity Model. Working Paper; 2006b.

O'Marah, K. Why DDSN matters: supply chain professionals set the course for profitable growth. *AMR Research Outlook*; 2004 June 2.

Sabourin, E., Srivastava, A. The i2 agile business process platform blends with a heterogeneous IT environment and existing applications. *Supply Chain Leader*; 2006 Spring, pp. 25–26.

PART III:
CHANGE MANAGEMENT

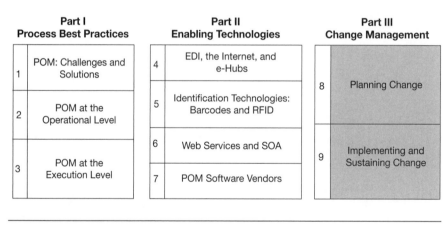

Part I Process Best Practices	Part II Enabling Technologies	Part III Change Management
1 POM: Challenges and Solutions	4 EDI, the Internet, and e-Hubs	
	5 Identification Technologies: Barcodes and RFID	8 Planning Change
2 POM at the Operational Level	6 Web Services and SOA	
3 POM at the Execution Level	7 POM Software Vendors	9 Implementing and Sustaining Change

Figure 1. Organization of Part III.

I am all for progress—it's the change I can't stand.
Mark Twain

In Parts I and II focus has been on technology and the operations-process aspects of POM. In Part III attention will turn to the human processes—or the "people" aspects—of change (see Figure 1).

Effective change management requires planning, implementing, and sustaining change to support business strategy. The focus of Part III will not be on whether or not to make a change. We will assume the decision for the change has already been made. The focus in Part III will be on how to plan, implement, and sustain change. The emphasis will be on getting people to "buy-in" to and use their new "tools."

Chapter 8 will focus on the planning phase of change management. Although change planning is always critical, planning is especially challenging in POM changes because the interests of stakeholders outside of the organization must also be considered. Chapter 8 will discuss the three most popular approaches to organizational change and how to apply them to POM change.

Chapter 9 is devoted to the implementing and sustaining phases of change management. Even the best-planned change may stall during the implementing and sustaining phases. Therefore, critically important is that change leaders be aware of the psychological, sociological, cultural, educational, and political reasons for resistance to change.

PLANNING CHANGE

INTRODUCTION

Planning for purchase order management (POM) change is more challenging than other types of organizational change because POM changes frequently involve hundreds, sometimes thousands, of supplier organizations. The buyer organization might be experienced with driving change internally, but not externally. The organization may also have a reward system in place to implement and sustain change in-house, but not be able to ensure buy-in from outside organizations.

Effective organizational change, of any kind, requires three phases: planning, implementing, and sustaining. Most organizational change efforts are doomed to failure long before the implementation phase begins. Therefore the critical importance of the planning phase for POM change cannot be overemphasized. Diagnosis and planning should always precede implementation.

In Chapter 8, three popular change models will be discussed: the Beitler Strategic Change Model, the Besaw Five-Step Change Model, and the Kotter Eight-Step Change Model. All three of these models emphasize the importance of the planning phase of change.

BEITLER'S STRATEGIC CHANGE MODEL

The "Targets for Change" model places emphasis on the importance of having all organizational changes aligned with a strategic plan (Figure 8.1) (Beitler 2006). POM changes, as well as other process changes, are only justified by an explanation of how the change will help implement the organization's strategic plan. (*Note*: Although the strategic planning process is beyond the scope of this book, strategic planning is clearly a critical management responsibility.)

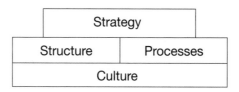

Figure 8.1. Targets for Change.

Once the link between the POM change and organizational strategy has been made clear to management, the linkage must be communicated to the individuals who will be responsible for implementing and sustaining the change, which requires developing a communication plan that expresses the importance, urgency, and strategic linkage of the change. After considering the strategic relevance of the POM change, looking for structural, cultural, and human process support for the change is then necessary.

This discussion will begin by looking at why effective organizational change must be strategy driven.

Strategy-Driven Change

The time to discuss the link between a proposed POM change and the company's strategic plan is when a proposed change is first considered. Change requires a commitment of organizational resources such as time, energy, and money. The expenditure of these resources can only be justified by showing how the expenditure will further the mission and strategic plan of the company. Every organizational member who will be involved in implementing and sustaining the change must clearly understand the strategic relevance of the change: "The strategy-driven approach to organizational change assumes that every organization is more effective when 'all the horses' are pulling in the same direction" (Beitler 2006, p. 6).

Structural Support

Once the strategic relevance of the POM change has been established, looking at the structural support for the change is necessary. If the structure is deemed to be inadequate, then restructuring becomes necessary. Restructuring interventions range in degree from minor adjustments to large-scale, organization-wide changes that affect virtually every member of an organization. Large-scale restructuring is commonly referred to as "reengineering."

Reengineering involves a fundamental rethinking of how the organization makes and delivers its products and services, which questions the shared underlying assumptions about the organization's operational and human processes. Questioning the basic assumptions about how the organization does business can be deeply disturbing to an employee's sense of security. Therefore managers, project leaders, and consultants must become familiar with the psychosocial aspects of change.

When a POM change involves downsizing, the change will be especially disturbing for all workers. Downsizing can involve early retirement, attrition, redeployment, delayering, divestiture, and/or layoffs. Regardless of how downsizing is accomplished, it always means one thing—fewer people. The ultimate result of fewer people is disturbing for terminated employees as well as for the survivors. Downsizings, especially in the form of large layoffs, can produce dramatic short-term cost reductions, but can also result in large long-term opportunity costs. Therefore short- and long-term effects must be analyzed during the change planning phase.

In his textbook, Muchinsky (2005) discusses the impact of downsizing on the "psychological contract" in an organization. A psychological contract is an unwritten list of expectations that employees have concerning their job security and promotion opportunities. In essence, employees perceive that they have a reciprocal agreement with the organization—their hard work and loyalty will give them the "right" to have job security and promotion opportunities.

Muchinsky (2005) believes that terminated employees and surviving employees see downsizing and layoffs as a "fundamental violation" of their psychological contract with the organization. Although senior management members may not agree with this thinking, they must remember that workers will see it that way. Motivating surviving employees in a postdownsized organization is very difficult (Beitler 2006). Violation of psychological contracts result in an organizational culture becoming less relational and more transactional (Robinson, Kraatz, and Rousseau 1994).

Surviving employees of a downsizing will question the necessity of the downsizing, the criteria used for termination, and the caretaking activities such as severance pay, outplacement counseling, etc. (Beitler 2006, Chapter 8). Keep in mind that, although considerable attention has been given to the terminated employees, the success of any change and the ongoing profitability of an organization will depend on the surviving employees. Frequently an organization's best employees will update their resumes and/or "jump ship" after a downsizing.

Cummings and Worley (2001, pp. 304–306) believe that cross-functional teams should follow reengineering steps:

- Identify and analyze core business processes (e.g., improving company efficiencies by outsourcing noncore processes).
- Define performance objectives. (These objectives should be based on customer requirements or on "benchmarks" and the best practices of industry leaders.)
- Design new processes to create a competitive advantage.
- Restructure the organization around the new processes.

Cummings and Worley (2001, p. 303) correctly add, "The business strategy should determine the focus of reengineering and guide decisions about the business processes."

Cultural Support

POM change (as well as any other type of organizational change) requires cultural support within an organization, but organizational culture by its very nature resists change. Yet organizational culture does change over time, either indirectly or directly, because of other types of change that occur (Beitler 2006, Chapter 9).

Whenever strategic, structural, or process changes occur in an organization, organizational culture is affected. An example of a strategic change would be a decision by management to enter a high-end niche market. The organizational culture, which has formerly supported the low-cost, high-speed production of standardized products, will resist any sudden changes to the POM and supply chain systems. Additionally, the organizational cultures of upstream suppliers will resist the new supplier-customer interactions.

Although structural changes may come in different forms, structural changes will invariably affect the organizational culture. Changes in reporting authority or decision-making authority are typically resisted by cultures that reward old behaviors and punish new ones. Always review the existing reward system to ensure that the desired new behaviors will be reinforced.

Changes in workflow between individuals and teams also have psychological and social effects that must also be considered during planning for POM changes. Failure to diagnose and plan for resistance to these changes will lead to resistance and other issues when trying to implement and sustain the change.

Organizational processes (both operational and human) are inextricably intertwined with organizational culture. To attempt a process change without considering the organizational culture in which the process is embedded is foolhardy. Therefore diagnosing the culture of the departments and divisions affected by the change is necessary during the change planning phase.

Human Process Support

Assuring that human process support will be available for a POM change is a critical step in the change planning phase. In discussing process change in this context, do not confuse *human* processes with the *operational* processes that were discussed in Parts I and II. In this context, "Human processes in an organization involve *how* things get done" (Beitler 2006, p. 139). Changes in strategy, structure, or operational processes will invariably require changes in human processes—*how* people get their work done.

Although a detailed discussion of all human process interventions is beyond the scope of a book on POM change, discussing the human process interventions that will be required to effectively implement and sustain POM changes is still important. The range of human process interventions that must be considered for POM changes include:

- Team building
- Conflict management
- Organizational learning
- Knowledge management
- Leadership development
- Training and skills acquisition

Teams. Although significant time and energy are frequently devoted to team building interventions for intact teams, team-building exercises should also be considered for new teams during the change planning phase.

Conflict. Conflict management interventions should be used whenever conflict is being inappropriately handled. Yet conflict should not be eliminated. Although different viewpoints and different ways of doing things (i.e., diversity) give effective teams strength, conflict must be managed if POM changes are to be effectively implemented and sustained.

Learning. Organizational learning and knowledge management interventions are necessary in virtually all POM changes. Because change requires learning, new knowledge must be acquired, captured, and transferred. Plan how these processes will be implemented and sustained.

Leadership. Leadership development must be considered in the planning phase because some of the individuals who will be responsible for the POM change will likely have little or no leadership experience. How leadership experience will be acquired requires serious consideration.

Skills Training. POM changes invariably require new KSAs (knowledge, skills, and attitudes). The proper allocation of resources for acquisition of knowledge and skills is critical to the success of POM changes. New learning requires a commitment of organizational resources—time, energy, and money.

A strategic approach to organizational change should be the foundation for the planning phase of POM changes (Beitler 2006).

BESAW'S FIVE-STEP CHANGE MODEL

John Besaw's approach to organizational change is visual and therefore is very helpful for a management team throughout all three phases of a change process—planning, implementing, and sustaining. The change model by Besaw (2006) describes "where we are" (*as is*), "where we want to go" (*to be*), and "how we are

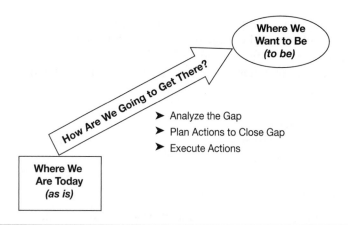

Figure 8.2. Visual of the Organizational Change Process.

going to get to where we want to be" in an organizational change process (Figure 8.2).

According to Besaw (2006), an organizational change process should be seen as a journey, not as an event. The left side of Besaw's figure represents the current status, "where we are today." The right side represents the desired future state, "where we want to be." The distance between the two represents the gap between "where we are today and where we want to be." Change planning requires an understanding of how an organization will get from where it is today to where it wants to be in a timely and efficient manner.

There is no one best method or "one-size-fits-all" solution for achieving successful change. An organization is best served when change is customized to meet the unique needs of the organization. Therefore the change process should be adaptive, not imposed.

Besaw envisions a closed-loop, iterative process, which is broken down into five steps:

Step 1. Where we want to be (*to be*)
Step 2. Where we are today (*as is*)
Step 3. Gap analysis
Step 4. Preparing an action plan
Step 5. Leading the way

The Besaw process is intended to be flexible. Therefore combining several steps or doing multiple steps in parallel rather than sequentially may be useful to meet an organization's particular needs. The Besaw approach should be empowering, not restricting.

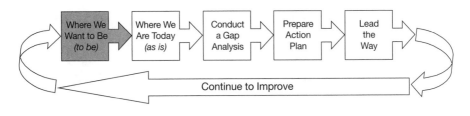

Figure 8.3. Where We Want to Be.

Step 1. Where We Want to Be (*to be*)

Step 1 is to determine where the organization wants to be (Figure 8.3). Begin with the end in mind. Having a clear description of where the organization is going is essential to any change process. Therefore, begin with defining where the organization wants to be. Note that using the word "vision" has been intentionally avoided. The term "vision" often leads to long unproductive discussions about the differences between vision statements, mission statements, and purpose statements.

According to Besaw, the *to be* is simply a short statement that provides direction for the process. This short statement (or the "elevator speech") is a concise description of where the organization wants to be in the future. Ideally, a *to be* statement should be presented in the time it takes for an elevator to go from the top floor to the first floor or vice versa. Simplicity and clarity are the goals. Detailed planning will be worked out later in the process. Examples of elevator speeches for a POM could be:

- We will be the industry leader in rapidly deploying technology to realize quantifiable benefits in purchase order management.
- Our POM system will minimize information/transaction costs throughout the organization.

A business leader should not make the mistake of coming up with the elevator speech and then simply delegating accomplishment of it to someone else. Too often doing so will add to or create resistance during the implementation phase. Developing the elevator speech should be an early part of the change planning phase. The individuals most impacted by the change should participate in development of the elevator speech. Early involvement of the individuals most impacted by the change will add to their commitment and buy-in to the change.

One of the best ways to develop an elevator speech is through a formal group process, possibly facilitated by an independent consultant. *Remember*: The sophistication of the words is not necessarily important. What is important for commitment and buy-in is the early involvement of the individuals who will be most impacted by the change. Trust the process and the words will come.

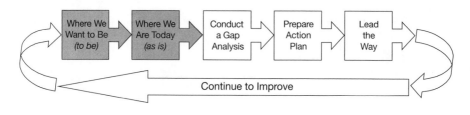

Figure 8.4. Where We Are Today.

Step 2. Where We Are Today (*as is*)

Step 2 is to analyze where the organization is today (Figure 8.4). After setting the direction with the *to be* elevator speech, make a complete analysis of where the organization is today, often called *as is*.

Members of an organization are typically more willing to spend time on where they want the organization *to be*, than on exploring where the organization is today. However, without a complete understanding of *as is*, the organization will likely be unable to get to *to be*.

The people doing a job know best how the job is done. Therefore their involvement in describing current reality (the *as is*) is essential. Several questions will help guide the discussion:

- How do processes operate today?
- What is important?
- What is measured?
- What skills are required for effectiveness?
- Who are the key players?
- What are the rewards?

Step 3. Gap Analysis

Step 3 is gap analysis, which is a critical step in the Besaw approach (Figure 8.5). Gap analysis provides the foundation for action planning. Realistically assessing the gap between *to be* and *as is* is necessary. This "needs analysis" must consider all of the following critical elements to have a successful organizational change (see the discussions of the elements in Parts I and II and the Beitler Strategic Change Model):

- Strategic alignment
- Structural support
- Cultural support
- Human process support
- Operational/technical process support

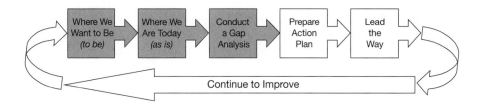

Figure 8.5. Gap Analysis.

Gap analysis will typically reveal deficiencies in current KSAs (knowledge, skills, and attitudes). Training may be the answer for some but not all of these deficiencies (Beitler 2005). Some of the required KSAs for POM change may be so far beyond the organization's current core competencies that outsourcing or hiring must be considered.

Step 4. Preparing an Action Plan

Step 4 is preparing the action plan. The action plan in a change planning process must be built on the results of a thorough gap analysis (Figure 8.6). If gaps are not uncovered during the planning phase, addressing these gaps afterward will require considerably more time in the implementing and sustaining phases.

The action plan must be customized for an organization. Following the action plan of another organization, even if it is referred to as "benchmarking" or "best practices," is often short-sighted. Every action plan for change must consider the uniqueness or "quirkiness" of the organization.

Step 5. Leading the Way

Step 5, leading the way, is ultimately the responsibility of senior management (Figure 8.7). The involvement of organizational leaders cannot be overemphasized. Organizational leaders must be visible during the planning, implementing, and sustaining of POM change efforts. If the leaders are not visible, organizational

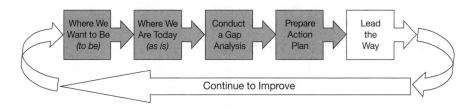

Figure 8.6. Preparing an Action Plan.

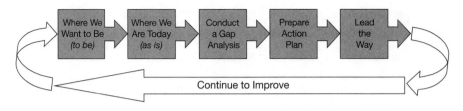

Figure 8.7. Leading the Way.

members will assume that the change is not important. Once a change effort stalls, getting it moving forward again is difficult. Leaders must be visible.

Leading change is best accomplished by using a path-goal leadership approach. Path-goal leadership (perhaps a more accurate term is "goal-path leadership") starts with a highly collaborative change planning process that involves leaders and workers. The path becomes the focus after a collaboratively developed change plan has been completed. The responsibility of leaders during the implementation phase is to clear the path so that the workers can accomplish the goal.

KOTTER'S EIGHT-STEP CHANGE MODEL

A popular model for planning, implementing, and sustaining change is the Eight-Step Change Model by John Kotter (1996). The Kotter model breaks down the organizational change process into eight steps:

Step 1. Establish a sense of urgency.
Step 2. Create a guiding coalition.
Step 3. Develop a vision and strategy for the specific change.
Step 4. Communicate the vision and strategy for the specific change
Step 5. Empower the employees for action.
Step 6. Generate short-term wins.
Step 7. Consolidate gains and produce more change.
Step 8. Anchor the new changes in the culture.

The eight-step approach of Kotter offers simple, straightforward guidance for change planning. Let us take a closer look at each step.

Step 1. Establish a Sense of Urgency

Kotter (1996) believes that the critical first step in any change effort is to establish a sense of urgency. (*Note*: The authors agree.) Managers are busy people. To get the attention and commitment of the organizational managers, the change leader must convince busy managers of the importance—the urgency—for the change.

Kotter (1996, p. 36) states, "With urgency low, it's difficult to put together a group with enough power and credibility to guide the effort or convince key individuals to spend the time necessary to create and communicate a change vision." Even with the leadership of the best CEO, "If many others don't feel the same sense of urgency, the momentum for change will probably die far short of the finish line."

With the guidance of an independent change consultant, according to Kotter (1996), senior management should consider ways to counteract "sources of complacency." He lists the nine reasons for complacency:

- The absence of a major and visible crisis
- Too many visible resources
- Low overall performance standards
- Organizational structures with narrow functional goals
- Measurement of the wrong performance metrics
- Lack of feedback from external sources
- A "kill-the-messenger-of-bad-news" culture
- Denial of problems
- Too much "happy talk" from senior management

Kotter (1996) offers a valuable reminder: "Never underestimate the magnitude of the forces that reinforce complacency and that help maintain the status quo." Every situation (the current status quo) is supported by resisting forces.

Raising the urgency level involves a response by senior management to each source of complacency. Some responses include:

- Provide "visuals" of what will happen without the change.
- Establish "stretch" goals for everyone in the organization.
- Create cross-functional teams with cross-functional goals.
- Reevaluate how the organization measures "success" (the things that are measured by senior management get the attention of employees).
- Actively seek feedback from external sources (customers, suppliers, distributors, industry analysts, etc.).
- Reward the messenger who has the courage to reveal problems.
- Openly discuss organizational weaknesses.
- Have senior managers demonstrate realistic, problem-confronting communication.

Step 2. Create a Guiding Coalition

For the past few decades, our society has created mythological heroic characters from successful CEOs, in a similar way in which the myths about military heroes were created in earlier societies. CEOs such as Jack Welch (GE), Lee Iacocca (Chrysler), Sam Walton (Wal-Mart), and Lou Gerstner (IBM) deserve much credit for their accomplishments. Yet the heroics of a single person will not be enough to lead tens of thousands of employees. Senior management must create a strong coalition of organizational leaders to guide the POM change effort.

The issue is not executive knowledge. Everyone knows some extremely knowledgeable executives. Instead the issue here is "buy-in." Without buy-in from key players, a change effort will fail. Kotter (1996, p. 57) suggests four key characteristics of members of effective coalitions:

- Position power: the coalition needs key players, including members of the board and line managers.
- Expertise and diversity: the coalition needs the expertise and diversity necessary to make informed, intelligent decisions.
- Credibility: the coalition must have credibility, which is based on the reputation of members, to be taken seriously.
- Leadership: the coalition must have proven leaders.

Kotter (1996) also recommends avoiding selecting certain types of people as team members. He recommends avoiding big egos and "snakes."

Egos. Big egos can destroy a talented and committed coalition. Members of a coalition must be talented leaders who have a realistic sense of their own limitations. Effective teamwork is impossible when a few overinflated egos dominate the team.

Snakes. Snakes undermine the work of a coalition. Snakes can destroy the trust that is essential for a strong, influential coalition.

There must be a coalition or team of committed leaders leading the change effort in various parts of the organization. These team leaders must pass along essential information to organizational members. Team leaders must immediately confront rumors and provide inspiration for their teams. These leaders must "know how to encourage people to transcend short-term parochial interests" (Kotter 1996, p. 65).

Step 3. Develop a Vision and a Strategy for the Specific Change

Every organization should already have a clear vision and a well-crafted strategic plan (emphasized previously in the discussion of the Strategic Change Model of Beitler). Additionally, when leading a specific change effort, developing a vision and strategy for that *specific* change is important. (Note that this is Step 3, instead of Step 1 in Kotter's approach, which is significant.)

No leader, regardless of talent, should single-handedly develop the vision and strategy for a specific change effort. Even if the leader is capable of developing a grand vision and a well-crafted strategic plan, the issue of buy-in is more important.

Therefore a change leader should actively elicit participation from all coalition members. Their participation provides valuable input into the decision-making process. Additionally participation provides coalition members with a sense of ownership in the plan.

The vision for the specific change effort must inspire organizational members. A vision makes decision making easier by eliminating many of the possible distracters. A shared vision is helpful throughout the organization. According to Kotter (1996, p. 70), "With clarity of vision, managers and employees can figure out for themselves what to do without constantly checking with a boss or their peers." Kotter considers that including the following six characteristics is essential in an effective vision:

- Imaginable
- Desirable
- Feasible
- Focused
- Flexible
- Communicable

Imaginable and desirable. An imaginable and desirable vision will "paint a picture" of a future that is very appealing. Kotter (1996, p. 73) correctly states that the vision must "appeal to most of the people who have a stake in the enterprise: employees, customers, stockholders, suppliers, community." Obviously, a vision cannot please all the people all of the time, but the vision and strategic development process for every substantial POM change should consider the long-term interests of all stakeholders. If stakeholders consider that they have been forced to make unreasonable sacrifices, resistance to the POM change may be insurmountable.

Feasible. Feasibility is a crucial issue in any vision or strategic plan. Ambitious goals must be doable. "Stretch" goals are motivating, but unrealistic goals actually "de-motivate." Employees will not have buy-in and will lose respect for management if goals are unrealistic.

Focused and flexible. Having focus and flexibility requires a delicate balance. The focus must be narrow enough to harness limited resources such as time, energy, and money, but be flexible enough to take advantage of peripheral opportunities.

Communicable. An effective vision must be communicable, which will be discussed in Step 4.

Step 4. Communicate the Change Vision and Strategic Plan

The value of the vision and the strategic plan for any organizational change effort is the guidance that each provides in goal setting and decision making. To provide guidance, the value of the vision and the strategic plan must be clearly communicated throughout the organization.

Kotter (1996) warns managers about "undercommunicating" and sending "inconsistent messages." Senior managers must think beyond communicating only to their immediate subordinates. A plan must be developed to communicate the vision and the strategic plan to every stakeholder inside and outside of the organization. Undercommunicating often occurs if information about the vision becomes lost in "a river of routine communication" (Kotter 1996, p. 88). Employees become distracted by hundreds of messages, which appear to be important or urgent. Frequently these distracting messages obscure the truly important communication. Kotter (1996) offers several suggestions for effectively communicating organizational change:

- Simplicity
- Metaphor, analogy, or example
- Multiple forums
- Repetition
- Leadership by example
- Explanation of seeming inconsistencies
- Give-and-take

Take a look at each suggestion.

Simplicity. Simplicity is avoiding jargon and "techno babble." Employees will not be inspired by a vision that they do not understand. A metaphor, analogy, or an example will provide a more understandable picture.

Forums. Multiple forums and repetition are crucial for successful communication. The vision and strategy should be communicated through training sessions, meetings, memos, press releases, the company intranet, etc. Repetition, through using various forums, is necessary to make the message stick.

Leadership. Leading by example is very important. In fact, leading by only talking-the-talk is difficult. If senior managers do not walk-the-walk, employees will not take the message seriously.

Explanations. When leading by example, managers invariably exhibit some apparently inconsistent behaviors. Any apparent inconsistency must be addressed.

Give-and-take. Give-and-take is necessary to maintain an open, interactive organizational culture. Senior managers should actively solicit feedback and make adjustments as necessary.

Step 5. Empower Employees for Broad-Based Action

Empowering employees is based on a leadership principle known as path-goal theory, which was discussed earlier in the Strategic Change Model (Beitler 2006).

Empowering employees involves a management style that is dramatically different from the management style of micromanaging and controlling. In an empowering management style, managers serve as facilitators. Managers seek ways to acquire the resources that their employees need to reach their goals, which may include time, money, personnel, and/or training.

New knowledge, skills, and attitudes will be required when major changes are initiated (Beitler 2005, 2006). Meeting these requirements may require considerable training. Plan for new knowledge, skills, and attitude requirements.

POM changes may also require changes in human resources (HR) policies such as selection, compensation, performance evaluation, promotion criteria, etc. HR policies must be supportive of operational process changes (POM or any other type).

Step 6. Generate Short-Term Wins

Executives who have ignored this step have paid with their jobs (or careers!). Organizational stakeholders, especially in the United States, look for short-term results. Although having long-term plans for success is important, no change leader should ignore the importance of providing some short-term wins.

Remember: When leading change, leaders will always encounter resisting forces and driving forces. Keeping the driving forces committed to the cause is important. All managers are under pressure to present short-term wins. Therefore, the coalition leaders must have wins—something to show for their efforts.

Short-term wins do not have to be earthshaking, but they need to be big enough to inspire the driving forces and to silence the resisting forces. Short-term wins build the credibility of a POM change plan. Kotter (1996, pp. 121–122) provides three characteristics for an appropriate short-term win:

- It is visible.
- It is unambiguous.
- It is clearly related to the change effort.

Short-term wins with these three characteristics should be woven into the timetable for the change plan. "Six months" is recommended for small companies and "eighteen months" is recommended for big organizations (Kotter 1996). Short-term wins let organizational members know that the sacrifices are worth it. They "turn neutrals into supporters" (Kotter 1996, p. 123). According to Kotter (1996, p. 123), "The more cynics and resisters, the more important are short-term wins." Building and maintaining momentum for the change effort is important (implementing and sustaining change will be discussed in Chapter 9).

Step 7. Consolidate Gains and Produce More Change

In Step 7, after achieving some short-term wins, leaders must continue to diligently monitor the progress of the POM change effort. *Remember*: Resisting forces are "waiting for an opportunity" to make a comeback. Whenever leadership "lets up" before the job is done, critical momentum can be lost and a change effort can stall. According to Kotter (1996, p. 140), "The credibility afforded by short-term wins [can be used to] push forward faster, tackling even more or bigger projects."

During large transformation efforts, multiple changes may be taking place at the same time. Sequencing these changes to maximize the use of resources such as time, energy, and money may be necessary. Guiding coalition members should agree on the sequencing or scheduling of events.

Step 7 requires the best efforts of senior management to not only maintain momentum, but also to build momentum for the change. During this step, add new members to the coalition that was created in Step 2 (Beitler 2006).

Step 8. Anchor the New Change in the Culture

The eighth step is the same concept that Kurt Lewin termed "refreezing" in his well-known "Three-Step Model of Change" (Lewin 1947). Once positive change occurs, management must work to make this positive change part of the organizational culture. Any new organizational change must be reinforced by the policies for recruiting, selecting, promoting, compensating, evaluating, and training. (See the discussion of the importance of organizational culture support for change efforts as presented earlier as part of the Beitler Strategic Change Model.)

THE AUTHORS' APPROACH TO CHANGE PLANNING

The approach of the authors of this book to change planning includes aspects of the Beitler (2006), Besaw (2006), and Kotter (1996) models as described earlier and involves asking several questions:

1. How does the proposed change help fulfill the organization's mission?
2. How does the proposed change align with the organization's strategic plan? (Is the change strategically relevant?)
3. Which stakeholder groups (internal and external) should be represented in the guiding coalition?
4. What ideally does the organization want from the change?
5. What is the current situation?

6. What are the changes (strategic, structural, cultural, and process) that are necessary to implement and sustain the change?
7. Who is responsible for writing the change plan?
8. Who has the authority to approve or veto the change plan?
9. How will the change plan be communicated?
10. How will the change leaders be empowered to implement the plan?
11. What short-term wins must be accomplished to keep the change on track?
12. How will the change be sustained or "anchored" in the culture of the organization?

Each of these questions must be seriously debated during the change planning phase. These questions provide only general guidelines for discussion. Ask additional questions to facilitate the planning of every unique POM change.

CONCLUSION

By customizing a change plan to fit the uniqueness of the particular POM change and its stakeholder interests, management can dramatically improve the possibilities for POM change success. If a POM change has been properly planned (e.g., based on the suggestions offered in this chapter), implementing and sustaining the change becomes easier. Yet even when POM change planning has been accomplished in a thorough and systematic manner, inevitably problems will arise during the implementing and sustaining phases. These problems can derail even the best POM change plan. Implementing and sustaining change problems and how to overcome them will be discussed in Chapter 9.

REFERENCES

Beitler, M.A. *Strategic Organizational Learning*. Greensboro, NC: Practitioner Press International; 2005.

Beitler, M.A. *Strategic Organizational Change, Second Edition*. Greensboro, NC: Practitioner Press International; 2006.

Besaw, J. Personal correspondence; 2006.

Cummings, T.G. and Worley, C.G. *Organization Development and Change, Seventh Edition*. Cincinnati, OH: South-Western; 2001.

Kotter, J.P. *Leading Change*. Boston: Harvard Business School Press; 1996.

Lewin, K. Group decision and social change. In *Readings in Social Psychology*. Newcomb, T.M. and Hartley, E.L. Co-Chairmen of Editorial Committee. New York: Henry Holt; 1947, pp. 340–344.

Muchinsky, P.M. *Psychology Applied to Work, Eighth Edition*. Belmont, CA: Wadsworth Publishing; 2005.

Robinson, S.L., Kraatz, M.S., and Rousseau, D.M. Changing obligations and the psychological contract: a longitudinal study. *Academy of Management Journal*. 1994; 37: 137–152.

IMPLEMENTING AND SUSTAINING CHANGE

INTRODUCTION

Although the change planning phase is critical, typically the implementing and sustaining phases of change are considerably *more* difficult. Stakeholders such as workers, suppliers, and customers may sometimes be calm and rational during the change planning phase, but then these same stakeholders may experience strong negative emotions during the implementing and sustaining phases.

EMOTIONAL ROLLERCOASTER

Because all individuals experience intellectual and emotional responses differently, all individuals will also experience change differently. Even when an individual knows a change is coming, and understands it intellectually, the change can still produce an intense, negative emotional reaction (Besaw 2006). The "fear of loss" is often manifested in various types of behaviors, which can then be interpreted as resistance. Some individuals may become defensive, angry, confused, or disoriented and then behave in a wide variety of unproductive ways. Unproductive responses are simply a predictable part of the change-adjustment process. Withdrawal, denial, and feelings of helplessness may take time for some individuals to work through. Even though there are individual differences, the process is quite predictable.

An emotional response is not a linear process. Therefore Besaw (2006) has depicted the emotional adjustment process as an emotional rollercoaster (Figure 9.1). His emotional rollercoaster model is based in part on a model that is used

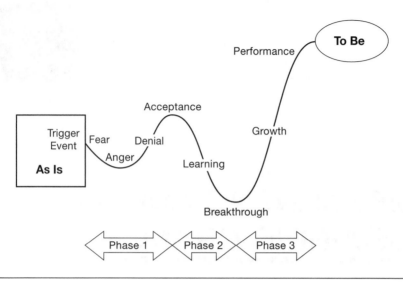

Figure 9.1. The Emotional Rollercoaster.

for dealing with death (Kübler-Ross 1997). Typically, after a triggering event in an *as is* situation, first there will be *fear*, which is followed by *denial*, then *acceptance*, and then an *opportunity for growth*. Obviously significant individual variations may exist in this process. The three phases therefore are a triggering event, the acceptance of change, and growth and performance. All individuals and organizations may not experience each phase, the phases may be different, and the length of time that each phase lasts can vary.

Phase 1. Trigger Event

In Phase 1, a trigger event initiates the change. A trigger event may be as simple as a rumor of an impending change or the initial proposal of a possible change. The initial response to the trigger event is often varying degrees of fear and denial. Some individuals begin to act defensively almost immediately and avoid all aspects of the change. Time and energy are subsequently expended in discussing the impending change, which distracts these individuals from their work, and productivity declines. Many individuals have difficulty in "letting go" of old patterns, behaviors, and processes. For some of these individuals, "letting go" is often just as difficult as learning a new set of skills. Yet the sooner these individuals "let go," the faster they will be able to move ahead.

Change is often resisted because people are busy. Leaders must provide opportunities for individuals to feel more in control of what is happening. Feeling more in control will be facilitated by involving stakeholders in the planning. Perceived losses will lead to fear and perceived irrelevance will lead to denial.

Stakeholders such as workers, suppliers, and customers must therefore be told by leaders *how* they will be affected by the change and *why* the change is necessary. Before the acceptance phase can begin, stakeholders must understand the benefits for the organization and for themselves. What problems will the POM change solve? What is the advantage over the "old way?"

During Phase 1, fighting fear and denial with information is important. An informed stakeholder has a greater sense of control and a greater sense of control leads to less resistance to change.

Phase 2. Acceptance of Change

In Phase 2, stakeholders begin to accept (but not necessarily like) the change. During Phase 2, stakeholders should be involved in ongoing operations as well as in the rollout of the change. In terms of productivity and job satisfaction, before things become better, things will become worse. This downturn in productivity will continue until workers master the new learning curve. Therefore management must provide learning opportunities and reward early adopters in as many forms as possible during Phase 2. (*Note*: More will be said about the role of learning in POM changes later in the chapter.)

Phase 3. Growth and Performance

Phase 3 is a period of growth and performance. From Besaw's emotional rollercoaster model, a breakthrough must occur before growth and higher performance can be achieved. A breakthrough is only achieved after significant levels of confidence, security, and new skills have been obtained. Management must remain visible, measure the change with appropriate metrics, and reward new behaviors during Phase 3.

CHANGE ADOPTION RATES

Change leaders must anticipate resistance and be prepared to deal with various change adoption rates because virtually all organizational changes, including POM changes, will meet with resistance during the implementing and sustaining phases. For many years, marketing experts have been aware of an adoption curve for new ideas and fashions. Similarly various adoption rates also exist in organizations that are introducing POM changes. Figure 9.2 depicts six different categories of employees and the respective variation in their adoption of change rates.

Although an entire stakeholder group could possibly fall into one of the six categories, this situation would be highly unlikely. Typically the individual members of a stakeholder group are dispersed across all of the six categories, which will require having a specific implementation plan for each category.

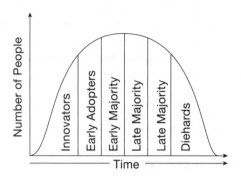

Figure 9.2. Change Adoption Rates.

From a strategic perspective, focus on innovators and early adopters first. The innovators are the most open to change and will be the first to embrace change or a new process. Early adopters will follow soon after. Getting innovators and early adopters onboard as quickly as possible is important. The good news is that having everyone onboard initially is *not* necessary. According to research, adoption of a change requires acceptance by only 5 to 10% of the employees for the change to become "imbedded" in the organization. An adoption rate of 20 to 25% makes the change "unstoppable" (Scott and Jaffe 1995). Although some may disagree with these percentages, the important point is that having 100% buy-in initially is not necessary.

Adoption rates vary based on who adopts the change first. If senior leadership and opinion leaders are the first to adopt, lower acceptance numbers will be sufficient for implementation of the change. If senior leadership and opinion leaders are not early adopters, larger acceptance numbers will be necessary for implementation.

The focus of change leaders should not be on the late majority or the late adopters because they will follow the innovators and early adopters. Because "diehards" will refuse to accept the change, they must be warned, transferred, or dismissed. Rarely is it wise to spend limited resources on diehards.

A rate-of-adoption model offered by Besaw (2006) suggests a 20%-60%-20% model (Figure 9.3). According to Besaw, anticipate that 20% of the employees will be early adopters, 60% will be in a wait-and-see category, and 20% will be cynics. Questions to ask employees in the "majority" or the "wait-and-see" group (depending on the preferred model) include:

- What is being resisted?
- Who is resisting?
- How can the resisters be reassured?

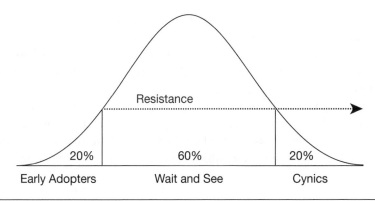

Figure 9.3. The 20%-60%-20% Model.

FIVE SPECIFIC GUIDELINES

Five specific guidelines that should be considered in all POM change efforts during the implementing and sustaining phases include:

- Putting a respected person in charge of the change
- Creating transition management teams
- Providing new knowledge and skills training
- Bringing in outside help
- Acknowledging and rewarding people

Putting a respected person in charge of a POM change effort is critical. Each significant organizational change needs a champion. POM changes invariably involve learning curves and unexpected obstacles. A respected advocate or champion must be available for stakeholders during times of frustration and setbacks.

The transition team. Creating a transition management team is recommended by Bridges (1991). His concept can be applied to virtually all POM changes. Representing the interests of internal stakeholders (e.g., organizational members in various departments and locations) and the interests of external stakeholders (e.g., suppliers, distributors, and customers) on the transition management team is important. Knowing who can provide assistance during times of frustration is also important. Members of the transition management team should provide emotional as well as technical support.

Training. Providing training for new knowledge and skills cannot be overemphasized. Having a feeling of incompetence is a major reason for resistance to change (Beitler 2006). Having adequate resources to help everyone achieve a feeling of competence with a new skill set is therefore important.

Consultants. Bringing in outside help is often critical to keep a process "on track." Independent consultants who specialize in human process consulting have helped many clients through a change process (Beitler 2006, Chapter 3). Independent consultants are not emotionally involved and are therefore in a better position to offer objective guidance.

Acknowledgment. Acknowledging and rewarding new positive behaviors are essential leadership functions during the implementing and sustaining phases. Using new skills involves risk—particularly the risk of failure. Acknowledging and rewarding those who use the new skills encourages others to do the same.

FEAR OF LOSS

The fear of loss is a powerful "de-motivator." Five types of loss must be considered during a POM change:

- Security
- Competence
- Relationships
- Sense of purpose
- Territory

Security. Security is important to all people. Obviously loss of security in the form of a possible job loss will be resisted with every possible tactic. Even the hint of the possibility of being replaced by software, hardware, or another person will be vigorously resisted.

Competence. No one enjoys feeling incompetent. Competency is the very essence of professional pride. Any time that an employee is asked to exchange a current set of skills for a new set of skills, the employee is being asked to endure a period of incompetence. Training and support must be provided to shorten that period as much as possible.

Relationships. Humans are social creatures. Even the most task-oriented workers value relationships. Because relationships make work more rewarding, the threat of losing valuable relationships will be met with resistance.

Purpose. A sense of purpose is another highly valued benefit that is received from work. Everyone wants to be the "go-to person" or "expert" in a certain field. If the purpose or "reason for being" is threatened, workers will resist a proposed change.

Territory. Humans are territorial, a characteristic that does not apply only to animals. "Territory" such as parking spaces, an office with a good view, and workspaces will be fiercely defended. Threats to the "territory" that one "owns" will be met with resistance.

Understanding these five types of loss will give change leaders valuable insight into why individuals and groups are being resistant during the implementing and sustaining phases.

LEARNING AND CHANGE

Each POM change will require learning new skills. Learning can be experienced in a variety of means—traditional training, computer-aided training, self-directed learning, and one-on-one coaching. Most people usually think of learning new skills as being provided in the form of a traditional, instructor-led workshop. This type of traditional instructor-led training is certainly appropriate when the number of trainees is large, if declarative knowledge is required, and if training time is limited, but numerous other choices of training methods are available for acquiring new skills and knowledge, such as computer-aided training, self-directed learning, and one-on-one coaching. The key to successfully implementing and sustaining POM change is *to choose the most appropriate method* for acquiring the necessary new learning.

In each POM change, acquiring some degree of declarative knowledge (often a significant amount) is required. Declarative knowledge involves facts and figures—the basic building blocks of higher levels of knowledge. If a large number of stakeholders require the acquisition of declarative knowledge, typically an instructor-led workshop is appropriate. Simply getting stakeholders such as employees, suppliers, and customers in a room and providing an instructor with all the resources necessary to facilitate learning the required declarative knowledge can be highly effective and efficient. Yet when an instructor-led workshop is impractical or inappropriate, creating and supporting computer-aided training, self-directed learning, or one-on-one coaching may be more beneficial for the organization.

CAT. Computer-aided training (CAT) has become very sophisticated and can provide not only declarative knowledge, but also skills training in a self-paced format. CAT with a self-paced format can facilitate learning for a wide variety of stakeholders with different levels of knowledge and different learning speeds. Considering CAT to facilitate learning POM-related knowledge is highly recommended.

SDL. Self-directed learning (SDL) is not necessarily the same thing as CAT and may actually not involve any computer technology. SDL typically involves providing stakeholders with books, manuals, workbooks, audios, and/or videos. Similarly to CAT, SDL provides a self-paced format. Before using SDL, using the Guglielmino Self-Directed Learning Readiness Scale is recommended (Guglielmino 1978, 1997). Because of the nature of SDL, not all organizational stakeholders are "ready" for SDL (Beitler 2005, Chapter 4).

Coaching. One-on-one coaching is often appropriate after a trainee has acquired basic declarative knowledge. Coaching can be provided on the job by a supervisor, peer, or vendor (known as on-the-job training or OJT). OJT has the advantage of high "transferability." Transferability is always a training concern because a significant amount of classroom-type training does not "transfer" well to a real-world job. Concern about transferability is eliminated by using OJT.

KNOWLEDGE MANAGEMENT AND CHANGE

All organizations must be able to acquire, capture, and transfer knowledge, which is a capability that has become more important than ever with the twenty-first century emphasis on knowledge-driven organizations. The previous section has discussed *acquiring* new knowledge. This section will discuss *how* organizations can capture and transfer critical knowledge.

Virtually all POM changes require the capture and transfer of explicit and tacit knowledge. Two distinct knowledge management (KM) systems exist for the capture and transfer of explicit and tacit knowledge—codification and personalization systems (Beitler 2005, Chapter 5).

Codification systems. A codification KM system is designed to capture and transfer explicit knowledge. Explicit knowledge is knowledge that is easy to articulate in the form of steps, procedures, or best practices. A codification KM system typically utilizes an electronic database to store explicit knowledge and to facilitate its transfer to other organizational members. When large amounts of explicit knowledge are needed to successfully implement and sustain a POM change, a codification KM system is a necessity.

Personalization systems. A personalization KM system is appropriate for the transfer of tacit knowledge. Tacit knowledge is knowledge that is not easy to articulate. Tacit knowledge is the knowledge acquired from many years of experience. Tacit knowledge stubbornly eludes capture and codification. Although many attempts have tried to make tacit knowledge explicit, typically those attempts were futile exercises. Tacit knowledge is "stored" in the mind of a highly experienced practitioner. Unlike explicit knowledge, separating tacit knowledge from the practitioner is impossible. Personalization KM systems invest resources to bring practitioners together for the exchange of tacit knowledge. Computers are used in personalization KM systems to locate an individual who has the knowledge, not to locate the knowledge itself. A powerful type of personalization KM system is a community of practice. A community of practice is a group of practitioners who meet to share their knowledge and experience. This group is *not* a project team.

The practitioners voluntarily meet for only one reason—to share their knowledge and experience. They share problems, frustrations, and new ideas and provide encouragement and support. An organization's management team cannot mandate participation in communities of practice, but it can identify and support the ones that already exist. If communities of practice already exist, the task of management is to identify and nurture them.

POWER AND POLITICS

Political Savvy

A fact of organizational life is that politics influence virtually everything that happens in an organization. Leaders, especially change leaders, must therefore develop "political savvy" (Beitler 2006, Chapter 4). Unethical behavior is not advocated, but leaders are advised to consciously refine their awareness of existing organizational politics. Organizations will always have different individuals, groups, and coalitions that are vying for scarce resources. Each group is attempting to maintain or enhance its self-interests. Many change leaders underestimate these powerful forces.

Invariably any attempt to implement and sustain organizational change will be threatening to individuals, groups, or coalitions who have self-interests. Because organizational change is typically accompanied by conflicting interests and emotional turmoil, change leaders must learn to navigate the "dangerous waters" of self-interest.

Power and Change

The word "power" has positive and negative connotations. In this section, the concentration will on the positive, ethical uses of power. According to Burke (1982, p. 127), "For change to occur in an organization, power must be exercised."

When attempting to implement or sustain change, it is helpful to consider Richard Emerson's Power-Dependency Theory. Emerson's (1962) theory depicts a social relationship between two parties in which scarce resources (commodities and rewards) are controlled by one party and desired by another. Thus, power is inherent in any social relationship in which one person depends on another.

The "commodities" in power-dependency theory include social commodities, such as respect, praise, influence, and information. French and Bell (1999, p. 284) state, "We enter into and continue in exchange relationships when what we receive from others is equivalent to or in excess of what we must give to others."

Power Bases

A change leader must be able to recognize the bases from which individuals, groups, and coalitions exert power in the organization. French and Raven (1959) provide five bases of power:

- Reward power: based on the ability to reward another
- Coercive power: based on the ability to punish another
- Legitimate power: based on the holder's position
- Referent power: based on charisma or popularity
- Expert power: based on knowledge or expertise

Mintzberg (1983) provides five additional bases of power:

- Control of a critical resource
- Control of a critical technical skill
- Control of a critical body of knowledge
- Legal prerogatives (e.g., exclusive rights)
- Access to any of the other four bases

Additionally, according to Mintzberg, an influencer must have both the "will and skill" to use his or her base(s) of power.

Salancik and Pfeffer (1977) have contributed valuable insights into the understanding of power in organizational settings. They view power as a positive and necessary force for change and progress in an organization and believe that power bases can be created by the placement of allies in key positions.

Using Political/Power Skills

For change efforts to succeed, POM change leaders must develop and use power skills:

Analyze the current political situation. The first required skill is an ability to analyze the current political situation. Failure in this assessment phase invariably leads to frustrated change efforts. According to French and Bell (1999, p. 286), "One gains a quick understanding of the overall political climate of an organization by studying its methods of resource allocation, conflict resolution, and choosing among alternative means and goals."

Assess power levels. According to Greiner and Schein (1988), change agents must be able to assess their own power and to identify key stakeholders. Only after assessing their own power bases can change agents determine how to use them to influence others. A power assessment will also reveal areas in which the enhancement of power is necessary. Weaker areas can be strengthened by developing allies within the organization (Beitler 2006).

Beer (1980, pp. 258–261) suggests strengthening allies in an organization by:

- Demonstrating competence
- Cultivating multiple relationships with key power figures
- Acquiring multiple top-level sponsors
- Scoring early successes for credibility
- Gaining control of valuable resources
- Working toward group support

According to French and Bell (1999, pp. 292–294), several "rules of thumb are implied by the fact that power accrues to persons who control valued resources or commodities:"

- Become a desired commodity—be perceived as competent and trustworthy.
- Serve the needs of multiple people and groups.
- Create win-win solutions.
- Help managers (the sponsors) succeed.
- Be an expert in the process, not the content.
- Fulfill the role of facilitator.

Comment: The authors are of the opinion that developing political skills or partnering with individuals who have these skills is a critical activity for POM change leaders.

LEWIN'S FORCE FIELD ANALYSIS

Lewin's (1951) "Force Field Analysis Model" is often used during the change planning phase as a diagnostic tool (Figure 9.4). During change planning, Lewin's model is used to identify the driving forces and the restraining forces so that plans can be made to *leverage* the driving forces and *reduce* the restraining forces. (Using force field analysis during the implementing and sustaining phases is also recommended.)

As the status quo (represented by the dotted line) is being moved toward "where we want to be," it is wise to periodically reassess the driving forces and restraining forces. Certain restraining forces that existed on the launch date of the change are possibly driving forces now (or more realistically—they are now neutral forces).

Unexpected changes occur in driving forces and restraining forces during every organizational change. Force field analysis will be a valuable exercise throughout the implementing and sustaining phases because it creates a visual that indicates the best places to focus organizational resources at any given point in time. The implementing and sustaining of a POM change can be greatly improved by taking advantage of these changes in forces. (*Note*: The authors rec-

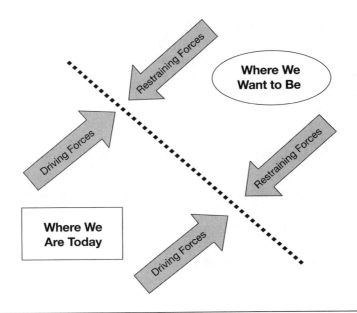

Figure 9.4. Force Field Analysis.

ommend the use of force field analysis during the periodic meetings of the transition management team.)

RETURN ON INVESTMENT

Measuring return on investment (ROI) is crucial for securing the buy-in from upper management that is necessary to implement POM process improvement. An effective ROI model can be of tremendous help in selecting the best initiative from several competing process improvement initiatives. An effective ROI model can also help answer questions about the justification of the IT investment and whether the required benefit and competitive advantage can be achieved.

Measuring ROI is also critical for sustaining a POM process change successfully. A positive ROI will mean continuous support and commitment from upper management. An effective ROI model will also help identify the factors that actually impacted the company's recent performance and reveal how much can be attributed to the POM process improvement. Conversely measuring ROI can also initiate root cause analysis if objectives are not achieved or if a lower than expected ROI is revealed.

Using traditional ROI models such as cost-benefit analysis, net present value (NPV), ROI financial, internal rate of return (IRR), etc. only in IT transformation programs (e.g., a POM process improvement) will result in the occurrence of many challenges, such as an inability to consider soft (operational) benefits, that cannot be easily converted into financial benefits. Another challenge is that specialized skills are required to understand and apply the appropriate ROI techniques, particularly when considering the number of methods and techniques that are available for selection (ranging from simple to very complicated).

Sabri and Rehman (2004) have developed an ROI model that addresses these challenges, which recommends bottom-up approach. The model begins with capturing all of the operational benefits that are usually generated by addressing the current "pain points" in a process. (*Note*: Pain points are key areas that have been identified as the best areas of focus for improvement that will provide an improved ROI.) For example, an operational benefit could be an increase in inbound material quality or an improvement in on-time delivery. These benefits and their equivalent metrics must be monitored on at least a monthly basis. Then operational benefits will be converted into financial ones, if possible. An example of a financial benefit would be a reduction in transportation costs. Financial benefits and their equivalent metrics must be monitored at least quarterly.

In many cases, it is not possible to convert certain operational benefits into financial benefits. Yet just because operational benefits cannot be used in traditional ROI models does not mean that they should not be captured and monitored.

Two primary reasons justify capturing operational benefits. One is that operational benefits may become financial benefits in the future (e.g., once data is available). For example, an increase in customer satisfaction is an operational benefit that is difficult to quantify, but in time and with the availability of more data, it will become clear that more business/revenue has been generated from existing customers because of a specific process change. At that point, a new financial benefit has been generated. The second reason is that capturing operational benefits will help to justify continuing the investment if no financial benefits have been generated by a certain time or to make a comparison between two competing initiatives with similar financial benefits.

All cost elements such as hardware, software licenses and upgrades, consulting costs for process changes and technology implementation, internal resources, integration costs, ongoing maintenance and support, and training must be captured and monitored closely. There are two categories of costs—initial costs (needed at the beginning of the implementation) and ongoing costs (needed to maintain the new process).

All financial benefits and costs should be considered in the ROI financial calculation (in which the difference between benefits and costs divided by costs is equal to the ROI of the process improvement). Operational benefits that are not quantifiable in financial terms should be also captured and communicated. A detailed breakdown of benefits and costs should be provided to indicate the magnitude of the project. Sabri and Rehman (2004) provide the following guidelines when computing ROI:

- No overlap is allowed in financial benefits or metrics. (*Note*: A metric is a measure of a benefit). For example, if premium freight cost is considered to be a financial metric, logistics cost should not be considered as another financial metric because premium freight is a subset of logistics (i.e., double counting of the benefits would occur).
- Consider a comprehensive set of metrics. At times improvements in one area will be achieved at the expense of another area. For example, an increase in the fill rate might occur at the expense of increasing inventory levels.
- Adopt an ROI model that can be sustained by the existing skills set in the organization. Additionally, the simpler the ROI model, the easier it will be for the model to be maintained.
- Computing ROI should not be a one-time exercise, which is done only at the beginning of the implementation to justify the implementation. Computing ROI should be an ongoing process.
- Optimize the level at which metrics data must be captured. At times the effort and time required to capture data will exceed the benefits. Automating capture of data is also recommended.
- Analyze benefits in six major areas—revenue increase, cost reduction, process lead-time reduction, asset reduction, customer benefits, and supplier benefits. The revenue increase and cost reduction areas are considered to be traditional financial areas, but analyzing only these two areas is no longer sufficient in today's competitive environment. Therefore it is critical to capture data from operational areas such as process lead-time reduction and asset reduction because sometimes the only benefits of a certain process improvement may be the flexibility of producing a wider range of products or improving the ability to respond quickly to changing demands. Although customer and supplier benefits areas are not always tangible or easy to measure and quantify, their roles and importance should also not be downplayed. Customer benefits can lead to greater business and revenue increases, long-term retention, and IT coinvestment to support a common process. Supplier benefits can lead to potential price reduction and IT coinvestment.

SUSTAINING CHANGE

The literature on the sustaining phase of change management is poorly developed and contradictory. Definitions of sustainability vary widely across the literature and disagreement exists as to whether sustaining change is good or bad for an organization.

Also relatively little research exists concerning sustaining change in organizations. Buchanan et al. (2005, p. 190) offer reasons for the lack of research on sustaining change: "Researching *change* is more interesting than studying *stability* and, for most managers, the next initiative promises more career value than continuing with established routines" and "sustainability requires longitudinal study and resources to which many researchers do not have access."

Buchanan et al. (2005) make an important point about the nature of sustaining organizational change. Although planning and the initial implementation of change may occur relatively quickly, sustaining change will involve a significant period of time. Maintaining a sense of urgency, or even a significant level of interest, therefore will be difficult over a long period.

The definition of sustainability varies based on the type of change initiative that a particular author has in mind. Miller (1982) speaks in terms of evolutionary, revolutionary, or quantum changes. Stace and Dunphy (1994) contrast incremental adjustments with company-wide transformations. Pettigrew (1985) focuses on issues that are particular to large-scale, risky reorganizations. Clearly the scale and complexity of a change will determine how sustainability is defined.

Another related issue when discussing sustainability of various change initiatives is the concept of an "improvement trajectory." Sustaining a change at a particular level is not the goal of many organizational changes. For example, to apply Lewin's (1951) concept of "refreezing" to a new, quality-improvement initiative could be a serious mistake. In a quality-improvement initiative *what* must be sustained (or "frozen") is the philosophy of quality improvement, not a *particular level of quality.* "What is to be sustained?" is therefore a critical question when the improvement trajectory is more important than a particular level of performance.

Is sustaining change good or bad for an organization? Many authors assume that it is good, but many do not. As Buchanan et al. (2005, p. 190) state, "Sustainability has been widely regarded … not as a condition to be achieved, but as a problem to be solved." Sustaining change becomes a problem when it blocks the need for new or additional change. At times a change initiative should just be allowed to "decay."

The initial excitement generated by a planned change is often squelched by the first few frustrating roadblocks. Cummings and Worley (2001, p. 168) correctly state, "A strong tendency exists among organizational members to return to what is learned and well known unless they receive sustained support and reinforcement for carrying the changes through to completion." It is important for changes to become part of the organizational culture (i.e., "how things get done around here"). Yet the process of organizational changes becoming a part of the organizational culture can take months or years in many organizations. Cummings and Worley (2001) list five activities for sustaining change:

- Provide resources for change.
- Build a support system for change agents.
- Develop new competencies and skills.
- Reinforce new behaviors.
- Stay the course.

Resources. Implementing change often requires substantial resources such as time, money, and human resources. Change leaders must devote considerable time and effort to acquiring these resources. Organizational leaders typically underestimate the amount of resources required to implement and sustain a change. Worley, Hitchin, and Ross (1996) recommend a separate "change budget" that earmarks resources for training and other related needs.

Support. A support system for the change agents is very important. A system of mutual learning and emotional support for change leaders should not be ignored. Cummings and Worley (2001, p.170) recommend using "trusted colleagues as 'shadow consultants' to help think through difficult issues with clients and to offer conceptual and emotional support."

Competency. Developing new competencies and skills is essential in every change effort. Cummings and Worley (2001, p. 170) recommend using "traditional training programs, on-the-job counseling and coaching, and experiential simulations, covering both technical and social skills."

Reinforcement. Reinforcing new behaviors involves providing the rewards that individuals need to continue their efforts. "Management can use extrinsic or intrinsic rewards, as long as the rewards are valuable to the recipients" (Beitler 2006, Chapter 4).

Leadership. Management must remain available and lead by example.

LEADING VERSUS FACILITATING CHANGE

Making a distinction between leading change and *facilitating* change is important. Leading change is the responsibility of management in an organization. These in-house change leaders must be intimately familiar with the *content* issues and the *company-specific* issues related to the POM change.

Facilitating change is typically the role of an external (independent) consultant who specializes in facilitating (guiding) the process of change. Any substantial POM change will benefit from an independent facilitator. The facilitator should be a person who is concerned only with the change *process* itself. The facilitator should also have no stake in the final outcome. Therefore, hiring an independent consultant to act as the change process facilitator is important.

Comment: Although perhaps sounding self-serving, the authors, who are independent consultants, recommend considering an independent change consultant in most POM change efforts. Because change is a process that follows a relatively predictable pattern, a knowledgeable, independent facilitator can add considerable value to a POM change initiative.

CONCLUSION

Although the change planning phase is critical, the implementing and sustaining change phases should never be taken for granted. Change leaders must be familiar with the psychological, sociological, cultural, educational, and political issues that are involved in implementing and sustaining change. Lack of knowledge about these issues can be very costly to an organization and to the career of a change leader.

REFERENCES

Beer, M. *Organizational Change and Development: A Systems View*. Santa Monica, CA: Goodyear; 1980.

Beitler, M.A. *Strategic Organizational Learning*. Greensboro, NC: Practitioner Press International; 2005.

Beitler, M.A. *Strategic Organizational Change, Second Edition*. Greensboro, NC: Practitioner Press International; 2006.

Besaw, J. Personal correspondence; 2006.

Bridges, W. *Managing Transitions: Making the Most of Change*. New York: Perseus Books; 1991.

Buchanan, D., Fitzgerald, L., Ketley, D., Gollop, R., Jones, J.L., Lamont, S.S., Neath, A., and Whitby, E. No going back: a review of the literature on sustaining organizational change. *International Journal of Management Reviews*. 2005; 7(3): 189–205.

Burke, W.W. *Organization Development: Principles and Practices*. Boston: Little, Brown, & Co.; 1982.

Cummings, T.G. and Worley, C.G. *Organization Development and Change, Seventh Edition*. Cincinnati, OH: South-Western; 2001.

Emerson, R.M. Power-dependence relations. *American Sociological Review*. 1962; 27: 31–40.

French, J.R.P. and Raven, B. The bases of social power. In D. Cartwright, E., Ed. *Studies in Social Power*. Ann Arbor, MI: Institute for Social Research/University of Michigan; 1959, pp. 150–167.

French, W.L. and Bell, C.H., Jr. *Organization Development, Sixth Edition.* Upper Saddle River, NJ: Prentice-Hall; 1999.

Greiner, L.E. and Schein, V.E. *Power and Organization Development: Mobilizing Power to Implement Change.* Reading, MA: Addison-Wesley; 1988.

Guglielmino, L.M. Development of the Self-Directed Learning Readiness Scale. Doctoral dissertation, University of Georgia, 1977; *Dissertation Abstracts International.* 1978; 38, 6467A.

Guglielmino, L.M. Reliability and validity of the Self-Directed Learning Readiness Scale and the Learning Preference Assessment. In Long, H.B. & Associates. *Expanding Horizons in Self-Directed Learning.* Norman, OK: College of Education, University of Oklahoma; 1997, pp. 209–222.

Kübler-Ross, E. *On Death and Dying, Reprint Edition.* New York: Scribner; 1997.

Lewin, K. Field theory in Social Science. New York: Harper & Row; 1951.

Miller, D. Evolution and revolution: a quantum view of structural change in organizations. *Journal of Management Studies.* 1982; 19: 131–151.

Mintzberg, H. *Power In and Around Organizations.* Englewood Cliffs, NJ: Prentice-Hall; 1983, pp. 24–26.

Pettigrew, A.M. *The Awakening Giant: Continuity and Change in ICI.* Oxford, England: Basil Blackwell; 1985.

Sabri, E. and Rehman, A. ROI model for procurement order management process. In *Proceedings of Lean Management Solutions Conference*, Los Angeles; 2004.

Salancik, G. and Pfeffer, J. Who gets power—and how they hold on to it: a strategic-contingency model of power. *Organizational Dynamics.* 1977; 5: 3.

Scott, C.D. and Jaffe, D.T. *Managing Change at Work, Revised Edition.* Menlo Park, CA: Crisp Learning; 1995.

Stace, D.A. and Dunphy, D. *Beyond the Boundaries: Leading and Re-creating the Successful Enterprise.* Sydney, Australia: McGraw-Hill; 1994.

Worley, C., Hitchin, D., and Ross, W. *Integrated Strategic Change: How OD Helps Build Competitive Advantage.* Reading, MA: Addison-Wesley; 1996.

INDEX